REFLECTIONS ON STALINISM

A VOLUME IN THE NIU SERIES IN

Slavic, East European, and Eurasian Studies
Edited by Christine D. Worobec

For a list of books in the series, visit our website at cornellpress.cornell.edu.

REFLECTIONS ON STALINISM

Edited by J. Arch Getty
and Lewis H. Siegelbaum

NORTHERN ILLINOIS UNIVERSITY PRESS
AN IMPRINT OF
CORNELL UNIVERSITY PRESS
Ithaca and London

Copyright © 2024 by Cornell University

All rights reserved. Except for brief quotations in a review, this book, or parts thereof, must not be reproduced in any form without permission in writing from the publisher. For information, address Cornell University Press, Sage House, 512 East State Street, Ithaca, New York 14850. Visit our website at cornellpress.cornell.edu.

First published 2024 by Cornell University Press

Library of Congress Cataloging-in-Publication Data

Names: Siegelbaum, Lewis H., editor. | Getty, J. Arch (John Arch), 1950– editor.
Title: Reflections on Stalinism / edited by Lewis H. Siegelbaum and J. Arch Getty.
Description: Ithaca [New York] : Northern Illinois University Press, an imprint of Cornell University Press, 2024. | Series: NIU series in Slavic, East European, and Eurasian Studies | Includes bibliographical references and index.
Identifiers: LCCN 2023035811 (print) | LCCN 2023035812 (ebook) | ISBN 9781501775543 (hardcover) | ISBN 9781501775550 (paperback) | ISBN 9781501775567 (epub) | ISBN 9781501775574 (pdf)
Subjects: LCSH: Totalitarianism. | Communism—Social aspects—Soviet Union. | Communism and culture—Soviet Union. | Communism—Soviet Union—History.
Classification: LCC JC480 .R44 2024 (print) | LCC JC480 (ebook) | DDC 320.53/22—dc23/eng/20230812
LC record available at https://lccn.loc.gov/2023035811
LC ebook record available at https://lccn.loc.gov/2023035812

For Arya, Augusta, Wiley, Immi, Julian, Niels, and Saila

Contents

Acknowledgments ix

Introduction: Reflecting on Reflections
J. ARCH GETTY AND LEWIS H. SIEGELBAUM   1

PART ONE: THE SOCIAL   13

1. Personal Reflections on Stalinism and Social History LEWIS H. SIEGELBAUM   15

2. Revisiting Stalinist Social Mobility
   SHEILA FITZPATRICK   33

3. Marxism and the Study of the Stalinist System DONALD FILTZER   46

PART TWO: MASS REPRESSION/TERROR   65

4. Stalinism, the Terror, and Social History WENDY Z. GOLDMAN   67

5. Lost and Found Revolutions: Between Emancipatory Dreams and Mass Terror in the Soviet Union
   GÁBOR T. RITTERSPORN   84

6. Wrestling with Aspects of Interwar Stalinism WILLIAM J. CHASE   100

PART THREE: BELIEFS AND EMOTIONS   117

7. Affective Dispositions, Bolshevism and Stalinism: The Rational Actor in His Emotional Environment
   RONALD GRIGOR SUNY   119

8. Fear, Belief, and Stalinism J. ARCH GETTY   136

PART FOUR: THE IDEOLOGICAL — 159

9. Stalin as Historian and Legalist
   ALFRED J. RIEBER — 161

10. Stalin as Revolutionary Social
    Democrat LARS T. LIH — 177

PART FIVE: THE SPACIAL — 197

11. Power, Violence, and Rurality in the
    Soviet Union in the 1930s LYNNE VIOLA — 199

12. How I Learned to Read Stalin's Time
    in Space KARL SCHLÖGEL — 210

About the Contributors 227

Index 229

Acknowledgments

As senior citizens, we dedicated this book to our grandchildren, who are the future generation. As senior scholars, we are also conscious of past generations who left the stage too soon. So here we would like to remember those who influenced us and who are no longer with us: Ken Bailes, Stephen Cohen, Jerry Hough, Moshe Lewin, Robert H. McNeal, Roberta Manning, Nadezhda V. Muraveva, Andrei K. Sokolov, and E. P. Thompson.

REFLECTIONS ON STALINISM

Introduction
Reflecting on Reflections

J. ARCH GETTY AND LEWIS H. SIEGELBAUM

Stalin has been dead for seventy years, more than twice as many years as he ruled, and the Soviet Union he built has been gone for more than three decades. Yet popular and scholarly biographies, sometimes multivolume tomes, continue to appear regularly, along with journal and newspaper articles and real or imagined memoirs. Why anyone should pick up another volume about Stalinism is a fair question. What is there left to say?

This collection has a unique perspective. Here, senior historians at or near emeritus status look back over our shoulders and reflect on the Stalin period of Soviet history based on decades of research and writing about it. We daresay that few scholars in any other field of history have lived through such important developments as the establishment of Soviet history as a field worthy of study accompanied by sharp political polemics, an unprecedented revolution in archive access and the disappearance of the country we studied. It seems valuable to present our personal reflections and distillations as salient aspects of the Stalin period.

We decided to title this volume *Reflections on Stalinism* for two reasons. First, to emphasize the contemplative, that is, our thoughts when we think not only about the past but about the ways we and others have written about that past. Second, we chose "Stalinism" because despite the absence of biography here, it is the term that emerged at the early stage of our careers, in preference to the older Cold War-inspired characterization of totalitarianism or the broader and more anodyne Soviet history.

We think that part of the reason that Stalin's ghost still haunts us has something to do with the all-too-common equivalencies being made between the Soviet dictator and the current occupant of the Kremlin. Since Russia's invasion of Ukraine, one needn't go far to encounter pundits proclaiming that Stalin "remains omnipresent ... imprinted everywhere in the state structure" (*History News Network*, March 9, 2022); that he and Putin are "two men with the same mindset" (*The New European*); and that "isolated [and] paranoid," Putin is "ever more like the Soviet dictator" (*Foreign Affairs*, no. 8, 2022). By emphasizing historic specificity, the multiplicity of actors and factors that went into the making of Stalinism, and the importance of Marxism, our volume can help to counteract the dangers of such facile comparisons and, dare we hope, avoid policies derived from them.

A better reason for historians' continued interest in the Stalin period is the sheer magnitude of what occurred in those years. The dramatic transformation of an underdeveloped peasant country into a superpower, the scale of domestic bloodshed, and the dominance of the Soviet Union in the largest war in human history all need explanation in their own right, even without a Putin.

In their attempts to grapple with the Stalin era, polemicists and scholars traditionally have wondered about its place in Russian history, its origins. In one way or another, almost all of them have asked, "where did it all go so wrong?" or "who or what is to blame?" Their answers were often colored by politics. For many Russian conservatives, the answer was easy. Stalinism was inherent in Leninism which, in turn, was the natural result of socialism; the original sin was Marx's. Things first went off the rails in February 1917 when the monarchy was overthrown. Western conservatives also pointed to long Russian traditions of autocracy, patrimonialism, and violence as roots of Stalinism. For liberals, Russia was on course to democratic modernization but was derailed by the accident of World War I, which led to a political crisis and brought fanatics to power in 1917. Things went particularly wrong in October when the Bolshevik coup highjacked the (good) February Revolution and hopes for democracy.

Socialists had (and have) a variety of explanations in their efforts to rescue socialism from Stalin. Some of them were at pains to save Marx from Lenin, whom they regarded as an ideological usurper of Marx's ideas and whose inherently undemocratic theories implied both dictatorship and violence. Other leftists sought to save the Russian revolutions from Stalin. They welcomed 1917 as a positive democratic and egalitarian step forward and wondered how the

Revolution could have gone so wrong in twenty years. Their answer was Stalin usurped it. Many of them argued that whatever one might think of Lenin, after his death there were many possibilities; the Stalinist path was not inevitable.

Our contributors here approach the "how did it go wrong?" question in a variety of ways. Wendy Goldman stresses the immense difficulties the Bolsheviks faced in implementing their revolutionary and modernizing vision in an undeveloped impoverished society. Lynne Viola focuses on that impoverished peasant society, seeing rurality as the site of much of the problem. Donald Filtzer shows that Stalin was able to coopt the workers' language of class to blunt their ability to organize or protest. Sheila Fitzpatrick points to the enormous social mobility the Stalinist policies enacted, leading to considerable support for the regime. Unlike others, Gábor Rittersporn does not accept the Stalin regime as coherent on any policy level, but rather chaotic, with efforts at repression misfiring in ways that rounded up and executed thousands of innocent people. Ronald Suny and Arch Getty explore the emotional side of Stalin and his leadership, seeing Stalin and Stalinists as products of environment and experience. Lars Lih and Alfred Rieber show the importance of Stalin's ideological and historical views.

Any attempt to answer "why did it go wrong?" implies an understanding of what exactly was "it" once Stalin took over. That is, how can we define Stalinism? For a hundred years since 1923, polemicists and scholars have attempted a definition using biography, psychology, social and political history, subjective consciousness, and aesthetics. The huge volume of books and articles on the subject and their sharp political charge already imply the difficulty of defining it. Stalin's name is attached to this dramatic period of change, but how much of it boils down to one man rule? Do individuals make history or vice versa? What about ideology, backwardness, social class, Russian traditions, hostile foreign neighbors, and a legacy of violence? How do we weigh the remarkable accomplishments against the almost incalculable violence?

One is reminded of the cliché about blind people touching different parts of the elephant, with each of them claiming to have found the main thing. The Stalinist elephant is huge, and its scale defies any single definition. It is hard to imagine any other thirty-year period in history during which so much happened so quickly, so violently. This compression should make it easier to define, but the opposite is true. It rather makes for such complexity that no single definition could capture it all or even enough of it to be satisfying. So, without intending to offend the visually impaired or elephants, we are tempted to say that the best we can do is present a selection of learned reflections on different aspects of the phenomenon, with no claim to total definitions. We hope that this will contribute to an ongoing process of definition and understanding.

People residing in the countries of the former Soviet Union are bound to relate to its Stalinist past differently. Most Russians surveyed still think he played a positive role in their history. Russian polls over the past thirty years put him in the top three most significant leaders in world history; in 2021 he came in first. But a sharp debate about Stalin, posed in stark terms of good and evil, persists. Partisans and defenders of Stalin openly and publicly make their case that he did more good than bad, while critics are just as firm and dug in when they argue that his evil is the main lesson of the period and it is the job of historians to expose and condemn it. There seems to be little overlap between the two camps partly because the Stalin period was part of their history, the histories of their families and of their culture, and thus has an immediacy that is lacking for us. The debate there is complicated further by the attributed, explicit relevance of Stalin to current governments and policies. Sometimes it seems that the polemical tail wags the analytical dog.

Considerations of relevance also affect historians in the West. Their works are often interpreted as judgments on socialism, whether or not the historian so intended. And there are still echoes of Cold War partisanship when historians' works are said to have implications for rehabilitating Stalin or using language that does not condemn him enough. But Western historians are at least free from having their works put to use by politicians seeking either to restore Stalinism or to drive a stake through its heart, as is the case in Moscow. We don't have any skin in that game.

This brings us to the question of paradigms. Standard representations of our field chart its evolution in three stages. First came totalitarianism stressing a hyper-authoritarian state dominating an intimidated atomized society. Then came revisionism which posited rivalries, conflicts, and contradictions among party and state officials. The next phase was postrevisionism, which incorporated the linguistic, poststructuralist, and subjectivist turns in the social sciences and humanities.

This apparent progression of paradigms, as Lewis Siegelbaum discusses below, may provide useful benchmarks, but it also oversimplifies the variations in research at different times. It also can obscure the significance of contributions that do not fit neatly into the schema. Social history, as Siegelbaum argues, was one; the significance of empire-nationality dynamics was another. And then there are sui generis studies whose elusiveness in terms of classificatory convenience might be an indication of creativity. As Thomas Kuhn noted, paradigms by their nature do not encourage thinking "outside the box" of currently accepted styles and approaches.

Paradigm battles in the field of Soviet history were particularly charged and bitter because of Cold War politics. These paradigmatic swings saw criticisms that were sharper and more ad hominem than might otherwise have been the case and sometimes enforced a less-than-useful conformity. In his study of scientific revolutions, Kuhn also argued that criticisms of work whose conclusions fall outside reigning paradigms are often as personal as they are substantive. With the collapse of the Soviet Union, politicized debates seem to have faded, but conformity—and its cost—has not. Graduate students and younger scholars still worry about how their mentors and elders will receive a dissertation or first book that doesn't fit a prevailing paradigm. Some of our generation will remember the self-defense mechanism used by our Soviet colleagues: the "Lenin sandwich," in which one started and ended one's work by praising Leninism and socialism but in between argued something else. One still sees similar censor-avoiding mechanisms in Western scholarship when in introductions or footnotes scholars criticize a school of thought while supporting it in their research. As the reader will see, our contributors' reflections are free from such requirements.

In Soviet times during which the contributors to this volume labored early in their careers, the law required all incoming flights from abroad to be met by border guards who were visibly armed and generally humorless, and whose mission was to defend the motherland against invasion by jetway. Figuratively and literally, archive entryways were also guarded by an armed policeman. Before the Gorbachev era, archives were closed to foreigners except for those lucky enough to have a patron to intervene for them (a familiar Russian phenomenon even today). Our careers saw the demise of the Soviet Union and the opening of Soviet-era archives that began during its last years. This archive revolution unfolded in slow motion. It began hesitantly; this was new ground in the USSR. Contrary to archivist training in the West, Soviet archivists had been taught that their first duty was guarding and protecting; facilitating access was a distant second if it figured at all. For several years, scholars' access depended on the sometimes-arbitrary decision of the archive's director who in most cases was a political appointee put in place to defend Soviet secrets. We foreigners had to carefully craft a *tema* outlining one's project, and the archival guardians in the reading rooms would often deny giving out a document if it fell outside one's subject area or their interpretation of it. We were seated in special reading rooms under the stern gaze of a room monitor and unable to consult catalogs or inventories (*opisi*). Our requests for documents had to go through an invisible layer of experts in the back rooms who decided whether or not to approve the request.

When the Yeltsin regime fired the top two or three layers of management in many institutions in an attempt to purge them of communists, the archival doors swung wide open. Professional historians replaced party hacks as archive directors. But even then, change did not come overnight. It often took explicit decrees to the reading rooms from new archive directors that withholding a document because it didn't strictly fall within the text of one's research statement was not legitimate, or as they put it, *eto ne argument* ("this is not an argument"). And even then, we Westerners faced public criticisms from politicians complaining that well-funded foreign researchers were crowding out Russian researchers who were in dire economic circumstances: "foreigners are buying our history." Archivists often had to gauge such political winds and the new classifications of secret documents in deciding what to give out. One was heard to say that nobody had even been fired for saying no to a foreigner. If anything, that cautious attitude is enjoying a comeback under Putin, who now concerns himself with patriotic and "correct" interpretations of history. It is possible that our contributors will have seen archives that were closed suddenly open, only to close once again. The border guards at the jetway are now plain clothes with concealed weapons, and the policemen who guard archive lobbies at least hide their pistols, but figuratively they are still there.

It has become commonplace to refer to the "archive revolution" of the 1990s, and to be sure, the new access to archival sources certainly changed the methodology of doing Soviet history. Thirty years on, we are still processing the new materials. But just how revolutionary was the archive revolution? Thus far, few bombshells have emerged, and more than one scholar found that the new archives did not radically change the overall picture that had resulted from the careful use of published sources. Paging through classics like E. H. Carr's volumes shows how much we can learn from published sources. The new archives became the indispensable Bible for Soviet historians, but as with the Bible one can find citations there to support any point of view. When the archives revealed themselves, defenders of all points of view claimed vindication.

Even before the archival revolution, historians had staged their own implicit revolt against political science's totalitarian models. In the 1970s, works by Moshe Lewin and Sheila Fitzpatrick showed that it was possible to write Soviet social history; works by Stephen Cohen and others did the same for political history. Studying the Soviet Union as history is no longer in question, and the sharp ad hominem polemics of the past are also gone.

It may not seem worthy of note to younger generations, but for those who began their professional careers in the turbulent 1960s and 1970s to admit that emotional attachments shaped interest and even conclusions would have seemed like committing professional suicide. Indeed, objectivity would remain something of a fallback position for a while longer, particularly in response to accusations of political bias. Hence, the stories told here of youthful longings and affiliations have a somewhat revelatory quality, as if the authors were unburdening themselves. Reinforcing this point is the use of the first person singular. Perhaps this is a consequence of the post-modernist tilt toward subjectivity or the result of the call for reflections. Whatever the case, one would have difficulty finding examples of the use of "I" in earlier works of ours, at least before the new millennium, except in the prefaces and acknowledgments of our books.

We gave our contributors the freedom to write on whatever they chose in any format. Our idea was to allow them full flexibility to reflect, to write about how Stalinism looks at this point in their careers. The chapters they produced cross styles, disciplines, periodizations, and interpretive boundaries in ways that only senior scholars feel free to do. As editors, we resisted the temptation to enforce conformity to any style or format. Some of the contributions are more personal or autobiographical than others. Inevitably, certain topics and approaches get less attention than others; their absence in no way reflects our view of their value. Some, such as gender and sexuality, largely postdate the contributors' intellectual formation and sustained pursuits. Others, such as empire and nationality, have featured prominently in the works of at least one contributor and have figured in those of several others, but here the focus lies elsewhere. Finally, questions of foreign policy, including war strategy, wartime and postwar negotiations with British and American leaders, as well as relations with China, remain subjects for future investigation and assessment.

Lewis Siegelbaum's contribution begins a group of chapters on social history by asking what does it have to offer to the study of Stalinism? His historiographic overview of Anglophone literature considers the impulses for such works and the impact they had in the 1970s and 1980s, suggests why the social-historical approach faded toward the end of the millennium only to make a strong comeback in the last two decades. Like other contributions, his reflections are personal, not only in the sense that they represent his inevitably subjective judgments but because they (critically!) address some of his own contributions and motives for undertaking them.

Sheila Fitzpatrick's numerous contributions to the social history of Stalinism were groundbreaking both in their use of archives and their interpretations. Her chapter in this volume reflects on her motivations for taking up social mobility, specifically "proletarian promotion," as a theme and the "strong criticism" it provoked from both the Marxist left and "the totalitarian-model right." She then looks at what happened to the Soviet promotees in terms of access to universities and thence professional and managerial jobs in the late Stalin years and under Khrushchev in the late 1950s and early 1960s. She invokes Jerry Hough's observation that the end of large-scale upward mobility in the 1980s doomed the regime launched by Stalin. Thus, the theme of affirmative action Soviet style—which, as Fitzpatrick points out, had peasant, women, and "backward" nationality components—not only retains its historical cogency but finds broader contemporary applicability.

Donald Filtzer's chapter deploys Marx's concepts of the social relations of production and class antagonisms to enhance our understanding of the Stalinist system. After considering why Marxism (or "marxism" as he prefers to call it) fell out of fashion in the late twentieth and early twenty-first centuries, Filtzer applies several of Marx's insights into the nature of capitalist society to the Soviet Union. He argues, much as Hillel Ticktin did in the 1970s, that the objective condition of workers as providers of labor power alienated from them by a ruling elite is the key to understanding the nature of Soviet society, its inefficiencies, waste, shortages, and other characteristic features. Forged in the Stalin era, the structural antagonisms between the creators of the surplus product and the expropriators help explain the long-term decline of the Soviet system and its eventual collapse.

Just as social and political history are inseparably intertwined, any discussion of Stalinism sooner or later touches on the question of violence. Influenced by social history and insights from the study of other fields, several of our contributors shed different lights on Stalinist bloodshed. While not denying Stalin's role as author of the Terror, Wendy Goldman, Lynne Viola, and Gábor Rittersporn argue that Stalin's personality cannot alone explain the violence. They look elsewhere: Viola to the village, Goldman and Rittersporn to social conflicts. They draw our attention to the ways agency, power, and input existed on many levels and were important components of the 1930s violence. Officials and ordinary people from all walks of life were neither unwitting pawns nor initiators of terror, but they were part of it. Without making a facile argument about terror emanating from below, our contributors argue that local participation or acquiescence were key elements of the violence, contexts that help explain how it unfolded as it did.

Goldman's chapter begins by providing a personal overview of her trajectory as a historian of Stalinist society and politics. Beginning in the early 1990s, her immersion in the archives demonstrated that Stalinism could best be understood as a dialectical process involving social pressure, state response, and new realities, which posed their own problems in turn. Like Filtzer and Rittersporn, she is interested in social antagonisms. For Goldman, the interplay of broad social forces and state policies "produced a propulsive dialectic that determined the beginning, escalation, and end of the Terror." Similarly, her more recent work has stressed not only state policies like wartime evacuation, rationing, deportation, and labor mobilization, but their dynamic relationship to people's material needs, the flourishing black markets, and widespread disobedience of draconian labor laws.

Rittersporn also explores the contradictory relationship between violence and power. Like Filtzer, Goldman, and Viola, he highlights social antagonisms that were inherently part of the Stalin system. He argues that between the February and October revolutions of 1917, there was an even larger social upheaval, which he calls the "April Revolution," when peasants seized the land. It was the April Revolution that peasants remembered and later defended against Stalinist collectivization. During the Stalinist forced transformations of the 1930s, villagers and workers resisted the demands of the state, and like the managerial cadres in the state itself, they devised strategies to cope with and resist the demands of that state and its leaders. Rittersporn argues that paradoxically the state could not function without these dysfunctional schemes and conflicts, and that Stalin's attempts to enforce obedience were therefore bound to fail. Stalin was a powerful dictator but one who could not always control the outcomes of his actions in an "inherently confused and inefficient dictatorship."

In offering perspectives on Stalinist violence, William Chase's contribution shows how *Ezhovshchina*, *Stalinshchina*, Great Terror, and Great Purges are each inadequate to describe what happened in the 1930s. Chase provides striking new information on the show trial of 1936 and reminds us how much of the standard view of Stalinism comes from Lev Trotsky. Even though Trotsky publicly denied any operational connection to underground followers in the Soviet Union, it turns out that he and his son Sedov were actively engaged with them, and in the murky world of émigré politics in the 1930s, with others connected to Nazis. These connections, even twice or thrice removed, provided the background for Stalin's claims that the oppositionists were German agents.

Stalin perhaps inevitably has provoked efforts by scholars to explain his psychological makeup. Ronald Suny and Arch Getty depart from this tradition by connecting Stalin with broader political and social practices. Suny's chapter plumbs the emotional states induced by the October Revolution and what followed. He seeks to account not only for Stalin's own individual "affective disposition" as he passed through periods of intense revolutionary activity, civil war, intraparty squabbling, and the immense challenges of collectivization and the hunting down of suspected conspirators but also popular attitudes, enthusiasms, resentments, and fears as they danced dialectically with efforts to shape consciousness and commitment from above.

Getty also discusses emotions, specifically the roles of fear and belief in the unfolding of Stalinist violence. He argues that Stalin and the Bolsheviks' experience caused them to fear for the fragility of their regime, and that "fear-induced aggression" was an important precipitant of the violence of the 1930s. He argues that Stalin's fear of conspiracy was not something he invented or inflicted on society but was rather a widely shared belief from top to bottom of party and society, stemming from class conflict, Russian "underground" traditions, and Civil War experience.

Many scholars have studied Stalinist ideology as part of a debate on continuity: how close was Stalin's ideology to Lenin's or Marx's? Here Alfred Rieber and Lars Lih offer fresh perspectives. Rieber's chapter shows how Stalin "followed Lenin's path, but not always in his footsteps." While following Marx's basic schema, Stalin expanded the theoretical role of the superstructure, making it a tool of transformation rather than simply a function of the economic base. Rieber is thus able to link Stalin's views on socialism in one country, the autonomy of language, the heroization of the Russian people, a history of great men rather than impersonal economic forces, the end of class conflict, and a strict legalism in foreign policy, all into a consistent (and for Stalin, convenient) theoretical whole.

That Stalin had more in mind than simply inflicting violence, that he took himself seriously as a Marxist and Leninist, and that we should do so as well is the thrust of Lih's characteristically contrarian contribution. Lih's methodology is as straightforward as it is rare: give close readings of texts and do not be swayed by prevailing orthodoxies. In this case, he nails Stalin for "exorcising" in his *Foundations of Leninism* (1924) the German Social Democrat Karl Kautsky, assigning to Lenin Kautsky's role as "authoritative spokesman of revolutionary Marxism," and he finds Stalin in 1938 desperately seeking to occupy the role of the "Lenin of today" to justify collectivization post hoc as the new October.

Viola suggests a spatial dimension with respect to the other major social constituency of Stalinist society—the peasantry. She uses Stathis Kalyvas's concept of "rurality" to examine the consequences of "under-government" in the Soviet Russian countryside, namely the campaign-style policy implementation of dekulakization, collectivization, and the mass operations and the violent explosions this method of governing produced throughout the 1930s. Contrary to long-held assumptions about violence as the expression of power, Viola follows Hannah Arendt in suggesting the opposite: that violence stems from a lack of power.

Karl Schlögel goes further and argues for a focus on space rather than time as a historical narrative. His iconoclastic chapter challenges the utility of a sequential temporal approach in general, the almost exclusive fixation on the temporal dimension. "There is no history of 'Stalinism' beyond the violent transformation of spaces." Contradictory events such as terror and enthusiasm, destruction and construction, old and new building styles, and states of emergency and normality all happened in one place, and we should think more in terms of spatial simultaneity than sequential progression. To grasp the co-existence of extremes, he argues, we need a stereoscopic-panoramic overview of what happened because events took place not only in time but also in places.

We hope the reader will find all these contributions equally panoramic. They offer the reader reflections based on long experience and thought while at the same time contributing both new and refined insights.

Part One

The Social

CHAPTER 1

Personal Reflections on Stalinism and Social History

LEWIS H. SIEGELBAUM

It is all perfectly clear now. It is a story told before, many times. First came the "totalitarianists," the Cold Warriors, those who identified the Soviet Union as a repressive, stultifying country whose leaders sought global domination in the name of anti-imperialism and, ultimately, communism. These scholars overwhelmingly situated in political science departments, some with government service in their pasts, got their start during the upsurge of Soviet studies in the 1950s, when first Columbia, then Harvard, then other august institutions lent their prestige to the founding of Russian institutes and the Department of Defense (previously, the Department of War) granted its dollars.

Born of the late Stalin period and the turbulent years that followed, the theory of totalitarianism saw a self-aggrandizing state swallowing society, its purpose being nothing more than self-perpetuation via monopolizing the reins of power. Similarly, continuity from the October Revolution (if not before) on was stressed when looking back to origins. The Bolsheviks under Lenin were incipient totalitarians. Their antipathy toward democracy and markets impelled them to seize and hold onto power in the name of the proletariat. Politics, insofar as they existed in Soviet-type polities, consisted of inner-party struggles that barely broke the surface—and even then, visible only to the discerning eyes of Kremlinologists—until, like lava, blood flowed from the volcanic eruptions of purges.

Not until the 1970s, the story goes, would the stranglehold of totalitarian theory weaken. Credit belongs to a younger generation of scholars, including political scientists and political historians. Thanks to them, Stalinism, a term used up to that point pejoratively by Trotsky and his supporters, entered the scholarly vocabulary. It referred to a whole complex of state practices, ideological principles, and discursive tics that permeated the lives of Soviet citizens from the late 1920s until 1953 and, in some respects, for years thereafter. For the so-called revisionists, a term that took hold by the mid-1980s and has persisted to the present, the theory of totalitarianism rested on erroneous assumptions about how both the Communist Party and the Soviet state functioned, vastly exaggerating Stalin's power to realize his aims or even know what was going on down below. This is not to say revisionists soft-pedaled the lethality of the Great Terror or other bouts of state violence under Stalin. On the contrary, the impression one got from much of Arch Getty's work, for example, is that something approaching the Hobbesian state of *bellum omnium contra omnes* existed, at least during the late 1930s (Getty 1985). Yet somehow revisionists occasionally were accused of being soft on Stalin, if not on communism.

This story is not wrong, but it is incomplete. It effaces one of the main currents of research on the Soviet Union's history from the October Revolution until the Great Patriotic War, namely, social history. Because I contributed to that current—not consistently, but for a major part of my career—I will be reflecting on my work as well as that of many others, almost all of whom I have known personally, some as close friends. This is to say that there is a strong subjective element to these reflections, but it is at least somewhat critical and especially self-critical.

In 1978, Sheila Fitzpatrick noted that "Stalin's Russia is still almost uncharted territory for the historian." She then proceeded to employ a profoundly social historical interpretation of the upheavals of the late 1920s and early 1930s that she labeled "cultural revolution." She argued that they stemmed from the "unleashing" of social groups that had been agitating for "more militant and radical policies," that Stalin's revolution from above depended on a "revolution from below," and that the cultural revolution was a "class war . . . waged on behalf of the proletariat" (Fitzpatrick 1978, 6–7, 8–40). In a monograph published a year later, she took up the process that made it possible for what Moshe Lewin had referred to as "newcomers from the popular classes" to arrive in positions of higher social status and authority, namely, the massive, organized promotion of workers and communists to institutions of higher education (Fitzpatrick 1979). Fitzpatrick argued that *vydvizhenie* was essential to the making of Milovan Djilas's "New Class." It also not incidentally produced broad support among its beneficiaries for the Stalin regime and what the émigré sociologist Nicholas Timasheff had called "the Great Retreat," the restoration of traditional norms and values after the turbulence of the Cultural Revolution. Fitzpatrick's book drew on materials from three different state archives in Moscow that would remain out of the reach of other Western researchers for nearly another decade.

By the mid-1980s, she could discern three distinct approaches in published work by and informal discussions among historians that, to a greater or lesser degree, revised the old state-centered, from above perspective on Stalinism. One, represented in work on criminal justice and the prosecution of collectivization, stressed the tenuousness of central party control over local organs and the latter's improvisation and radical initiatives. A second pointed to the ways that social pressures of both a critical and supportive nature "must to some degree shape, constrain and modify the actions of the party leadership." Practitioners of this approach, such as Arch Getty and Gabor Rittersporn, linked the Great Purges of 1936–38 to tensions "within the bureaucracy as well as popular grievances against the new Soviet bosses." The third and most radically revisionist approach had yet to be fleshed out but seemed to emanate from Fitzpatrick's own hypothesis of "revolution from below." As for an agenda for future research, she suggested, quite controversially as it turned out, that historians consider discarding "the assumption that the only significant social relations in the Soviet Union are those in which society relates to government" and "try turning their attention elsewhere." She also recommended somewhat contradictorily that social historians turn their attention to the Great Terror, albeit without moralizing or counter-moralizing (Fitzpatrick 1986, 371, 373, 410–11).

Fitzpatrick's article inspired four responses that appeared along with it in the October 1986 issue of *The Russian Review*. A year later, indicative of the seriousness of the issues raised by the exchange, the same journal published comments by eleven specialists in the field, six from the new cohort of social (aka revisionist) historians, and five from more senior scholars. Above versus below, models and epistemologies, interpretation and methodology, political subtexts and subjectivities, (quasi-)Marxist and liberal inspirations, the 1920s versus the 1930s—reactions ran the gamut. This was just before a veritable flood of historical work on the Soviet interwar period began to appear in print. Part of this outpouring, thanks to Mikhail Gorbachev's policy of glasnost, had to do with the granting of access to pertinent archives. Partly, it reflected the ever-expanding appeal of social history not only among Russianists but in the historical profession at large, both in the United States and elsewhere. And within social history, labor history, previously channeled into institutional accounts or dammed up entirely, contributed mightily to the flood.

It would be left to a younger generation, those who earned their PhDs in the 1970s, to construct a narrative about what happened to workers after the revolution the Bolsheviks made in the name of workers' emancipation from the shackles of capitalist oppression. Among the questions they addressed were: Did the proletariat disintegrate during the civil war as Lenin complained at the time and some Western historians would later contend? Did the opening of the party to masses of new workers during the Lenin levy of 1924 lead to the party's dilution? Was there a crisis of proletarian identity among older, skilled (male) workers toward the end of the 1920s as comparatively raw youths without any direct experience of the revolution and increasing numbers of women entered the industrial workforce? In light of the persistence of patriarchal relations in the villages, rural ties among workers, and the particularism of work culture among workers in different industries and regions, does it make sense to speak of an all-embracing class consciousness?

These questions represented efforts to understand the Stalinist outcome of inner party struggles by analyzing what was going on down below. That is, they embodied a social dimension to a story hitherto told almost entirely from above. Seeking answers to them meant wading into and trying to make sense of the world of work as it existed half a century earlier. It meant reconstructing the technologies of the time and the shopfloor arrangements—skill definitions, wage rates, disciplinary procedures, and much else—that managerial-technical staff deemed appropriate to fulfilling the tasks assigned by neophyte planning agencies. But that was not enough. One had to dig deeper to try to recover the everyday lives of workers and their families and in the process determine, as Diane Koenker would in *Republic of Labor*, her marvelous book about printers in Moscow, the often-subtle differences between the cultures—working-class, socialist, and proletarian—that competed for their affinities (Koenker 2005).

One had to do this conscious of seeking a moving target. During the 1920s the Soviet industrial workforce underwent significant demographic changes. It then changed on an even greater scale and more profoundly during the First Five-Year Plan years (1928–32) thanks to the massive influx of peasants fleeing collectivization and starvation, the egress of cadre workers upward via factory schools into management and party positions, and outward via relocation to new industrial installations. One had to learn the peculiarities of party-speak—*obezlichka* (depersonalization), *krugovaia poruka* (passing the buck), *lzheudarnichestvo* (phony shock work), *uravnilovka* (petty bourgeois egalitarianism), and so on—to get at the subterranean war the party waged against the institutions and practices that workers often informally organized to protect themselves from the vagaries of the individual piece-rate system and other Taylorist-inspired measures then in vogue.

Here, I will shift from the anonymous indefinite pronoun ("one") and references to other individual practitioners to recall my own contributions to this literature. My first effort, appearing in a then-obscure Australian journal, concerned "shock work" (*udarnichestvo*) and "socialist competition" (*sotssorevnovanie*, for short) during the 1920s and early 1930s. It was all about young workers, inspired by the Komsomol and the prospect of being showered with prestige, pledging to fulfill, or better still overfulfill their quotas and encouraging others to emulate their example. It was about the triumph of productivism, which (and I quote from the conclusion) "socialist competition both reflected and promoted." The article included references to the production collectives and communes that workers formed, particularly in the metalworks and textile industries, but did not ponder their significance. By 1986 when I published an entire article devoted to them, I had decided that their relation to socialist competition was "problematic." They were, rather "fortresses erected by workers to defend themselves from the depredations caused by forced-pace industrialization and collectivization, even while those policies elicited much support among them. Behind these fortresses, collectivists and communards set high standards for themselves, maintained their own forms of labor discipline, and generally exhibited high productivity." But their independence from both managerial and party supervision doomed them, and these fortresses were successfully stormed, with Stalin denouncing them at the Seventeenth Party Congress in 1934 as "infantile egalitarian exercises" (Siegelbaum 1986, 65, 84).

What was I trying to do here? Ron Suny, a dear friend, observed that I was using social history as a means of trying to rescue socialism from Stalin. I do not know if that observation is correct. I might have been trying to save Soviet workers—retrospectively—from the obloquy of having succumbed to their own pacification. I would repeat that effort in subsequent years by investigating other working-class-based institutions and practices, such as the trade union-organized comrades-disciplinary courts of the early Soviet period, decrying the role that output norms and foremen played in imposing labor discipline, and deploring the upsurge and then concealment of industrial accidents. This is part of what I later referred to as "the late romance of the Soviet worker" (Siegelbaum 2006).

To be sure, I was not alone in that affair. Much of the labor history from the 1970s and 1980s could be said to have been motivated, consciously or unconsciously, by a desire to save the working class, if not from Stalin, then, in E. P. Thompson's immortal phrase, from "the enormous condescension of posterity." The aspirations of Soviet workers may have been casualties of Stalinism -much like those of their English predecessors were of the original Industrial Revolution—but rediscovering their struggles and celebrating the strategies they employed in them could nonetheless be inspirational. Donald Filtzer, at least in my reading of *Soviet Workers and Stalinist Industrialization* (1986)—the first of four he published on the industrial working class under successive political administrations, was trying to do the same thing.

We—and others—were both fascinated and appalled by what was done in the name of building socialism during those decades. We were drawn to industrial work sites because of the Soviet romance with steel and coal and probably also because of our own materialist assumptions. Mesmerized by the Stalinist regime's success in expropriating labor, our gaze rarely left the shop floor. We thus tended to ignore or refer only in passing to such dimensions of workers' identities as nationality, gender, and familial relations because they did not appear to impinge on the production process. We cleaved to collective subjects because, as labor historians, we believed that it was through them that individuals obtained social agency.

The opening of Soviet archives in the 1990s made it possible to get closer to the shop floor and follow the process of class formation as it occurred in specific enterprises. Two monographs published in that decade by David L. Hoffmann and Kenneth M. Strauss used such material to analyze how Moscow's factories forged new Soviet workers out of peasant migrants. That the books differed markedly in their interpretations of the degree of integration—Strauss seeing the factory as a "social melting pot" and "community organizer" in contrast to Hoffmann, who (perhaps channeling Lewin) argued that the in-migrants turned Moscow into a "peasant metropolis"—made for more than a few stimulating conference panel discussions and reviews.

The social history of Stalinism consisted of more than labor history, and its practitioners had many different objectives and perspectives. Lewin, the godfather of the field throughout the 1970s and 1980s, marshaled social history to underscore the inappropriateness and the tragedy of "the superstructure rushing ahead," that is, the Stalin revolution that produced, in his inimitable terms, "the quicksand society" and "the ruralization of the cities" (Lewin 1985). Sheila Fitzpatrick took a different approach. In *Stalin's Peasants*, she exploited her access to Soviet archives to highlight everyday life in the countryside—kolkhoz organization, *otkhodniki* (seasonal workers), religious practices, crime and violence, and so on. The book, as its subtitle announced, was essentially about "survival in the Russian village after collectivization." The subtitle also mentioned "resistance," which overwhelmingly consisted of "hidden transcripts" and other forms of subterfuge (Fitzpatrick 1994).

The theme of surviving Stalinism through subterfuge might well be considered one of the lodestones of social historical analysis of the period, in no small measure thanks to Fitzpatrick. In *Stalin's Peasants* and its urban equivalent, *Everyday Stalinism*, she sought to explain how everyday-life stratagems—petitioning and patronage, exchanging favors, pretending, and otherwise playing the government's game—helped ordinary Soviet Russians survive. She would go on to produce an entire book about the artifice of imposture—mostly concerning the Bolsheviks' obsession with identifying people according to social class or, as she provocatively argued, ascribing class as a means of determining obligations and entitlements, thereby enabling individuals to play off this obsession by inventing working-class backgrounds (Fitzpatrick 1999, 2005).

Others had yet another take on the ways ordinary citizens reacted to—or interacted with—the Soviet state. For example, in *Magnetic Mountain* Stephen Kotkin adapted Michel Foucault's understanding of power in the modern world to explore the "little tactics of the habitat" among Magnitogorsk's hastily assembled workforce. These tactics involved "learning the rules of daily life" so that they could be bent to the new inhabitants' advantage by "realigning, even if only slightly, . . . the landscape of possibility." In successive chapters, he examined living space, the proper discourse to discuss one's work and oneself (famously characterized as "speaking Bolshevik"), consumption, and participation in the state's politics, including the Terror (Kotkin 1995).

Magnetic Mountain's subtitle was "Stalinism as a Civilization." This is not unlike Fitzpatrick's *Everyday Stalinism* or the book I coedited with Andrei Sokolov, which we called *Stalinism as a Way of Life*. Containing 157 translated documents from 1929 to 1940, that book found resistance accompanying "every major state initiative of the 1930s," though it also cited adaptive behaviors "between the extremes of resistance . . . and abject compliance" (Siegelbaum and Sokolov 2000, 11, 14). Among these, I would like to single out labor activism because I earlier had devoted an entire book to precisely that phenomenon. Published in 1988, that is, before most of the works I have been discussing, my study of Stakhanovism defined it as "both a state policy and a social phenomenon," and sought to determine whether the enthusiasm evinced by leading Stakhanovites for raising their own productivity was genuine and if so, whence it came (Siegelbaum 1988, xii).

Amazingly, two other books on Stakhanovism, one in Italian and the other in German, appeared in print within a three-year span (Benvenuti 1988; Maier 1990). Like me, Francesco Benvenuti and Robert Maier were searching for hidden meanings and motivations while also pursuing implications and consequences. But they posed their questions mostly about the leading party and technical personnel. Evidently, they found it impossible to imagine that workers could believe that increasing their productivity would redound to their and their fellow workers' benefit. Why was I willing to entertain that possibility? Could it have been that I was trying to save these workers' reputations after decades of their pummeling as stooges of party and managerial bosses?

Only once more did I track down these types—the Stakhanovites, or as they were referred to in correspondence that I discovered in the archives among the materials of an obscure trade union, "notables" (*znatnye liudi*)—this time, rural-based prize-winning livestock and dairy state farm workers. I published an article on them under the title "Dear Comrade, You Ask What We Need." This time, I claimed to be investigating what I called "socialist paternalism," as manifested in "the politics of distribution." What really animated the project was coming into close proximity with these prize-winners whose trade union had asked them what they needed. This, after all, is the privilege of doing social history—of encountering such people on their own turf and listening to what they have to say. Of course, this was an illusion. Of course, what these people wrote in response to their trade union's solicitations was constrained. And yet, when the historian encounters a "noted milkmaid" from a state farm in Pridneprov'e reporting that since the death of her husband three years ago, she had "become a human being," stood on her own feet, was raising her children, and was "twice as happy as any man," or when, by contrast, another prize-winning milkmaid complained that she had to look after her two children, ages two years and eight months, because there was no daycare, that she had to prepare food because there was no cafeteria, that there was nothing in the shops and that "from a Stakhanovite of production, I have become a slave of the kitchen," well, then, you sit up and take notice and maybe even sympathize (Siegelbaum 2000, 247–48).

The same volume in which "Dear Comrade" appeared also contained a contribution from Jochen Hellbeck. "Fashioning the Stalinist Soul" introduced what would become a significant advance in thinking about, as the opening line put it, "how members of Soviet society subjectively experienced the Stalinist system." This "subjectivity school," most fully elaborated in *Revolution on My Mind* (Hellbeck 2006), represented a clear departure from social history and, ultimately, the loss of its prestige. It challenged social history's animus and conceptual frameworks in three significant ways: its primary subjects were not collective social actors but rather the magnetic influence of the revolutionary project and its discourses on individuals and their sense of "self"; it stressed the growing importance of professional expertise in the human sciences and other indices of "modernity"; and it recast the relationship between Bolshevism and Stalinism largely in terms of continuity, thereby returning, albeit via a different route, to an earlier historiographic position.

One can find antecedents of the idea of a distinctly Soviet (or totalitarian) subjectivity in some of the work of Sovietology's founding fathers, as well as that of such literary scholars as Katerina Clark, Vladislav Todorov, and Thomas Lahusen. Still, the argument that Stalinist Manichean categories exercised a monopolistic influence over Soviet citizens' subjectivity sparked considerable polemics in the early years of the new millennium. It also clashed with the perspective on Soviet identity that Sheila Fitzpatrick advanced in *Everyday Stalinism*—that of the pragmatic, rational actor, the materially obsessed *Homo Sovieticus*—as well as his/her more playful cousins, the trickster and the impostor. If Fitzpatrick was fascinated by Soviet individuals working *for* themselves, then the subjectivists insisted on their efforts to work *on* themselves.

Like social historians, subjectivists took seriously the Stalinist project of modernization but shifted the optic toward interiority. "In their works," write Choi Chatterjee and Karen Petrone, "modernization . . . happens at the level of the subject and, more pertinently, within the soul. Processes of industrialization, collectivization, the apparatuses of terror, and social formations play a limited role in these histories" (Chatterjee and Petrone 2008, 977) or none at all. Soviet subjects seek not so much to master the principles of Marxism-Leninism or navigate through the turbid waters of the state's repressive apparatus but rather, according to Igal Halfin, to read the hermeneutics of the soul, or in Hellbeck's terms, to perfect their revolutionary selves.

Chatterjee and Petrone are right to see the emphasis on subjectivity as part of a larger intellectual project that, inspired by Foucault by way of Kotkin, sought to place the Soviet experience within the pan-European framework of modernity, meaning attempts to reshape individual mentalities through state intervention and the application of science. In the analyses of such historians as Oleg Kharkhordin (1999) and David Hoffmann (2003, 2011), the masses are "cultivated" to adopt certain "behavioral and cultural norms" and discourses consistent with and derived from the Stalinist state's modernization project. These authors and others (Pinnow 2010, for example) stress the role of the social sciences—statistics, sociology, demography, psychology, criminology—no less than Marxism in advancing the "New Soviet Person." Comparisons with and the attribution of inspiration from Western practices are integral.

This literature has had considerable appeal. For one thing, it linked up with linguistic theory—all the rage in the humanities around the turn of the millennium—interpreting class as a discursive construct rather than a social category. For another, its emphasis on individual rather than collective subjects reflected and reinforced the shift away from collectivist thinking of all kinds toward individualism and identity politics, themselves perhaps connected to the collapse of state socialism in the East, the weakening of socialist parties and trade unions in the West, and the concomitant rise of neo-liberalism just about everywhere. This, then, is the story—the amended story—at least through the early years of the new millennium, by which time social history as a mode of historical analysis was exhibiting distinct signs of becoming passé. Added to this, studying the Stalin era began to lose its centrality as more and more historians looked to developments in the post-Stalin decades.

Except that the story did not end there. On the contrary, thanks in part to the infusion in the past few decades of new scholarly voices from outside the Anglophone world, the social history of the Stalin era has turned out to be greater in quantity and has made a larger contribution to understanding how the Soviet masses experienced Stalinism than what had appeared in print up to that point. And not only the Soviet masses. It surely would not be amiss to acknowledge here the importance of Central and East Europeanist historiography, particularly in labor history. Dissatisfied with both Cold War-inspired histories of betrayal as well as émigré intellectuals' philosophizing, Anglophone historians of East-Central Europe began turning out articles and monographs already in the 1990s on the complex relationship between working classes and communist parties during the relatively brief period between the end of the Second World War and the de-Stalinization of the mid-1950s. These few years saw respective east European parties adapting to their national situations policies honed by the CPSU over the previous three decades: nationalizing industry, disenfranchising landlord and bourgeois elements, extracting surplus value from peasants by price scissors followed by collectivization, and squeezing productivity from workers via Taylorist techniques and heroic efforts such as Stakhanovism.

But the emphasis of the new work was on the social history of these efforts, that is, treating workers not as objects of party bosses' directives but as agents capable of exercising their collective power, sometimes in support of party objectives and sometimes opposed to them, sometimes in the factory or on building sites and sometimes in recreation and consumption. Such an approach is evident in Padraic Kenney's *Rebuilding Poland* (Kenney 1997), which contrasted the effective resistance of Lödz textile workers to communists' attempts to appropriate their traditional institutions to the complaisance among rural recruits mobilized to rebuild the city of Wroclaw. Mark Pittaway would similarly frame *The Worker's State* (Pittaway 2012), his study of three different Hungarian industrial communities. A factory town near Budapest, a cluster of coal mining villages west of the capital, and oilfields located in a rural area along Hungary's southwestern border with Yugoslavia, each had its own socio-economic specificities and hence political ecology. Pittaway's book also partook of the history of emotions by repeatedly citing workers' "fury," "fear and resentment," and even "hysteria" sometimes against other workers (e.g., Stakhanovites) but also against the Hungarian Workers Party and the State Security Agency. In this sense, it represented the antithesis of *Unfinished Utopia* (Lebow 2013), Katherine Lebow's history of the founding and populating of Poland's Nowa Huta, which evoked workers' enthusiasm for effectuating the ballyhooed social transformation accompanying socialist construction.

In the meantime, social historians from the region itself began to enter the conversation. Several articles on "Labor in Postwar Central and Eastern Europe" were a harbinger when they appeared in the journal *International Labor and Working-Class History* in 2005. Introduced by Mark Pittaway, the special issue addressed party recruitment in Romania, working-class life in Sztálinváros (Hungary's equivalent to Magnitogorsk and Nowa Huta), a prize-winning female workers' brigade in a Hungarian hosiery factory, and Czechoslovak factory and mine workers' reactions to incentive schemes. Cross-fertilization thereupon followed, culminating in an outstanding volume on "the history of work" in the eastern bloc countries with contributions on finding a job, workers' rights, issues of safety and risk, and on-the-job protest and reform (Seifert 2020).

Here, I can briefly sketch out longer works by two of the contributors. Adrian Grama's ethnography of postwar Romanian industrial workers, his dissertation for CEU from 2017, skillfully adapted several well-known conceptual and methodological frameworks, including Carlo Ginzburg's *ricerca micronominativa*; Alf Lüdtke's *Eigen-Sinn*; Mark Pittaway's definition of legitimacy; and William Sewell Jr.'s "organization of difference." It demonstrated innovativeness as well in its construction of "fragmented biographies," incorporation of socialist realist fiction as part of the Romanian Communist Party's meaning-making activity, and emphasis on interstitial categories (Grama 2017). Also about Romania, Alina-Sander Cucu's *Planning Labour* is a Marxist-inflected historical anthropology of work in a state socialist setting—in this case, two factories in Cluj—with a strikingly original interpretation of central planning. For Cucu, the plan "had to be juggled against the multiple temporalities of primitive socialist accumulation"; it was both anticipatory and corrective, seeking to achieve increased productivity even while promoting new social differentiations. The choice of Cluj, "at the margins of postwar economic life," is counterintuitively brilliant, for it is here in central Transylvania, where class was "systematically hidden under ethnicized processes of identification," that class formation under socialism could occur de novo (Cucu 2019, 4, 24, 25).

This recent literature on postwar east-central Europe resuscitated some of the issues that had animated social historians of Soviet Stalinism in the 1980s and 1990s but did so on a more sophisticated theoretical foundation. The temporal disjuncture is striking, for when, after the new millennium, the second wave of social histories on the Soviet version of Stalinism emerged in the West, it was less marked by Marxist categories and less focused on industrial labor than both the first wave and the works appearing simultaneously among east-central Europeanists. There were exceptions. In 2005, two unambiguously Marxist histories of worker militance and its repression appeared in print: Jeffrey Rossman's *Worker Resistance under Stalin*, a fine-grained study of protests at a provincial textile factory in 1932, and Kevin Murphy's *Revolution and Counterrevolution: Class Struggle in a Moscow Metal Factory*, a forthright treatment of longer-term shopfloor conflict at the same Hammer and Sickle factory studied by Kenneth Strauss a decade earlier. But, by and large, new sensibilities made for new emphases—gender, above all, but also its intersection with class, nationality, and other identities—as well as what could be considered the new economic history.

Collectivization remained a pertinent topic though now with prominence given to deracination. Lynne Viola, for example, followed 2,000,000 dekulakized peasants to the special settlements established in remote regions of the country in the early 1930s. Utilizing archival records from the state's carceral institutions as well as published documents and memoirs, *The Unknown Gulag* (Viola 2007) contains a double narrative, alternating between the OGPU (Joint State Political Administration) as it tried to get ahead of the unfolding catastrophe of too many people and too few resources, and the peasants themselves, the appalling conditions to which they were subjected, and how they coped. Neither is represented in one-dimensional terms. Some of the "company men," Viola's term for the commandants, were more conscientious and humane than others. This approach to an occupational group that rarely has attracted any empathy would be repeated in her more recent monograph on *Stalinist Perpetrators* during the Great Terror in Ukraine (Viola 2017).

Collectivization comprises the spinal chapter in Sarah Cameron's gripping account of the forced sedentarization of—and subsequent famine among—Kazakh mobile pastoralists. Presented as a counternarrative to the better-known Ukrainian *Holodomor*, *The Hungry Steppe* offers new insight into Stalinism's merciless "modernization" of the Soviet East, read as a nation-making project (Cameron 2018). That project, Cameron is at pains to point out, included Kazakhs not merely as victims but also as participants/victimizers. Indeed, access to indigenous sources helps to expose the many internal divisions among Kazakhs as well as their multiple survival strategies.

But not all the revived social histories are about violence and responses to it. Consumption drew the attention of historians interested in everyday life, the service industry, gender, and social hierarchies based on special access to goods and services. Here, Elena Osokina's books from the 1990s paved the way. While Julie Hessler's *Social History of Soviet Trade* (Hessler 2004) covered the ground comprehensively from the revolution to Stalin's death, Amy Randall's *Soviet Dream World of Retail Trade and Consumption* (Randall 2008) focused on techniques to replace the drudgery of seeking desired goods and providing them during the 1930s with transactions between worthy "citizen-consumers" and cultured "Stakhanovite" sales personnel. Jukka Gronow's *Caviar with Champagne* meanwhile narrowed the focus even further to those two luxury goods that the Commissar of Trade Anastas Mikoian made "common," that is, accessible and within the price range of ordinary citizens, unlike in capitalist countries (Gronow 2003).

Diane Koenker, whose earlier exposure of discrimination by male printers of their female coworkers constituted a distinct departure from the aforementioned "late romance," decided to pursue workers on vacation as tourists and rest home residents. In a series of articles and then in *Club Red*, she examined "the struggle to balance purpose and pleasure," that is, the interface between the state's therapeutic and socializing regimes with workers' determination to relax and have fun. The book follows the evolution of the institutions serving these needs from the 1920s to well beyond the Stalin era. It demonstrates that what had originated as a "largely purposeful, medical, and state-oriented agenda" was transformed by the mid-1930s into "an experience emphasizing individual pleasure, comfort, knowledge, and even escape, . . . [which] neither the war nor the death of Stalin significantly altered"—a kind of happy middle ground productive of a lot of nostalgia (Koenker 2013, 284).

Around the new millennium, Wendy Goldman, like Koenker, focused on gender as the key variable, producing the influential monograph *Women at the Gates* (Goldman 2002) on women workers in the 1930s. But then she published two monographs on the Great Terror in the factories and the trade unions (Goldman 2007, 2011) that demonstrated the intimate connection between democratic and repressive practices, that is, the power struggles on and off the shop floor often inflected by class-based suspicions and resentments. *Inventing the Enemy*, the latter book, focused on ordinary people and their denunciatory practices in five Moscow factories, providing a microhistorical perspective from the bottom-up on a subject once dominated by political historians and novelists. More recently, Goldman coedited with Donald Filtzer a volume on food production and provisioning during the Great Patriotic War— the hierarchies of provisioning, the physiological dimensions of food deprivation, the pervasiveness of hunger, and the reality of starvation (Goldman and Filtzer 2015). And, in 2021, they crowned their collaborative efforts with a monograph on the home front. This, too, is social history of the expansive kind, covering evacuation, food distribution, illicit trade, labor both "free" and coerced, and healthcare (Goldman and Filtzer 2021).

Considered beyond the ken of social historical inquiry before its second wave, the Great Patriotic War now presents something of an embarras de richesses. Books on Soviet soldiers—Catherine Merridale's *Ivan's War* (2006), Anna Krylova's *Soviet Women in Combat* (2010), and Roger Markwick and Euridice Cardona's *Soviet Women on the Frontline* (2012)—blazed the path for others that have analyzed the role of the Komsomol in guiding Soviet youth through the war, and discussed in inventive ways the objects (mess kits, rations, helmets, boots, knapsacks, weapons, etc.) that soldiers used. When it appeared in 2009, *To the Tashkent Station,* Rebecca Manley's book on evacuation during the war broke new ground. Working with material from archives in Uzbekistan as well as Odesa, Vologda, St. Petersburg, and Moscow, Manley reconstructed the journeys to the east—primarily to the Uzbek SSR's capital—of Soviet citizens in danger of falling under Nazi occupation. In aiming "to reintegrate the war into the social, cultural, and political history of the Soviet Union," she reconstructed not only the Herculean effort of state authorities who made up the Evacuation Council and its regional offices, but evacuees' strategies when faced with their "organized redistribution" their relations with their hosts, and ultimately, their return home (Manley 2009, 6).

To date, the most comprehensive social historical treatment of the war is Goldman and Filtzer's book. Additional scholarship in article form or monographs still in the pipeline has benefited from the Center for the History and Sociology of World War II and Its Consequences at Moscow's Higher School of Economics. Under the directorship of Oleg Budnitskii, the center has sponsored post-doctoral fellowships and hosted conferences on such topics as "Europe 1945: Liberation, Occupation, Retribution" (2015), "Stalinism and the War" (2016), "The Second World War and Problems of Soviet History" (2019), and "Oral History of the Great Patriotic War: Practices of Compilation and Interpretation" (2019). Websites devoted to the memories of Red Army veterans and other survivors of the war (see, for example, "I remember/ia pomniu," www.iremember.ru) promise to enrich further publications.

When in 1998 Elena Zubkova published her monograph on everyday life in the post-war years, she had the field to herself. The book challenged Vera Dunham's thesis, derived from her reading of literary sources, of a big deal between the party-state and what Dunham termed the Soviet middle class—essentially mid-level bureaucrats, the scientific-technical and cultural intelligentsias. But it did more than that. Using a broader swath of sources that included state security assessments based on intercepted correspondence, diaries, memoirs, interviews, and literary fiction, Zubkova assessed "the public outlook," that is, the expectations and disappointments of overwhelmingly Russian workers, peasants, and other sections of Soviet society (Zubkova 1998). It thereby mapped the terrain on which others would situate their own work in years to come. Soviet trade practices, the repatriation of POWs and *Ostarbeiter*, war veterans as an interest group, monetary assistance, and currency reform are just some of the topics that other scholars, many of them trained at the University of Chicago under Sheila Fitzpatrick, have treated as social history. Not to be overlooked are Donald Filtzer's *Hazards of Urban Life* (2010), a characteristically hard-hitting investigation into the "health, hygiene, and living standards" of late-Stalinist Russian cities, and Juliane Fürst's lively cultural history of *Stalin's Last Generation*, replete with sections on being female and male after the war, and how, more generally, "Soviet society adopted new life and survival strategies, designed to make life more bearable and fun" (Fürst 2010, 269–83, 339).

So, what happened to saving socialism? When in about 2010 I reinvented myself as a historian of migration, I did not burden myself with this task. Rather, Leslie Moch and I used social history for what it is better equipped to do—emphasize the agency of both individuals and groups in circumstances not of their own making. In *Broad Is My Native Land*, we applied the conceptual framework of repertoires and regimes of migration and the myriad ways they interacted. If we gave "due importance to state plans and perspectives," the regimes of migration, we also insisted on the importance of "migrants' own practices, their relationships and networks of contact that permitted adaptation to particular migration regimes" (Siegelbaum and Moch 2014, 5). The Stalinist regimes figured centrally in each of the book's eight chapters, as did corresponding repertoires.

Popular agency, the coin of the Thompsonian realm, had its greatest purchase when industrial working classes were still thought to be potential counterweights to the dictatorship of capital. In that context, it was easy to succumb to the romanticism of equating popular agency with political virtue. Now, in the wake of the Trumpist assault on the citadel of American political democracy and an eerily similar mass action in Brazil two years later, one needs to be wary of such a temptation. To return to the Soviet masses, the ability of seasonal workers and itinerants of all kinds to bend regimes of migration to their own purposes may have staved off their own starvation but did not make them better people than those who went along with the rules, and the same could be said of workers on the shop floor, consumers searching for scarce goods, and others. It was one thing for masses of people, toiling and otherwise, to limit the power of the state, and even at times use it to their advantage, but quite another for their actions to bring genuine socialism any closer.

Besides, are we to assume that the grand designs of states always lack virtue? It remains true, as Moch and I noted in 2017, that "We live in an age when large undertakings by states are likely to inspire suspicion if not outright hostility," while "corporate and other private enterprises reap the whirlwind of profit and power from state retrenchment." In this and many other respects, we added, "the Soviet Union seems to be of another age," for it was made for big projects. One thinks immediately of the collectivization of agriculture, the industrialization of the economy, the deportation of whole categories of people deemed "enemies," the war effort including mobilization and evacuation, and postwar reconstruction (Siegelbaum and Moch 2017, 188). All of these enormous endeavors, of course, occurred during the Stalin era and helped to define Stalinism as a way of life. Each shook up the country involving not only massive displacement but social dislocation. As Lewin inimitably put it, referring to Stalin's "big drive," "For a while, before the dust settled, the whole nation became as if *déclassé*, some *déclassé* down, some *déclassé* . . . up" (Lewin 1985, 118).

Whether virtuous or not—and surely the record is mixed—these undertakings sparked all manner of enthusiastic participation, resistance, and avoidance. The simple point, then, about approaching Stalinism from the perspective of social history is that there was a lot of it, and it was so damned fascinating.

Works Cited

Benvenuti, Francesco. *Fuoco sui sabotatori! Stachanovismo e organizzazione industriale in Urss, 1934–38*. Rome: V. Levi, 1988.

Cameron, Sarah. *The Hungry Steppe: Famine, Violence and the Making of Soviet Kazakhstan*. Ithaca: Cornell University Press, 2018.

Chatterjee, Choi, and Karen Petrone. "Models of Selfhood and Subjectivity: The Soviet Case in Historical Perspective." *Slavic Review* 67, no. 4 (2008): 967–86.

Cucu, Alina-Sandra. *Planning Labour: Time and the Foundations of Industrial Socialism in Romania*. New York: Berghahn Books, 2019.

Filtzer, Donald. *The Hazards of Urban Life in Late Stalinist Russia: Health, Hygiene, and Living Standards, 1943–1953*. New York: Cambridge University Press, 2010.

Fitzpatrick, Sheila, ed. *Cultural Revolution in Russia, 1928–1931*. Bloomington: Indiana University Press, 1978.

Fitzpatrick, Sheila. *Education and Social Mobility in the Soviet Union, 1921–1934*. Cambridge, 1979.

Fitzpatrick, Sheila. "New Perspectives on Stalinism." *Russian Review* 45, no. 4 (October 1986): 357–73.

Fitzpatrick, Sheila. *Stalin's Peasants: Resistance & Survival in the Russian Village after Collectivization*. Oxford: Oxford University Press, 1994.

Fitzpatrick, Sheila. *Everyday Stalinism: Ordinary Life in Extraordinary Times: Soviet Russia in the 1930s*. Oxford: Oxford University Press, 1999.

Fitzpatrick, Sheila, ed. *Stalinism: New Directions*. London: Routledge, 2000.

Fitzpatrick, Sheila. *Tear Off the Masks! Identity and Imposture in Twentieth-Century Russia.* Princeton: Princeton University Press, 2005.
Fürst, Juliane. *Stalin's Last Generation: Soviet Post-War Youth and the Emergence of Mature Socialism.* Oxford: Oxford University Press, 2010.
Getty, J. Arch. *Origins of the Great Purges: The Soviet Communist Party Reconsidered, 1933–1938.* Cambridge: Cambridge University Press, 1985.
Goldman, Wendy Z. *Women at the Gates: Gender and Industry in Stalin's Russia.* Cambridge: Cambridge University Press, 2002.
Goldman, Wendy Z. *Terror and Democracy in the Age of Stalin.* Cambridge: Cambridge University Press, 2007.
Goldman, Wendy Z. *Inventing the Enemy: Denunciation and Terror in Stalin's Russia.* Cambridge: Cambridge University Press, 2011.
Goldman, Wendy Z., and Donald A. Filtzer, eds. *Hunger and War: Food Provisioning in the Soviet Union during World War II.* Bloomington: Indiana University Press, 2015.
Goldman, Wendy Z., and Donald Filtzer. *Fortress Dark and Stern: The Soviet Home Front during World War II.* Oxford: Oxford University Press, 2021.
Grama, Adrian. "Laboring Along: Industrial Workers and the Making of Postwar Romania (1944–1958)." PhD diss, Central European University, 2017.
Gronow, Jukka. *Caviar with Champagne: Common Luxury and the Ideals of the Good Life in Stalin's Russia.* Oxford: Berg, 2003.
Hellbeck, Johan. *Revolution on My Mind: Writing a Diary under Stalin.* Cambridge, MA: Harvard University Press, 2006.
Hessler, Julie. *A Social History of Soviet Trade: Trade Policy, Retail Practices, and Consumption, 1917–1953.* Princeton: Princeton University Press, 2004.
Hoffmann, David L. *Peasant Metropolis: Social Identities in Moscow, 1929–1941.* Ithaca: Cornell University Press, 1994.
Hoffmann, David L. *Stalinist Values: The Cultural Norms of Soviet Modernity, 1917–1941.* Ithaca: Cornell University Press, 2003.
Hoffmann, David L. *Cultivating the Masses: Modern State Practices and Soviet Socialism, 1914–1939.* Ithaca: Cornell University Press, 2011.
"I remember/ia pomniu." http://www.iremember.ru.
Kenney, Padraic. *Rebuilding Poland: Workers and Communists, 1945–1950.* Ithaca: Cornell University Press, 1997.
Kharkhordin, Oleg. *The Collective and the Individual in Russia: A Study of Practices.* Berkeley: University of California Press, 1999.
Koenker, Diane P. *Republic of Labor: Russian Printers and Soviet Socialism, 1918–1930.* Ithaca: Cornell University Press, 2005.
Koenker, Diane P. *Club Red: Vacation Travel and the Soviet Dream.* Ithaca: Cornell University Press, 2013.
Kotkin, Stephen. *Magnetic Mountain: Stalinism as a Civilization.* Berkeley: University of California Press, 1995.
Lebow, Katherine. *Unfinished Utopia: Nowa Huta, Stalinism, and Polish Society, 1949–56.* Ithaca: Cornell University Press, 2013.
Lewin, Moshe. *The Making of the Soviet System: Essays in the Social History of Interwar Russia.* New York: New Press, 1985.

Maier, Robert. *Die Stachanov-Bewegung, 1935–1938 der Stachanovismus als tragendes und verschärfendes Moment der Stalinisierung der sowjetischen Gesellschaft.* Stuttgart: F. Steiner, 1990.

Manley, Rebecca. *To the Tashkent Station: Evacuation and Survival in the Soviet Union at War.* Ithaca: Cornell University Press, 2009.

Murphy, Kevin. *Revolution and Counterrevolution: Class Struggle in a Moscow Metal Factory.* New York: Berghahn Books, 2005.

Pinnow, Kenneth M. *Lost to the Collective: Suicide and the Promise of Soviet Socialism, 1921–1929.* Ithaca: Cornell University Press, 2010.

Pittaway, Mark. *The Worker's State: Industrial Labor and the Making of Socialist Hungary, 1944–1958.* Pittsburgh: University of Pittsburgh Press, 2012.

Randall, Amy E. *The Soviet Dream World of Retail Trade and Consumption in the 1930s.* New York: Palgrave Macmillan, 2008.

Rossman, Jeffrey. *Worker Resistance under Stalin: Class and Revolution on the Shop Floor.* Cambridge, MA: Harvard University Press, 2005.

Siefert, Marsha, ed. *Labor in State-Socialist Europe, 1945–1989: Contributions to a History of Work.* Budapest: CEU Press, 2020.

Siegelbaum, Lewis H. "Dear Comrade, You Ask What We Need: Socialist Paternalism and Soviet Rural Notables in the Mid-1930s." In *Stalinism: New Directions*, ed. Sheila Fitzpatrick, 231–55. Routledge: London, 2000.

Siegelbaum, Lewis H. "Production Collectives and Communes and the 'Imperatives' of Soviet Industrialization, 1929–1931." *Slavic Review* 45 (Spring 1986): 65–84.

Siegelbaum, Lewis H. *Stakhanovism and the Politics of Productivity in the USSR, 1935–1941.* Cambridge: Cambridge University Press, 1988.

Siegelbaum, Lewis H. "The Late Romance of the Soviet Worker in Western Historiography." *International Review of Social History*, no. 41 (2006): 463–82.

Siegelbaum, Lewis H., and Leslie Page Moch. *Broad Is My Native Land: Repertoires and Regimes of Migration in Russia's Twentieth Century.* Ithaca: Cornell University Press, 2014.

Siegelbaum, Lewis H., and Leslie Page Moch. "Evacuation as Migration: The Soviet Experience during the Great Patriotic War." In *Migration and Mobility in the Modern Age: Refugees, Travelers, and Traffickers in Europe and Eurasia*, ed. Anika Walke, Jan Musekamp, and Nicole Svobodny. Bloomington: Indiana University Press, 2017.

Siegelbaum, Lewis H., and Andrei Sokolov. *Stalinism as a Way of Life: A Narrative in Documents.* New Haven: Yale University Press, 2000.

Strauss, Kenneth M. *Factory and Community in Stalin's Russia: The Making of an Industrial Working Class.* Pittsburgh: University of Pittsburgh Press, 1996.

Viola, Lynne. *The Unknown Gulag: The Lost World of Stalin's Special Settlements.* Oxford: Oxford University Press, 2007.

Viola, Lynne. *Stalinist Perpetrators on Trial: Scenes from the Great Terror in Soviet Ukraine.* Oxford: Oxford University Press, 2017.

Zubkova, Elena. *Russia after the War: Hopes, Illusions, and Disappointments, 1945–1957*, trans. Hugh Ragsdale. Armonk, NY: M.E. Sharpe, 1998.

Chapter 2

Revisiting Stalinist Social Mobility

Sheila Fitzpatrick

The collapse of the Soviet Union in 1991 was an exciting time for Western Soviet historians. It brought with it a sudden huge expansion in access to archives and other sources of information, and therefore of our database. We did not have the problem of our political science colleagues of explaining why we had not predicted the collapse since prediction has never been part of our job description. All the same, there was a sense of shock and even disorientation. I remember wondering if, in light of the Soviet Union's demise, I should still use "Soviet historian" as my professional descriptor, and indeed over the next few years it started to morph into "modern Russian." There was also the question of how well our previous interpretations would stand up in the light of the new data. So for us, as well as for former Soviet citizens, the shock of the new carried a degree of apprehension as well as invigoration.

Our reflections on Stalinism in this volume must inevitably reflect the impact of this cataclysmic event. Rather than trying to recapture this impact as a whole, I decided to take one particular strand of my work in the 1970s, the issue of worker "promotion" (*proletarskoe vydvizhenie*) into elite managerial and professional positions under Stalin. What I do in this chapter is in part historiographical, but I also examine how the topic waxed, waned, and evolved (in my mind as well as in its reception in the field) in response to changing external circumstances.

Worker promotion was part of a broader complex of "promotion" policies through which the new regime strove to increase opportunity for those formerly denied it, including poor peasants, members of "backward" ethnic minorities (*natsmen*), and women. These were launched in the wake of the October Revolution of 1917, but the policy of worker promotion, in particular, was prosecuted on a much larger scale and with greater intensity during the First Five-Year Plan (1929–32). The three main channels of promotion were recruitment to party membership (which opened the doors to appointment to leadership positions), direct promotion on the job (for example, from skilled worker to factory manager), and preferential admission to higher education, for which strict process of class selection to favor workers, poor peasants, and party and Komsomol members were put in place.

I came at this issue through working on the education policies of the People's Commissariat of Education in the first decade after the revolution (Fitzpatrick 1970, 1979) and being puzzled by recurring discussions of *proletarskoe vydvizhenie*. This was a vast if baffling topic in the commissariat's archive, involving massive collecting of data on social origin and current social position and constant skirmishing between the Commissariat and the universities and technical schools on their admissions policies. The only thing that seemed incontestable about proletarian promotion was that the intelligentsia disliked it. In the Western scholarly literature it was mentioned rarely, and then as yet another aspect of communist privilege (proletarian being understood as a euphemism for party). After a while, it became clear that the main intended and actual beneficiaries of *proletarskoe vydvizhenie* in education were workers and their children, although communists (particularly those from the working class) also qualified. I came to the conclusion that this apparently esoteric educational issue was a key *kto-kogo* question for the new regime. (*Kto-kogo* was Lenin's formulation of the issue of power: which of the opposing classes, the old haves and the old have-nots, is going to dominate the other and thus win the class war.) It was integral to one of the Bolsheviks' major claims, namely that their party represented the working class, and one of their major promises—to enable workers to become masters.

Affirmative Action (or Whatever You Want to Call It) under Stalin

Power to the workers was a key Bolshevik promise in 1917. According to Marxist-Leninist theory, the party was the proletarian vanguard, and on taking power it would establish a dictatorship of the proletariat. It did duly establish a one-party state and, in effect, a party dictatorship, which could thus be construed as a proletarian one. Many outside commentators, as well as internal socialist critics, have regarded the proletarian part of this claim to be a sham, concluding that the Bolsheviks failed to deliver on their promise of power to the workers and betrayed the working class. But, despite increasing controls on trade unions (the party's main surviving competitor as workers' institutional representatives in the course of the 1920s), Soviet workers themselves seemed less angry about the betrayal than might have been expected. I wondered why that was.

One possible explanation lay in the transformation of the working class through an influx of peasants entering the urban industrial workforce for the first time during the First and Second Five-Year Plans (1929–37), diluting what the Marxists liked to call "proletarian consciousness" and making the working class less assertive and more amenable to direction. This seemed plausible to me, but I thought it was not the whole story. My contribution to the discussion, arising out of my early work on education, was to suggest that, while the Bolshevik Revolution had not given power to the working class as a class (probably an impossibility in the real world), individual workers and their children had indeed been given the chance to become masters—via state programs of proletarian promotion, including preferential access to higher education, particularly in engineering, and the increased opportunities for upward mobility attendant upon rapid industrialization. In my 1979 article "Stalin and the Making of a New Elite," I argued that this had the effect of creating a class of beneficiaries who, based on their individual experience of being promoted into the elite status of cadres and specialists, saw the Bolsheviks as having delivered on their promise of power to the workers. This, I further argued, was a major factor in legitimizing and creating social support for the Stalinist regime.

All kinds of *vydvizhenie* were encouraged during the cultural revolution (the subject of an eponymous edited book that appeared in 1978), the boisterous youth movement accompanying collectivization and the First Five-Year Plan, whose central thrust was to challenge the dominance of the old bourgeois cultural establishment, aka the intelligentsia. The essence of cultural revolution, as understood at the time, was class war; and the campaign to promote proletarians ran in tandem with an equally energetic campaign to demote bourgeois specialists (noncommunist intelligentsia), often by ruthless, repressive measures—a cultural counterpart to the dual policies of collectivization and dekulakization running at the same period in the countryside.

In addition to proletarian promotion, there were similar programs—though none as intensive as the proletarian one—for the advancement of poor peasants (*bednota*), ethnic minorities, and women. Essentially, any disadvantaged group whose members might have seen their way forward blocked under the old regime was likely to benefit—and that included a surprisingly large number of children in state orphanages, free from the contaminating influence of bourgeois or traditionally minded parents. Peasant promotion, while quantitatively significant, was a more ambiguous phenomenon than its working-class counterpart because it was happening at the same time as collectivization and dekulakization hit the village (as peasants were being collectivized, many of their children were leaving the village, often for further education in the towns as *vydvizhentsy* [promotees]—a theme I pursued in the early 1990s in *Stalin's Peasants*).

Promotion of women was partially overshadowed as far as activist Bolshevik feminists were concerned by the simultaneous closing down of the Central Committee's Women's Department, where they had held sway in the 1920s. But it occurred nonetheless, both in education and at the workplace, and has been most visible to historians in the context of the mass entry of women into the urban labor force during the First Five-Year Plan. (Wendy Goldman has an interesting chapter in her 2002 book *Women at the Gates* on activism at the plant level to get women promoted into skilled industrial jobs.) Promotion of ethnic minorities—part of the broader policy of "indigenization" (*korenizatsiia*) was actively prosecuted by the party before, during, and after the First Five-Year Plan, but scholarly recognition of its significance had to wait for Terry Martin's work at the beginning of the 2000s.

The title of Martin's book is *Affirmative Action Empire*. In the rightly enthusiastic reception of his work, nobody objected to the use of the term "affirmative action," implying a family resemblance to American affirmative action policies on behalf of Blacks in the 1960s. But it had been different thirty years earlier when I used the same term in connection with the Soviet proletarian *vydvizhenie* of the Stalin period, seeking to find a way of making the policy comprehensible to contemporary readers. The term, as well as my use of the concept of "upward mobility" in a Soviet context, provoked strong criticism from American Sovietologists, both from the Marxist left (unhappy with the suggestion that workers might jump at the chance to move upward out of their class) and the totalitarian-model right (outraged at the use of social science terminology more usually associated with American phenomena regarded as quintessentially democratic). Even a centrist critic like Abbott (Tom) Gleason expressed concern in his book on totalitarianism, writing that "No doubt there are some similarities [with American affirmative action], but the gain in understanding is more than offset by what the phrase leaves out in its linking of quite disparate situations. Any such comparison must inevitably have an exculpatory ring"; and Martin Malia saw it simply as "advocacy for the enduring legitimacy, founded on 'social mobility' of the Soviet regime" (the criticisms are summarized in my 2008 article "Revisionism in Retrospect"). As for the Marxists, Ron Suny accused me in a 1988 exchange in *Slavic Review* of going on a "personal crusade" against Marxist class analysis, which was probably not inaccurate: I did regard my upward mobility arguments as essentially an anti-Marxist as well as antitotalitarian intervention and found it therefore doubly frustrating to be characterized as a pro-Soviet Marxist by the totalitarian side.

In the context of Soviet scholarship, the term "upward mobility" was equally unacceptable. *Riskovannyi* (risky) was the word my friend, the Soviet historian Vladimir Drobizhev, used when he read "Stalin and the Making of a New Elite," although he agreed with the general thrust. Upward mobility was not a permissible concept in Soviet social science until well into the 1980s, the problem being that it implied a hierarchy of classes, which was not supposed to exist in the Soviet Union. "Elite," similarly, was not an acceptable term as applied to the Soviet Union, which notoriously since the mid-1930s had officially possessed two nonantagonistic and nonhierarchical classes, the working class and peasantry, plus a nonantagonistic and nonhierarchical "stratum," the intelligentsia/white-collar group. At the same time, Soviet historians like Drobizhev knew a lot about *proletarskoe vydvizhenie* and thought it important. But what I called "upward mobility" they called *formirovanie sovetskoi intelligentsii*, achieved in large part through the advancement of workers, peasants, and ethnic minorities. When I went to the Soviet Union on exchange visits in the 1970s, "formation of the Soviet intelligentsia" was my official topic.

The big push to proletarianize the new elite/Soviet intelligentsia came to an end in the early 1930s, giving way to policies of conciliation of the old intelligentsia/bourgeoisie described by the Russian émigré sociologist Nikolai Timasheff as "the great retreat" and by Trotsky as "the revolution betrayed." But some of its consequences became dramatically visible during the Great Purges of the late 1930s, when worker and peasant vydvizhentsy, predominantly trained in engineering during the First Five-Year Plan, were at the forefront of the new men moving into top positions in party and government. This was part of my theme, but (as I discuss in "Hough and History" [2021]) I owed a lot to Jerry Hough, who incorporated working-class upward mobility in his revision of Fainsod's classic text and had party biographies at his fingertips.

New Soviet Intelligentsia: The *Kto Kogo*? Question Again

In the aftermath of the Purges, Stalin treated the making of a "new Soviet people's (*narodnaia*) intelligentsia" as an accomplished fact rather than an ongoing process. The worker and peasant vydvizhentsy, he told the Eighteenth Party Congress in 1939, "radically changed the contours of the intelligentsia, remaking it in their own image." Stalin's answer to the *kto-kogo* question with regard to the cultural-political orientation of the new elite was unequivocal: the proletarian/party side had won. This was a plausible contention, at least in the short term. From the mid-1930s to perhaps the late 1940s, the Soviet intelligentsia was not only politically docile—the terror of the purges played a crucial role here—but also apparently Soviet in its values. This is most often attributed to the patriotic upsurge of the Second World War, but the arrival in the intelligentsia of the vydvizhentsy cohort, soon to be followed by demobilized World War II veterans, was surely also a factor. This remains an under-researched topic, but the pro-Soviet attitudes of the Soviet intelligentsia in this period are obliquely acknowledged in one of the central arguments of Yuri Slezkine's *The Jewish Century*, namely that an unprecedented rapprochement between the historically dissident (and philosemitic) Russian intelligentsia and government was ruptured by the antisemitic campaign of Stalin's last years.

Viewed from another perspective, it looks more as if the old intelligentsia won the battle by imposing its values on the vydvizhentsy in exactly the way Lenin had feared, raising the *kto-kogo* question with regard to the old tsarist bureaucracy and the new communist cadres, in his report to the Eleventh Party Congress in 1922. This is the view of Vladislav Zubok and Ben Tromly, both writing about the immediate postwar student generation in the elite universities of the capitals. While both authors emphasize the strong Soviet loyalties of this cohort, they are equally impressed by the commitment of these Soviet students (of whatever social origin) to old intelligentsia values. Zubok, whose parents were of this generation at MGU, calls the cohort "Zhivago's children, in a spiritual sense," that is, "descendants of the great cultural and moral tradition that Pasternak, his protagonist Yuri Zhivago, and his milieu embodies" (Zubok 2009, 20). Among those students who, in Zubok's words, identified simultaneously with "Soviet collectivity" as well as with "humanist individualism," were Mikhail Gorbachev, upwardly mobile from a peasant family, and his future wife, Raisa Titarenko, daughter of a railway worker, both students at MGU in the early 1950s.

Zubok and Tromly treat the postwar cohort of students as a homogenous group of varied social origins but united in an embrace of the humanist values of the old intelligentsia. In an influential (if idiosyncratically biased) work of the 1970s, Vera Dunham (1976) postulated a "big deal" between the new Soviet "middle class" (closely related to Stalin's "new Soviet intelligentsia") and the Soviet regime, which involved the middle class's acceptance of Soviet power in return for the regime's acceptance of a debased version of intelligentsia values (*kul'turnost'*)—the debasement being the result of the arrival of vydvizhentsy from the working class attempting to ape the culture of their old intelligentsia betters. Slezkine sees a functional divide developing within the intelligentsia between apparatchiks, predominantly vydvizhentsy, and the pure intelligentsia in the professions, who saw themselves as the guardians of high culture. He notes that while the apparatchiks had the political advantage, most of them "tacitly recognized the primacy of the professionals insofar as they raised their own children to be professionals, not apparatchiks" (Slezkine 2004, 333). This last point can be extended to the Stalinist Politburo, who as parents consistently encouraged their children to go into the humanities rather than follow them into politics (Fitzpatrick 2015, 187–88).

Proletarian Promotion in the Later Stalin Period

While large-scale high-pressure affirmative action programs were dropped in the early 1930s, and the (completed) creation of a new Soviet intelligentsia affirmed in the latter half of the decade, this was not quite the end of the story. As John Connelly (2000) described, similar programs were exported after the Second World War to the East European states, now within the Soviet orbit, as part of a larger package of sovietization policies that included collectivization and centralized economic planning; and the same was true of the new territories incorporated in the Soviet Union in 1939, notably the Baltic republics. This throws an interesting light on the abandonment of such high-pressure policies in the "old" Soviet Union at the same period, confirming the sense that they were seen by the Soviet leadership as essential transformation strategies in the first phase of Soviet power that became less relevant only once the desired renovation of elites was accomplished.

The question remains of how completely proletarian promotion was dropped as policy and practice in the later Stalin period. That period was something of a black box for historians in the 1970s, given the inaccessibility of archives and the exceptional poverty of published sources. There were no high-pressure affirmative action programs (outside the newly acquired territories) on the pattern of the 1930s, and the obsessive collection of data regarding social origin characteristics of that period had ceased. Based on Khrushchev's public denunciation of the closed-caste attitudes of the intelligentsia in the late 1950s, it was generally assumed that not only was proletarian promotion discarded as policy and practice in the late Stalin period, but also that this signaled a complete abandonment (disapproved of by vydvizhenets Khrushchev) of the regime's original identification with the proletariat.

My work on the original affirmative action schemes was published in the early 1970s. A decade later, the question of how completely affirmative action had been dropped in the late Stalin period was niggling at me. Everyone, including me, said that it stopped, but nobody had any real data to prove it. I did some additional research on the question, mainly using recent sociological studies and fragmentary contemporary statistics, and produced an article ("Social Mobility in the Late Stalin Period," n.d.) that I did not publish. I assume this was because I was discouraged by the reception of my social mobility arguments, which remained hostile for the first fifteen years or so (after which they were generally tacitly accepted), as discussed in my 2008 "Revisionism" essay.

In the unpublished article, I stated my central purpose to be an investigation of what I saw as a scholarly consensus "that the policies of the late Stalin period were intended to limit upward mobility and to strengthen and perpetuate the privileges of the Soviet intelligentsia or 'new class'; and that these aims were achieved." I did not find any such policy articulated, even in euphemistic form, which was perhaps unsurprising, but what I did find was evidence in sociological studies of different intelligentsia cohorts made in the 1960s that students of working-class and peasant origin made up a substantial part of the cohort in tertiary education in the postwar decade. In M. N. Rutkevich's mid-1960s study of engineering-technical personnel in a Sverdlovsk industrial plant over 40 percent of those trained in the immediate postwar period were of working-class origin and almost one-third of peasant origin, making nonwhite-collar 72.7 percent of the total (Rutkevich 1967, 23). This meant that under 27 percent came from white-collar and professional families—not at all like the picture of caste-like domination suggested by Khrushchev ten years earlier. In the wake of the war, lower-class demobilized veterans could have inflated the blue-collar contingent. But Rutkevich, in what was presumably an implicitly anti-Khrushchev intervention, provided the useful information that in practice the problem of lower-class entry to higher education became acute only when secondary-school output became much larger than VUZ intake, and VUZ entrance became really competitive. This happened between 1954 and 1958; in other words, Khrushchev was reacting to a recent change. My conclusion in the unpublished article was "that Western scholars have been too quick to equate *embourgeoisement* of manners in the upper levels of the Soviet education system with *embourgeoisement* of recruitment." Rather than a conscious policy to favor white-collar children in university admissions, "it looks very much like a policy of laissez faire, in which the only real decision was the decision not to collect data and thus not to know what social groups the students were coming from" (Fitzpatrick, n.d.).

After Stalin

Khrushchev's attack on intelligentsia privilege in the universities was an interesting aspect of his touchy relations with a group that supported his Thaw initiatives while also seeing them as a license to resume the intelligentsia's historic role as critic of power. He was himself a product of Stalinist *vydvizhenie*, and held the idea of proletarian promotion dear. Unlike Stalin, he did not regard it as simply a one-shot exercise in elite transformation but a continuing process. He thought the Soviet intelligentsia had become self-serving and cut off from the broader society and that it restricted university admissions to preserve its privileges, regarding this (in Tromly's words) as a "malignancy in Soviet society."

As of the late 1950s, according to Khrushchev, the working class, which constituted 40 percent of the population, was only providing 28 percent of entrants to full-time tertiary education. In the higher educational institutions of Moscow, he said in 1958, "only 30–40% of the students are the children of workers and collective farmers. The remaining students are the children of white-collared workers and the intelligentsia. Of course, this situation is clearly abnormal" (quoted in Matthews 1972, 294).

To correct this situation Khrushchev pushed forward educational reforms designed to increase representation of children of blue-collar families in universities via the old path of large-scale affirmative action. To be sure, class membership was no longer the ostensible criterion but rather labor experience, which intelligentsia children could also acquire through a year or so in the factory between school and university. The program encountered stiff resistance from university students as well as faculty, however, and achieved comparatively little. As Slezkine has observed in *The Jewish Century*, the affirmative action programs of the Khrushchev era differed from their Stalinist precursors in one important respect: there was no concomitant repression of a bourgeois "class enemy." Thus, "because [the party] did not reintroduce massive repression against white-collar workers, it merely added to the resentment of the entrenched cultural elite without jeopardizing its ascendance (well protected by superior education and patronage)" (Slezkine 2004, 333).

Khrushchev's education reforms produced no spiritual renovation of the intelligentsia since the working-class and peasant students who entered seem usually to have absorbed the dominant culture of the institution. After the heady experience of the Thaw, when university students participated in passionate discussions of the very bases of Soviet society, this dominant culture included a belief in the intelligentsia's role of moral leadership in the society and right, even obligation, to act as loyal critic of government. This was to have important consequences in the future, as loyal criticism increasingly bordered on dissidence.

The affirmative action program was quietly watered down after Khrushchev's fall in 1964. However, the abandonment of large-scale formal affirmative action programs in the Brezhnev period did not mean the cessation of working-class entry into higher education. Curiously, the student body nationwide apparently became more socially diverse in the 1970s, partly as a result of the revival of rabfaks, the workers' preparatory colleges that were an instrument of "proletarianization" in the 1920s, though their graduates were often subject to mockery (*kolkhozniki*) by other students (Tromly 2014, 251).

Upward Mobility in Retrospect

The collapse of the Soviet Union at the end of 1991 meant that the classified sections of state archives became open to foreign scholars for the first time, as did formerly inaccessible archives like that of the party's Central Committee. At the same time, regional archives also became accessible—sometimes even KGB regional archives, although in general that institution, now renamed FSB, kept its control over its archives, in contrast to the Communist Party. There was an incredible influx of new information, opening up whole subfields whose source-based study had previously been almost impossible (for example, Gulag) and disclosing whole genres of information for social historians (for example, petitions and NKVD reports on the mood of the population) whose existence had been previously unknown. That is not even to mention the information on high politics that was also now available (though initially less used because political history was out of fashion within the historical profession).

I was lucky in that the opening of the archives did not significantly change the picture as far as proletarian promotion was concerned: this was not a topic where documents had to be classified (putting them beyond the reach of Western historians in Soviet times), and it was one that had been well covered in the press at a time (the late 1920s) when the press still gave a broad and variegated coverage of many issues.

But by the 1990s, the attention of historians (including my attention) had moved elsewhere. That remained the case when, almost thirty years after the Soviet collapse, I sat down to write *The Shortest History of the Soviet Union* (Fitzpatrick 2022). With the passing of the Brezhnev generation's dominance of the Politburo in the mid-1980s, the political salience of the Stalinist *vydvizhentsy* cohort of the 1930s had diminished. In Gorbachev's perestroika, the focus was on freedom of expression, democratization, and structural economic reform, not workers' issues or equality of opportunity. In the final collapse of the Soviet Union at the end of 1991, it went unremarked that the two leaders of the major Slavic republics who led their republics out of the Union—Boris Yeltsin of Russia, of peasant-worker background, and Leonid Kravchuk of Ukraine, from a peasant family—were essentially late-Stalinist vydvizhentsy, as was the man who job as president of the Soviet Union they abolished, Mikhail Gorbachev.

In my *Shortest History*, upward working-class mobility was a more prominent theme in the first half of the book than in the second. Jerry Hough gave it more play in his 1997 book on the perestroika and the collapses of the Soviet Union, *Democratization and Revolution* (for more on this, see my article "Hough and History" [2021]). As Hough presents it, the near-coincidence of the life span of the Stalinist cohort of vydvizhentsy and the Soviet state that had promoted them was no accident. It was the availability of the opportunity to rise that had bonded this cohort to the regime and the disappearance of that opportunity for their children and grandchildren that doomed it. "The fundamental problem with the communist industrial system is that it, not capitalism, developed the grave diggers about whom Marx had written. It was not the proletariat who served in this role but the children of the proletariat seeking upward mobility." By the 1980s, Hough's argument goes, large-scale upward mobility into the elite was a thing of the past, and this was a major reason for the increasing alienation from the Soviet project of the younger generation. The vydvizhentsy's grandchildren wanted better paid professional and managerial jobs, and "the most ambitious wanted the chance to enrich themselves in private business." (Hough 1997, 50).

For most scholars in the early post-Soviet period, however, nationality had replaced class as a prime object of interest—a natural consequence of the circumstances of the breakup of the Soviet Union. Here the late Stalinist story had more contemporary resonance. Affirmative action on behalf of ethnic groups in the backward category (that is, Uzbeks and Kirghiz, but not Ukrainians, Georgians, or Jews) was Stalinist policy, not just in the early 1930s but throughout, and it was also post-Stalinist policy. Many administrative and professional jobs were still held by Russians, though the proportion diminished over time, and Russian-speaking was a sine qua non for promotion. But as L. P. Koshelev and O. V. Khlevniuk (2013) note in their archive-based study of Soviet nationality policy in the late Stalin period, central and republican authorities were at one in supporting the expansion of secondary and higher education for students from the indigenous nationalities, with the specific aim of preparing national cadres for leadership in the republics; and this policy was equally warmly supported by the local intelligentsia.

Thus, Stalinist and post-Stalinist affirmative action deserves its place not only in the history of Russia but the history of the former Soviet republics that emerged as independent states in 1991. As in the case of Russia with Boris Yeltsin, many of the first leaders of these new states had started as vydvizhentsy. Kazakhstan's Nursultan Nazarbayev, born in 1940, joined the party as a steel worker in 1962, and was promoted up through Komsomol jobs. His near contemporaries, Turkmenistan's Saparmurat Niyazov and Uzbekistan's Islam Karimov, were both brought up in orphanages and trained as engineers. Understandably, the new Central Asian governments are telling their newly invented national histories in terms of oppression by Russian (Soviet) imperialists; and many have also launched their own programs for further indigenization of elites, generally strongly favoring the titular nationalities at the expense of Russians (who have moved out of the republics in droves) and smaller national minorities (Oh 2017, 114–15, 118). This is eminently predictable, but there is a bit of irony in the fact that so many first presidents of post-Soviet Central Asian states were themselves the beneficiaries of Soviet *vydvizhenie*.

Post scriptum: as I was writing this piece, an email arrived from the Australian publisher of *Shortest History* conveying a message from the Czech translator, currently working on the text, saying, "'Affirmative action' cannot be used for Soviet conditions—I translate as 'quotas.'" Presumably, this is because the Czech translator views "affirmative action" as carrying a positive load. *Plus ça change* . . .

Works Cited

Connelly, John. *Captive University. The Sovietization of East German, Czech, and Polish Higher Education, 1945–1956*. Chapel Hill: University of North Carolina Press, 2000.

Dunham, Vera S. *In Stalin's Time: Middle-Class Values in Soviet Fiction*. London: Cambridge University Press, 1976.

Fitzpatrick, Sheila. *The Commissariat of Enlightenment*. London: Cambridge University Press, 1970.

Fitzpatrick, Sheila, ed. *Cultural Revolution in Russia, 1928–1931*. Bloomington: Indiana University Press, 1978.

Fitzpatrick, Sheila. *Education and Social Mobility in the Soviet Union, 1924–1932*. Cambridge: Cambridge University Press, 1979.

Fitzpatrick, Sheila. "The Russian Revolution and Social Mobility: A Reexamination of the Question of Social Support for the Soviet Regime in the 1920's and 1930's." *Politics and Society* (Fall 1984): 119–41.

Fitzpatrick, Sheila. "Stalin and the Making of a New Elite, 1928–1939." *Slavic Review* 38 (September 1979): 377–402. (Republished in Fitzpatrick, *The Cultural Front. Power and Culture in Revolutionary Russia*. Ithaca: Cornell University Press. 1992.)

Fitzpatrick, Sheila. *Stalin's Peasants. Resistance and Survival in the Russian Village after Collectivization.* Oxford: Oxford University Press, 1994.

Fitzpatrick, Sheila. "Revisionism in Retrospect: A Personal View." *Slavic Review* 67, no. 3. (Fall 2008): 682–704.

Fitzpatrick, Sheila. *On Stalin's Team. The Years of Living Dangerously in Soviet Politics.* Princeton, NJ: Princeton University Press, 2015.

Fitzpatrick, Sheila. "Hough and History." *Kritika: Explorations in Russian and Eurasian History* 22, no. 3. (Summer 2021): 535–56.

Fitzpatrick, Sheila. *The Shortest History of the Soviet Union.* New York: Columbia University Press. 2022.

Fitzpatrick, Sheila. "Social Mobility in the Late Stalin Period: Recruitment into the Intelligentsia and Access to Higher Education, 1945–1953." Unpublished manuscript, n.d.

Gleason, Abbott. *Totalitarianism. The Inner History of the Cold War.* New York: Oxford University Press, 1995.

Goldman, Wendy Z. *Women at the Gates. Gender and Industry in Stalin's Russia.* Cambridge: Cambridge University Press. 2002.

Hough, Jerry F., and Merle Fainsod. *How the Soviet Union is Governed.* Cambridge, MA: Harvard University Press, 1982.

Hough, Jerry F. *Democratization and Revolution in the USSR, 1985–1991.* Washington, DC: Brookings Institution Press, 1997.

Koshelev, L. P., and O. V. Khlevniuk, comp. *Sovetskaia natsional'naia politika: Ideologiia i praktika, 1945–1953.* Moscow: ROSSPEN, 2013.

Martin, Terry. *The Affirmative Action Empire: Nations and Nationalism in the Soviet Union, 1923–1939.* Ithaca, NY: Cornell University Press, 2001.

Matthews, Mervyn. *Class and Society in Soviet Russia.* New York: Walker & Co., 1972.

Oh, Chong Jin. "Comparative Analyses of Nationalizing Processes in Kazakhstan and Uzbekistan: Uzbekization and Kazakhization." *International Area Review* 10, no. 2. (Fall 2007): 109–34.

Rutkevich, M. N. "Sotsial'nye istochniki popolneniia sovetskoi intelligentsii." *Voprosy filosofii,* no. 6. (1967).

Slezkine Yuri. *The Jewish Century.* Princeton NJ: Princeton University Press, 2004.

Suny, Ronald G. "Class and State in the Early Soviet Period: A Reply to Sheila Fitzpatrick." *Slavic Review* 47, no. 4. (Winter 1988): 614–19.

Timasheff, Nicholas S. *The Great Retreat. The Growth and Decline of Communism in Russia.* New York: E.P. Dutton & Co., 1946.

Tromly, Benjamin. *Making the Soviet Intelligentsia: Universities and Intellectual Life under Stalin and Khrushchev.* Cambridge. Cambridge University Press, 2014.

Trotsky Leon. *The Revolution Betrayed.* London: New Park, [1937] 1967.

Zubok, Vladislav. *Zhivago's Children: The Last Russian Intelligentsia.* Cambridge, MA: Belknap Press, Harvard University Press. 2009.

Chapter 3

Marxism and the Study of the Stalinist System

Donald Filtzer

Prefatory note: In what follows, I use "marxist" and "marxism" without the capital M to emphasize that marxism was a method of analysis and system of thought and not the product of an individual genius or guru, who, for all his genius, was not the final arbiter of all human mental activity. This is a legacy of my activist days in the 1970s and 1980s. Inconsistently, however, I use "Stalinism" rather than "stalinism," even though Stalinism was also stalinism, that is a system of social organization from which the USSR never really emerged.

Like several contributors to this volume, my interest in Soviet history derived from my marxist politics. Each of us may come from a different political and intellectual tradition within marxism, and no doubt we differ in how we analyze Stalinist society and the conclusions we draw, but there would probably still be broad agreement among us that marxism as broadly construed has an important contribution to make to our understanding of the Soviet system.

In my contribution I explore some of the social phenomena which, for different, although in some ways interconnected, reasons led to a seismic decline in analytical and theoretical approaches, which draw their frame of reference and methodology either directly from marxism or from intellectual and political currents that marxism has heavily influenced. I then argue that Marx's theory of the relationship between phenomena and essence, his use of abstraction, and his use of the concept of contradiction are important for our understanding of the nature of Stalinist society. Finally, I sketch out how the social antagonism between workers and the Soviet elite, an antagonism put in place through the process of Stalinist industrialization, led to the long-term decline of the Soviet system.

During the 1960s and 1970s marxism enjoyed an intellectual and political revival right across the capitalist world, and marxist discourse penetrated deeply into mainstream political culture, not least because of the alarm that waves of political unrest provoked among Western political and intellectual elites. People who did not live through this period might find it difficult to comprehend just how influential these ideas were, but this period saw a renaissance of left-wing publishing, and marxist books or books sympathetic to marxism reached a large audience, and not just on the university campuses of Western Europe and the United States. What this meant was that marxist concepts and categories enjoyed circulation and usage among far larger numbers of people than just those who were members of left-wing political parties and organizations. As the political Left went into retreat and decline—a phenomenon that requires lengthy investigation and explanation—so, too, did marxist ideas and methods of analysis. I suspect that much of postmodernism had its origins in this trend: large numbers of left-wing intellectuals felt betrayed and "let down" by a working class that failed to make a revolution (or even to show much interest in revolution), and instead of using their marxist tools to explain and understand this development (as Karl Korsch so powerfully did in the 1920s), they abandoned marxism altogether (Korsch 1970). From the point of view of this chapter, a long-term result has been that today it is relatively uncommon to find younger Soviet historians who are familiar with marxism, and even rarer still to find people who consider it useful or interesting to read Marx himself. Looked at more broadly, a feature of the period in which we are now living is that the surge in large-scale political activism across a wide range of issues—antiracism, campaigns against male sexual violence, the fight to protect the planet, and struggles to reverse capitalism's grotesque inequalities—has not led to a commensurate rekindling of interest in marxism, or even in socialism, on the scale that we saw in the 1960s and early 1970s.

Where analysis of the Soviet Union is concerned, the situation since the 1960s has been more complicated, for while the 1960s and 1970s saw the emergence of rich veins of inquiry into postwar capitalism and imperialism, the Soviet Union remained a blind spot for the Left. Overtly marxist studies of Stalinism and of Soviet society in general were few and far between. The first intellectual challenge to postwar Totalitarianism theory came not from marxists but from liberal advocates of "interest group" theory (Skilling 1971; Solomon, ed., 1983). They were the first to point out the heterogeneity not just of Soviet society but also within the ruling elite. Similarly, the two leading studies of Soviet industrial managers during the Stalin years were by two mainstream economists, Joseph Berliner and David Granick, neither of whom was in the least sympathetic to marxism (Berliner 1957; Granick 1954). The marxist Left in the West had a much more difficult time coming to grips with Stalinism. That this was a problem for Western Communist parties is hardly surprising given their slavish obedience to Moscow and then, during their so-called Euro-Communist phase of the 1970s and 1980s, their reluctance to challenge the legitimacy of the Soviet system. A notable exception here was the Communist Party of Italy, where Giuliano Procacci encouraged a large group of scholars to learn Russian and do serious empirical research on Soviet history. Much excellent scholarship was to emerge from these scholars, but they did not develop a self-consciously marxist critique of Stalinism, even within the intellectual frame of reference of Italian Euro-Communism (Benvenuti 1988; Bettanin 1978; Pons 2002). Trotskyist and Maoist critics of the Soviet Union had their own difficulties, not the least being a surprising unwillingness to learn Russian and carry out systematic research into the workings of the Soviet system based on original Soviet sources. Almost without exception, Trotskyist organizations developed their analyses of Soviet society by first citing Trotsky's writings on the subject and then adjusting whatever information they gleaned from Western newspapers to fit into these prescribed formulae. What they failed to do was have their members learn Russian and follow the Soviet newspapers and academic journals to build up an immanent analysis based on empirical research. Those Trotskyist thinkers who labeled the Soviet Union "state capitalist" faced similar difficulties. They, too, had a preconceived formula into which all facts could be made to fit. And here, too, precious few of their members read Russian and studied actual Soviet reality.

A notable but underappreciated exception was the work of Hillel Ticktin at the University of Glasgow's Institute of Soviet and East European Studies. As a young white South African Trotskyist, Ticktin was forced to flee the Apartheid regime. Being then stateless, he successfully applied for a Third World scholarship to study in the Soviet Union, the Soviets having accepted him on the assumption that he was Black. He remained in the Soviet Union throughout the early 1960s, studying economics and immersing himself in a close reading of the newspapers and journals. What was important was that he arrived in the USSR already with a well-formed conceptual framework through which to interpret his empirical findings and observations. When he left the USSR, he took up a post at Glasgow and in 1973 launched the journal *Critique*. In June 1973, a few months before beginning my PhD at the institute, I made a brief visit to Glasgow to meet the staff and fellow students, where Ticktin gave me a copy of the first issue of *Critique*, which contained his seminal article, "Towards a Political Economy of the USSR" (Ticktin 1973). I read it carefully, and when I returned home to Baltimore my friends and comrades asked eagerly, "What's his line, what's his line?" To which I replied, "As far as I can make out, his line is that there's no substitute for knowing what you're talking about." Of course, there was more to Ticktin's work than that. To the best of my knowledge, he was the first Western marxist to place labor power and the worker's relationship to the regime at the heart of his analysis of the Soviet system, a methodological orientation that I have adhered to throughout my career.

Ironically, the generally poorly informed critiques of Stalinism from the Trotskyist Left turned out to have certain benefits for the rapid development of the social history of the Soviet Union in the late 1970s and 1980s. This new field attracted a fair number of historians whose political and intellectual roots were on the Left, if not from marxism itself. By and large, these were politically independent or nonaligned scholars who could approach their subjects largely unencumbered by the dogmas of a party line. Some were motivated to study Soviet history to answer one of the most pressing questions of all for the Left after World War II, that is, why did the Russian Revolution fail? For socialists this was an immediate political, as well as intellectual question, for only a coherent and convincing answer to it would allow the Left to offer a credible answer to anticommunism. I cannot speak for other historians active in this period, but I know that when writing my labor histories, I also had in mind a hypothetical audience in the Soviet Union, who, if they could gain access to my books, might be able to use the work I had done to develop a marxist understanding and critique of Soviet society. Thus in its own small way (and I was fully aware that it was microscopically small) I hoped that my scholarship would make its own indirect and rather distantly mediated contribution to the eventual overthrow of the Stalinist system. This was not quite as fanciful an aim as it might sound. For when, during perestroika, it was possible to meet activists, they themselves made it plain that they relied almost exclusively on Western scholarship to discover the real history of the USSR.

The fact that the bulk of this Western scholarship, as high-quality and voluminous as it was, came from people who had no close political, organizational, or philosophical connections between themselves also meant that the long-term impact of the body of knowledge we created turned out to be somewhat less than the sum of its parts, precisely because it did not bequeath a coherent analytical tradition or method of analysis once class-based theory fell out of fashion.

The fate of class analysis inside the Soviet Union had different determinants. One huge obstacle was the sterility and banality of official Soviet "marxism."

This was also a problem in the West, insofar as Western Communist parties were by far the largest "marxist" parties, and the marxism that their members learned there was heavily influenced by Soviet tutelage. The Soviet elite's adoption of marxism as its legitimating ideology—an adoption that was forced upon it by the circumstances through which that elite took shape during the late 1920s and 1930s—was always fraught with risks because of the uncomfortable similarity between Marx's analysis of capitalist exploitation and what people observed as Soviet reality. Throughout the Stalin and Khrushchev periods, at least, quite a few Soviet citizens concluded that the system was a betrayal of socialism, although they were never more than a tiny minority of the Soviet population. The main point here is that "marxism" as formulated under Stalin and his successors was a sterile, mechanistic, sophistic, and frankly boring doctrine that had nothing in common with either the spirit or the content of what Marx and his more imaginative nineteenth- and twentieth-century followers wrote and fought for. Moreover, it was a doctrine whose content actually conformed to the needs of the emerging Soviet elite, insofar as—like the education system itself under Stalin—it specifically did not train people in critical thinking or how to use marxism to develop a critique of their existing (that is, Stalinist) society, but instead stressed the need to memorize by rote static (yet periodically and arbitrarily changing) formulae designed to stress conformity, ideological consensus, and passive acceptance of the Soviet regime.

If under Stalin and Khrushchev significant numbers of people tried to grapple with this doctrine and absorb its basic precepts, by the Brezhnev era it had become totally hollow, and no one took it seriously, even within the elite. This was especially true of the intelligentsia. I do not deny that some within the intelligentsia, and within society at large, tried to articulate a critique of the society using these tools, but censorship made this a difficult task. Sociologists and economists who studied and exposed the glaring inequalities within Soviet society, and class-based inequalities, in particular, could not articulate their findings into a fully developed critique, and certainly not a critique that identified the ruling elite as a ruling class that drew its privileges by expropriating a surplus created by an exploited working class. They had to use other categories, most notably, "social groups," and adhere to the fiction that the ruling *nomenklatura* was really the "most advanced stratum of the working class" (among the more prominent examples, see Shkaratan 1970; Klopov, Shubkin, and Gordon 1977). A more relevant observation is that the sociologists were a small minority within the intelligentsia, most of which was made up of engineers, and most of whom had a profoundly reactionary view of Soviet workers, whom they saw (and feared) as an uncultured dark mass just craving for a Stalin-like dictator. Their main complaint was that the system denied them the standard of living and the privileges to which they felt their superior training entitled them, and to rectify this injustice they sought salvation in the market. It was a great historical irony that with the advent of capitalism in post-Soviet Russia much of this intelligentsia suffered a calamitous loss in both income and status (or, as the adage goes, be careful what you wish for).

It is useful to review the relationship between Stalinist marxism and class struggle in the USSR. I would argue that Stalinist marxism as an ideology played a minor, but nonetheless important, role in suppressing class struggle in the Soviet Union. Of course, the dominant factor in suppressing class struggle was the splintering (atomization) of the working class through a combination of repression, hunger, and dilution with migrants from the countryside during the early 1930s. In the longer term, however, the sheer absence of any possibility of developing a radical critique of Soviet society (and I use the concept of "radical critique" in Marx's sense, a critique that can only realize itself through the radical overthrow of the object being criticized, in this case, Stalinism) almost certainly helped to blunt workers' ability to see themselves as a class with its own needs, the satisfaction of which could only be achieved by superseding Stalinist society. It equally deprived them of a language adequate for the articulation of such a critique. At the same time, this absence of class struggle, even in rudimentary form, impeded the development of a critical, marxist analysis of the society. In other words, had the Soviet Union witnessed even periodic or episodic upsurges of class conflict, I suspect that this might have facilitated the emergence of a wing within the intelligentsia (most of whose members were themselves of working-class origin) that both supported such struggles and looked to marxism as a way to understand and assist them. I am not naively ignoring the fact that repression made this impossible. That is precisely the point: repression served a dual function. It made class struggle impossible, and it made impossible the development of the concepts and language through which workers and intellectuals alike could have developed a true critique of the Soviet "mode of production."

We only need to contrast the situation in the USSR with postwar Eastern Europe to see the validity of this proposition. I do not pretend to have a deep knowledge of East European marxism, but we do know that marxism had a much stronger impact on both the critical intelligentsia and the working class in countries like Poland, Hungary, Czechoslovakia, and the DDR than it ever did in the Soviet Union. Thinkers such as Leszek Kolakowski, Agnes Heller, and Rudolf Bahro made a genuine contribution to twentieth-century marxism, valid in its own right and not just as an example of marxist dissidents operating under oppressive regimes (Kolakowski 1971; Heller 1976; Bahro 1981). The fact that they, like most of their colleagues, eventually moved rightwards politically (albeit to varying degrees) does not change that fact. But they were products of a rather different political landscape compared to the Soviet Union. We only need to recount the upsurges of worker protest and class struggle in postwar Eastern Europe to see this: the 1953 workers' rising in the DDR; the 1956 mass strikes and workers' protests in Poland, where workers formed factory committees and nearly toppled the Stalinist regime; the workers' councils that emerged during the Hungarian revolution of 1956 (and long outlived it); the independent factory committee movement in Czechoslovakia in late 1968 and early 1969; the strikes and demonstrations against food price rises in Poland in late 1970, including the lengthy occupation of the Szczecin shipyards; the 1976 strikes against food price rises in Poland and the formation of the Workers' Defense Committee following the arrest of the participants; and of course the Solidarity movement in Poland in 1980–81. I cannot provide a profound analysis of why such events could occur within Stalinist Eastern Europe but not in the Stalinist USSR. Surely some of it has to do with the fact that Stalinism had only recently been grafted onto these societies from outside, so that unlike the USSR, it had not grown up organically out of the degeneration of a workers' revolution; it also had something to do, I suspect, with the fact that workers still had living memory of non-Stalinist socialist parties and non-Stalinist trade unions from the prewar years. Clearly matters were more complex than this, and I do not have the knowledge to speculate further. What is important, however, is the idea that there was an organic link between the occasional outbreaks of working-class protest—and not just protest, but workers' self-activity—and the fact that at least some minority voices within the intelligentsia looked to marxism, rather than to Totalitarianism theory or other procapitalist conceptions, to formulate their criticism of their societies.

Where the former USSR is concerned, my larger argument is that this absence of any tradition of non-Stalinist marxism within the USSR meant that in the post-Soviet period only small, fringe currents within the intelligentsia or the independent labor movement have looked to marxism as a way to analyze either Soviet society or its post-Soviet successor. Thus, in the former Soviet Union, as in the West, new generations of highly talented historians have tried to analyze history and the historical experience through other theoretical-conceptual frameworks, which have largely excluded the concepts of class, class consciousness, class conflict, or class struggle.

The question arises, what is the significance of any of this now, when the Soviet Union has long since disappeared, and moreover disappeared not because it was overthrown by a revolutionary or rebellious population, but because it simply collapsed from within? Why worry about the method of analyzing the history of a society when that society itself has disappeared?

The answer is not simply to do with the advancement of academic knowledge, that is, historians of all societies have methodological, theoretical, political, and ideological disputes over how to conduct the practice of history and how to interpret its results, and it is at least partly through such intellectual conflicts that knowledge moves forward. The USSR was not just any society. It was the product of the world's first successful anticapitalist revolution, and understanding its fate and why Stalinism emerged retains vital relevance for people on the political Left. We are now in a period of prolonged and profound crisis in the world capitalist system, not just an economic crisis and a perilous sharpening of inter-imperialist rivalries and conflicts, but one which now calls into question the long-term survival of the human race. Capitalism will no doubt survive this crisis in the short term, but equally certain is that this crisis is not going to be the last. In little more than a decade we have seen popular uprisings overthrow authoritarian and corrupt regimes (the Arab Spring, Ukraine, Sudan), but nowhere were initial gains consolidated, and in most cases they have been substantially or totally reversed, largely because there was no plan, program, or organizational structure that could go beyond the removal of the dictator and build a new society. Yet we cannot dismiss the possibility that, at some point, these missing elements will be put in place, and there will be a successful revolution that overthrows not just a repressive political regime but capitalism itself. In such a case understanding why the Russian Revolution evolved the way it did will prove extremely immediate for any future attempts to create a viable, democratic, postcapitalist society.

If we move back to the here and now, what can a marxist critique of Stalinist society still bring to the field of Soviet history in general? We have now reached a point where only a relatively small minority of people in the field are old enough actually to have lived and worked in that country, even if only for brief periods (soon this will also be true of historians born in Russia and the former Soviet republics). They have no direct, experience-based memory of the poverty, the empty shops, the queues, the bureaucratic contempt for people's ordinary needs, the excruciating inefficiency, the appalling quality of manufactured goods, or of the transactional nature of most personal and social interactions (the latter a particularly damaging survival in post-Soviet Russia, especially among middle-aged and elderly Russians). Even those of us who began going to the USSR only in the late 1970s or early 1980s could still conceptually link what we observed and experienced directly back to the 1920s and 1930s and use these experiences to contextualize our historical studies. Scholars who began going to the former Soviet republics only in the 1990s do not have that experience. I am not being a philistine here and claiming that only those who have seen the USSR can truly understand its history. The preposterousness of such a proposition is obvious, for it would render all historical research of any society impossible, not to mention gloss over the problems that immediacy can create for one's historical judgment. What it does mean, however, is that we must acquire that context through other means, largely from reading the old Sovietology, the sociologists, the economists, the historians, the journalists, and even (dare I concede) the political scientists, and by looking not just at the documents we find in the archives, but at the Soviet academic and popular publications of the times.

This last proposition clearly has nothing to do with marxism per se or with its application. My argument is that, irrespective of the type of history we do, whether we investigate art, literature, nationalism, identity, or more mainstream areas of political and economic history, we all still need to contextualize our research with a knowledge of how the Soviet system functioned. This means not just its politics and institutions but also its underlying political economy. And it is here that marxism acquires its relevance.

By political economy I do not simply mean the "economy." I refer to the entire fabric of social relations through which the Soviet system as what we might call a "quasi-mode of production" produced its social product, and how this process of producing the social product reproduced these social relations independently of the specific individuals who carried out given roles at any given time. I stress this latter point because a lot of historians who have written about the Stalin period, in particular, have dwelt at length on the question of the extent to which the working class supported or did not support the Stalinist regime. This issue is obviously important, and we have seen some impressive scholarly research on the impact of social mobility, public opinion, and whether the Stalin period saw the formation of a specifically "Soviet identity" (see, for example, Fitzpatrick 1979; Davies 1997; Hellbeck 2006). The fact that historians do not and cannot reach an agreement on these issues indicates just how difficult these questions are. Even if we had the answers to these questions, however, they still would not necessarily tell us all that we need to know about the underlying social relations of the system, any more than studying the opinions of Republican-voting workers in the United States or Tory working-class voters in Britain tells us about the inner drives of capitalism. To put it crudely, the fact that large numbers of workers vote Republican or Tory tells us a great deal about the state of politics in the United States and Britain and about the state of class consciousness, but it in no way changes the essential fact that capitalism is a system based on the exploitation of labor, including the labor power of these same pro-Republican and pro-Tory workers.

So, too, in the Soviet Union. Irrespective of how individual workers perceived their place within Soviet society, they remained in the last instance the providers of labor power, the products of whose labor were alienated from them by a governing elite, which then decided how that surplus product would be used: how much to sustain the living standards of workers, how much would go to accumulation, and how much would go to the privileges of the elite itself (I leave aside for the moment the question of how we label this elite—some have called it a ruling bureaucracy, others a ruling class—or how we define its composition). Even rapid social mobility cannot change this fact. If, let us say, some 15 percent (to cite one estimate from the early 1980s) of workers left the bench for managerial jobs during the First Five-Year Plan, this still left 85 percent of the remaining workers on the shop floor, creating society's necessary and surplus product (Schröder 1984). Moreover, the shopfloor places vacated by this upwardly mobile 15 percent were soon taken by migrants from the countryside who then slipped into the same roles. Admittedly, from a sociological standpoint the Stalinist regime presented a seeming paradox. It was a regime whose leadership and social base (managers, the technical intelligentsia) increasingly came from proletarian and peasant backgrounds, but once having entered this elite they fulfilled the function of an exploiting class—not because of their personal qualities (we know from archive documents that many could be quite humane or even outraged at the conditions under which workers lived), but because of their place within the system of social production. This fundamental reality undermines any suggestion that this was somehow a workers' state or that workers were the main beneficiaries of this state. The working class played no role in determining what type of state this would be, no role in selecting its leaders, and no role in deciding on the policies the state would pursue. Within production they remained, as I have said, the creators of a surplus product, but politically they played no part in deciding how that product would be used or for what goals.

Behind this example lies a larger argument: that when we interpret such phenomena as belief, identity (whatever that may mean), participation in official rituals, letter-writing to the press, or conversely, attacks on shock workers or Stakhanovites, in the last instance we must remain aware that beneath these phenomena there was a specific system of social production with its equally characteristic social relations. The way in which we analyze the causal mediations that may link these social relations with these higher phenomena is admittedly a complex issue, although I would maintain that it is not unknowable. This does not mean that these phenomena are less real than the underlying social relations of production—any more than Marx considered ideology, religion, or culture to be less real than the social relations of capitalist production. On the contrary, together they form the ensemble of relations that constitute Stalinist (or capitalist) society at any given point in its development. We can better understand this point if we look at Marx's method of abstraction. In determining the analytical priority of the categories he used, Marx looked first for the most basic categories without which the capitalist system would not be the capitalist system. He identified these as the commodity and value since while developed capitalist production presupposes these categories, the latter do not automatically presuppose developed capitalism. From here Marx discerned those categories that were at the next level of concretion, that is, wage labor and the wage labor-capitalist relationship, from which Marx then derived the category of surplus value. In this way there is a logical relationship between the analytical categories that moves from the abstract (the essential) to the increasingly concrete (Rubin 1974, ch. 4). At the level of what Marx called superstructures we see society in all its manifest complexities, and indeed the outcome of any specific historical event will depend on what transpires here, at this level. The superstructure is not "unreal," but nor does it efface the underlying reality of the essential relationships that gave rise to these superstructural phenomena.

In the case of the USSR, how do we explain its chronic inability to coordinate production and the de facto hollowness of economic plans? How do we explain the consistently poor, and often unusable, quality of what industry produced and its huge waste of inputs and labor power (what one commentator during perestroika characterized as its ability to take high-quality imported Japanese steel and turn it into defective ball bearings)? These are not questions of interest only to economists and economic historians. They were key to all social life. They structured the domestic division of labor and the larger constellation of gender relations. They impacted the health and longevity of the population. They created that specific, transactional nature of personal relations between individuals, summarized in the concept of *blat* (the exchange of favors) and determined the specific hierarchies, both formal and informal, within the workplace. At a higher level they determined the distribution of privileges and the reproduction of social stratification. They were the foundation upon which people formed their political attitudes toward the regime, their expectations and discontents with the Soviet welfare state, and their views on the various ethnic and national groupings within the population.

Economists tried to explain the difficulties of the Soviet economy through the absence of markets, bureaucratic incompetence and infighting, clashes between interest groups, arbitrary decision-making within the leadership, and the poor quality of information, in short by invoking a limited cast of social actors: industrial managers, bureaucrats, and the political leadership. What this approach excluded from view was the existence of other, more fundamental, relationships that underlay these phenomena, namely the relationships—and antagonisms—between the direct producers and the elite and its agents.

The essential contradictions of the Soviet system, the contradictions which eventually led to its collapse, had their origins in Stalinist industrialization. There are several elements here. One was the creation of an elite that based its power on the hypertrophic development of heavy industry and the production of means of production. The second was the elimination of the market and market relations. This meant that the elite could not exercise control over the economy through titles to ownership over the means of production and could not extract its privileges from the sale of a privately owned expropriated surplus product. Instead, the means of production were state property, and decisions over the use of the social product—what to invest, what to allow the population for consumption, what to divert to the elite's own privileges—were made by the state. In other words, the elite could only ensure its control over the economy through its political control over the state. This explains the vicious nature of the Stalinist police state, for only a police state could guarantee the elite's continuance in power as a precondition for its receipt of privileges. It also explains the reluctance within the elite to grant even limited political reforms, for fear that such reforms, once granted, would lead to increasingly radical demands from the population and fatally undermine the elite's hold on power. This perception, in my view, was well-founded. It was certainly the pattern in Poland, Hungary, Czechoslovakia, and ultimately the USSR.

My own argument has always been that the elite that emerged during industrialization was only able to assert and consolidate its position by doing battle with two separate social forces. On the one hand, it had to crush the peasantry, a social group rooted in market relations, where many (but by no means all) of its members would have welcomed some form of restoration of capitalism. On the other, it had to put down opposition and resistance from the traditional working class, opposition that was in no way coordinated or political (in the sense of seeking to overthrow the regime) but which potentially could have shipwrecked Stalinist industrialization. The elite, therefore, had to erect a system that was neither market nor plan. It eliminated the market with collectivization and the end of NEP. By suppressing democracy and workers' involvement in political decision-making and enterprise management it eliminated any possibility of planning, which can succeed only if those drawing up the plan and those executing the plan are one and the same, and if there is a free flow of accurate information from the bottom upwards. On the contrary, the elite had to remove the working class from any contact with decision making, and had to eliminate the working class as a class (Filtzer 1986, chs. 2–4). This process I and others have termed "atomization," although I now think "molecularization" more accurately evokes what happened. Politically and socially workers were not totally "atomized," but they did have to fall back on very small family and friendship groups. Even within these narrow circles it was dangerous to trust anyone with their real opinions, much less take the risk of acting on them. This was most obviously the case during the Stalin period, but it remained true right up until Gorbachev (Filtzer 2006).

This political relationship took on a particular expression within the industrial enterprise, where workers, deprived of any collective means of asserting their influence or redressing the imbalance of power between the state and themselves and between themselves and management, had to resort to individual, largely depoliticized, reactions, in the form of high turnover, absenteeism, haphazard fulfillment of orders, and most important of all, by exploiting the chaos intrinsic in Stalinist bureaucratic industrialization to usurp a significant degree of control over the individual labor process. This, in turn, shaped the specifically Stalinist (or Soviet) nature of shopfloor relations. Managers, under intense pressures to meet impossible plan targets, became reliant on workers to minimize disruptions to production and even to assert their own ingenuity to rectify the myriad faults caused by the system. In order to ensure workers' cooperation managers granted numerous concessions, such as turning a blind eye to labor discipline violations; attenuating officially decreed rises in output quotas and cuts in wage rates; and accommodating workers' partial control over the intensity and speed of work (Filtzer 1986, pt. II).

As I have emphasized many times, this was not resistance. It was exactly the opposite—it was the reaction of a workforce that had lost contact with most residues of class consciousness and, thanks to state repression, could not have acted in a political way even if it had wanted. The other salient feature of this reaction was that the relationships that emerged between workers and managers within the production process became reproducible and were independent of the specific views and attitudes of the individuals involved. It was perfectly possible for workers to see themselves as loyal Soviet citizens, admirers of Stalin, and still contribute to the huge losses of work time, slow growth of productivity, and the production of massive amounts of defective output. These phenomena were not simply the result of worker alienation, as real as that was. Workers were also responding to what in effect confronted them as objectively given conditions within the enterprise. Workers lost vast amounts of time roaming the factory looking for scarce parts, materials, and tools, rectifying defective components, or waiting for a mechanic to come and repair a machine that had broken down for the umpteenth time. They had equally to cope with the notoriously irregular work rhythms within Soviet factories, where workers would spend weeks idled while waiting for supplies, then engage in a mad rush at the end of the month or quarter (so-called storming) as factory management desperately pushed them to fulfill the plan. It is no surprise that one of the major sources of disputes between workers and line managers was over the issue of how delays, stoppages, and defective output would be paid. If workers suffered a long stoppage was this because they were slacking or ignored production protocols, or because the parts and tools they needed were not there? If workers turned out defective parts, was it because of their own negligence, or because the components they were given or the machinery on which they were working were themselves defective (Filtzer 1992, 133–60)?

Because the different stages of production were interconnected, delays or defects in the output from one shop fed through to successive stages of production, whether it be within the same factory or in another enterprise dependent on the first enterprise for vital supplies. We can pose this another way: by responding subjectively (but logically) to what confronted them as objective conditions, workers created these same objective conditions for other workers in other stages of production, who then responded in the same subjective but equally logical manner, creating new objective conditions for another set of workers further down the chain. In this way waste and inefficiency circulated and were reproduced throughout the economy.

This gave rise to the phenomenon that Hillel Ticktin called "waste" (Ticktin 1973) and what I would call a process of self-negating or self-consuming growth. By this I mean the process by which the expenditure of means of production and labor power failed to translate itself into the production of a commensurate quantity of useable goods (use values if we follow the terminology used by Marx). On paper plans could be fulfilled and overfulfilled, but this did not mean that the economy received all the useful objects that it required to sustain or expand production. On the one hand, Soviet industry (and I use the term broadly here to include construction and transport) required far larger quantities of inputs—metal, coal, electric energy—to produce a given quantum of finished output than did Western industry. This was for three basic reasons: the original quality of the inputs was poor, so you had to use more of them; equipment was poorly designed and badly manufactured and required a greater quantity of inputs to produce a given unit of output; and the labor process itself tended to waste inputs through indifference or negligence (disregard for production protocols, poor storage). On the other hand, a large percentage of what industry produced was either totally defective, so that it had to be discarded and totally remanufactured, or of such poor quality that it required the diversion of substantial amounts of labor time to rectify or refashion these products so that they could be used. You only had to study the Soviet machine-building industry to see how this worked: machine-tool operators routinely had to take time out to refashion castings and parts because they came into the shop in the wrong shape or size. A huge amount of metal wound up on the floor as shavings—and not all of these were recovered for resmelting. Factories had vast machine shops devoted to nothing else but remaking defective parts or making spare parts because the original machine manufacturers did not supply them—and even then the new parts often did not work because the machinists had no drawings. Not all defective items were discarded or rectified: in a shortage economy factories had no choice but to use them with the defects going on to compromise the quality of successive stages of production (Filtzer 1986, 261–66; 1992, 160–76; 1994, 204–13)

It is this process of self-negating growth that helps explain the continued dominance of heavy industry within the Soviet economy. Advocates of "interest group theory" tried to explain this phenomenon by reference to the overriding political power that the commissars (later ministers) and managers in heavy industry held within the top leadership, power which they exercised to claim an inordinate share of resources for their own factories. This observation was certainly true, but it had an objective foundation. The waste of inputs was of such a scale that it required an overblown heavy industry sector just to keep the economy standing in place. If you waste 10, 20, or more percent of the coal that comes out of the ground, either because it is lost in transit, is overconsumed by poorly designed and poorly made blast furnaces, or has a high ash content and so you require more of it, you need more coal mines to mine more coal. This requires more coal mining equipment, more rails, more coal carts, more rolling stock on the railways, and more locomotives to take it to its final destination, not to mention the additional labor power needed to produce or operate all these things. If you produce too much substandard steel, construction sites and machine-building factories have to use more steel to build buildings or make machines. And so you need more steel mills, which in turn requires the manufacture of all the inputs that go into putting up and equipping a steel mill. If window glass is so thin that it breaks almost immediately as soon as you glaze the windows in a new building, you need a much larger number of glass factories to produce replacement window glass—which then also breaks and needs replacing. I could go on, but the idea is already clear. The Soviet Union's hypertrophy of Group A (Department I in Marx's schemes of capitalist reproduction) was not only an ideological fixation of Stalin and his planners (and all subsequent generations of planners), and it was not only the result of resource wars between the commissariats or ministries. It was the automatic result of an economic system that could not put to productive use a large part of what it produced. Waste, or self-negating growth in this way was both the driving force of the Stalinist system, the force that drove forward extensive economic growth, and at the same time a major cause of that system's long-term instability and eventual stagnation.

For Marx the antagonistic relationship between wage labor and capital expressed itself in the contradiction between use value and exchange value. Labor power was a use value, an object of use, which performed the useful task of labor, which transformed means of production into commodities for sale on the market; that is, it created value. In this act the useful properties of specific forms of labor were effaced, and labor became abstract or homogeneous labor: the labor power of one worker was interchangeable with the labor power of another, just as the commodities they produced were equally interchangeable on the marketplace as possessors of (abstract) exchange value. Commodities, of course, were useful objects, use values, but their use could not be realized unless they achieved sale on the market, that is, unless their exchange value could be realized on the market and the commodities transformed into money. If they failed to find a sale, their useful properties were lost, wasted. We see this particularly at times of acute capitalist crises, such as the Great Depression or the protracted aftermath of the 2007–2008 financial collapse. During the 1930s people went hungry while farmers had to slaughter livestock and bury them in mass graves because their price on the market could not cover the cost of feeding them. Factories and construction sites lay idle, while people desperately needed clothing, shoes, and housing.

In the Soviet Union, by contrast, industry did not produce goods for sale on the market, and goods possessed no exchange value. Goods were produced and distributed through the system strictly for their concrete, useful properties: as timber, steel, coal, peat, cloth, footwear, cement, or what have you. The contradiction lay not between use value and exchange value but within use value itself (Ticktin 1978, 48–53). If the commodity is the social form of the product under capitalism, Soviet industry produced what I call the deformed product, which was the social form of the product within the Stalinist system. It was a product that appeared to possess useful properties but could only partially be used for the purposes for which it was intended, and in many cases could not be used at all. Individual consumers acquired shoes or clothing because they needed to be shod and clothed, but the goods were of atrocious quality and often totally defective. They either wore out prematurely or proved wholly unusable. Under Khrushchev and Brezhnev, you had a curious situation where the population suffered from a serious shortage of shoes, but shoes—large numbers of them—remained unsold in the shops. The reason was not because of a lack of effective demand, that is, because there was no market for shoes, but because the quality was so bad that people simply saw no point in buying them. Within production, enterprises acquired metal, raw materials, machinery, but these, too, could not function as planned or designed. The deformed product was, I would argue, the social expression of the antagonistic relationship between the elite and the Soviet workforce.

The contradiction inherent in waste, or self-negating growth, was also expressed at a political level. The elite required an atomized (or molecularized) workforce to protect its hold on power and the continued maintenance of its privileges. This atomization, I have argued, expressed itself in the specific form of the labor process within Soviet production, which in turn gave rise to the deformed product and waste (self-negating growth). Yet waste was not a positive expression of workers' discontent. Workers themselves found it profoundly frustrating and demoralizing, as interviews during perestroika made abundantly clear. To this extent waste, insofar as it helped to perpetuate workers' demoralization and atomization, was itself a political precondition for the elite's ability to stay in power. At the same time, however, it was the process of self-negating growth that ultimately led to the Soviet system's collapse and the unraveling of the elite's domination (Filtzer 1994, 210–11).

Why was this the ultimate outcome and not the reformation of a revolutionary working class? For Marx the contradictions within the capitalist system could only be abolished through the abolition of the capitalist system itself. When he used the concept of the dictatorship of the proletariat, he did not have in mind that there would be a shift of power within capitalism, and that the proletariat would somehow displace the bourgeoisie as the top dog but maintain capitalist relations. Aside from the fact that this appeared to Marx as a total impossibility, it also would not solve the problem. The capitalist system had to be superseded and replaced by a qualitatively new form of social organization, where society would democratically determine its priorities and objectives and the means by which it would achieve them. Ownership would be social (which is not the same as ownership by the state), and the true measure of a society's wealth would be leisure time, not the production of material goods. For it was through leisure time that Marx saw the individual achieve her or his full potential as a human being (Marx 1973, 708, 712; Heller 1976, 104–5). When Marx wrote that the proletariat was a universal class, he meant that for the first time in human history a class had emerged which, to achieve its own liberation, had to put in place a system that would liberate all people, not just the proletariat itself. This process had its own prerequisites, among them the creation of a working class that was self-conscious of itself as a class not just as distinct from other classes and with its own interests but as a class capable of making this revolutionary transformation of superseding class society as a whole. There was nothing automatic or deterministic about this process, as the experience of the workers' movement under both capitalism and Stalinism has shown. Rosa Luxemburg (who claimed to have taken the expression from Engels, although it probably originated with Karl Kautsky) put it succinctly and clearly when she said the choice was between socialism or barbarism. Luxemburg had in mind the carnage of World War I, although the twentieth century would go on to produce still greater horrors that even Luxemburg could not have imagined. Now, in the twenty-first century, humanity again faces calamities that capitalism has created but cannot solve. There is no guarantee that socialism will prevail, but if it does not the future will be bleak indeed.

Works Cited

Bahro, Rudolf. *The Alternative in Eastern Europe*. London: Verso, 1981.
Benvenuti, Francesco. *Fuoco sui sabotatori! Stachanovismo e organizzazione industriale in URSS, 1934–38*. Rome: V. Levi, 1988.
Berliner, Joseph S. *Factory and Manager in the USSR*. Cambridge, MA: Harvard University Press, 1957.
Bettanin, Fabio. *La collettivizzazione delle campagne nell'URSS: Stalin e la "rivoluzione dall'alto" (1929–1933)*. Rome: Editori Riuniti, 1978.
Davies, Sarah. *Popular Opinion in Stalin's Russia: Terror, Propaganda, and Dissent, 1934–1941*. Cambridge: Cambridge University Press, 1997.
Filtzer, Donald. *Soviet Workers and Stalinist Industrialization: The Formation of Modern Soviet Production Relations, 1928–1941*. London: Pluto Press, 1986.
Filtzer, Donald. *Soviet Workers and De-Stalinization: The Consolidation of the Modern System of Soviet Production Relations, 1953–1964*. Cambridge: Cambridge University Press, 1992.
Filtzer, Donald. *Soviet Workers and the Collapse of Perestroika: The Soviet Labour Process and Gorbachev's Reforms, 1985–1991*. Cambridge: Cambridge University Press, 1994.
Filtzer, Donald. "Atomization, 'Molecularization,' and Attenuated Solidarity: Workers' Responses to State Repression Under Stalin." In *Stalinistische subjekte–Stalinist subjects–Sujet staliniens: Individuum und system in der Sowjetunion und der Komintern, 1929–1953*, ed. Brigitte Studer and Heiko Haumann, 99–116. Zurich: Chronos Verlag, 2006.
Fitzpatrick, Sheila. *Education and Social Mobility in the Soviet Union, 1921–1934*. New York: Cambridge University Press, 1979.
Granick, David. *Management of the Industrial Firm in the USSR: A Study in Economic Planning*. New York: Columbia University Press, 1954.
Hellbeck, Jochen. *Revolution on My Mind: Writing a Diary under Stalin*. Cambridge, MA: Harvard University Press, 2006.
Heller, Agnes. *The Theory of Need in Marx*. London: Allison & Busby, 1976.
Klopov, E. V., V. N. Shubkin, and L. A. Gordon. *Sotsial'noe razvitie rabochego klassa SSSR: Rost chislennosti, kvalifikatsii, blagosostoianiia rabochikh v razvitom sotsialisticheskom obshchestve: Istoriko-sotsiologicheskie ocherki*. Moscow: Nauka, 1977.

Kolakowski, Leszek. *Marxism and Beyond: On Historical Understanding and Individual Responsibility.* London: Paladin, 1971.

Korsch, Karl. *Marxism and Philosophy.* London: New Left Books, 1970.

Marx, Karl. *Grundrisse: Foundations of the Critique of Political Economy.* Harmondsworth, Middlesex: Penguin Books, 1973.

Pons, Silvio. *Stalin and the Inevitable War, 1936–1941.* London: Routledge, 2002.

Rubin, I. I. *Essays on Marx's Theory of Value.* Detroit: Black & Red, 1972.

Schröder, Hans-Henning. "'Neue' Arbeiter and 'neue Bürokraten. Gesellschaftlicher Wandel als konstituierendes Element von 'Stalinismus' in den Jahren 1927–1934." Unpublished discussion paper, University of Bochum, 1984.

Shkaratan, O. I. *Problemy sotstial'noi struktury rabochego klassa SSSR.* Moscow: Mysl', 1970.

Skilling, H. Gordon, and Franklyn Griffiths, eds. *Interest Groups in Soviet Politics.* Princeton: Princeton University Press, 1971.

Solomon, Susan Gross, ed. *Pluralism in the Soviet Union: Essays in Honour of H. Gordon Skilling.* London: Macmillan, 1983.

Ticktin, Hillel H. "Towards a Political Economy of the USSR." *Critique* 1, no. 1 (Spring 1973): 20–41.

Ticktin, Hillel H. "The Class Structure of the USSR and the Elite" *Critique*, no. 9 (1978) 37–61.

Part Two

Mass Repression/ Terror

Chapter 4

Stalinism, the Terror, and Social History

Wendy Z. Goldman

Historians, like writers and artists, often choose their subjects for deep political, emotional, or familial reasons. For many in my generation, the attraction to certain topics was political. As a teenager in New York City in the early 1970s, I frequently skipped school to participate in left-wing political meetings. The city at that time was pulsing with revolutionary energy: hippies, anarchists, Maoists, Black Panthers, Young Lords, radical feminists, and other groups—all convinced that "the System," as we then called it, was on the verge of collapse. My memories of those smoke-filled meetings have long faded, but the electric excitement of one in which a large group of passionate young people debated the issue of monogamy is still vivid. The main positions emerged quickly: Should we, as revolutionaries, marry and commit to long-term faithful unions, or should we reject the patriarchal institution of marriage and practice sexual freedom without binding ties? As young people, we were riveted by the subject. No one considered the issue as a personal choice but rather as part of a revolutionary program to be determined collectively. Many participants in the meeting were involved with left-wing organizations that flaunted the slogan "Smash Monogamy." But those still committed to this slogan mounted a weak defense. The momentum was now on the other side. Women were tired of men who took advantage of free love to reject commitment and responsibility. A radical feminist movement had recently emerged within the New Left with a furious critique of male sexual and organizational behavior (Piercy 1969). Those hoping to build a disciplined revolutionary party declared that free sexuality was antithetical to the morality of the working class, a group deeply entrenched within our political imaginary but less known in reality. In short, the free love of the counterculture was on the way out, and party building was on the way in.

Over the next decade, the National Liberation Front defeated the mighty United States army in Vietnam, and the revolutionary wave receded. Some committed activists went into the factories to organize, a few joined small terrorist groups, and others returned to school or work. I made the decision to enter graduate school to study Soviet history. By the mid-1980s, I was sitting in a library in Moscow reading stenographic reports of women's congresses and juridical articles from the 1920s. Here, in the records of the early Soviet revolutionaries, I discovered, with a shock of delighted recognition, the same passionate debates, the same hopes for freedom, and many of the same arguments that so animated my political comrades in the early 1970s. The main difference was that we had possessed little more than outsized hopes. The Soviet revolutionaries held power and were debating the future of family law for an entire country. Many party activists, women, and jurists argued for an end to marriage; others expressed the same disgust with male behavior that would be taken up by American women of the New Left half a century later. These sharp and freewheeling debates seemed to belie the dominant totalitarian model that experts used to explain Soviet society. Moreover, as I soon discovered, the Stalinist retreat from free love in the mid-1930s was widely supported by Soviet women who were struggling to collect child support from their newly emancipated partners. Was the Soviet retreat from free love a result of pressure from below? Did the state use this social discontent to push through other laws, like the prohibition of abortion, which most women did not support? What was the relationship between the Stalinist state and society (Goldman 1993)? The primary sources pointed to two aspects of Stalinism that the Cold War totalitarian model ignored. First, the role of classes and social groups in forging state policy, and second, the contingent, reactive nature of many of the state's critical decisions.

Like many members of my generation, I was inspired by the world's first socialist revolution and baffled by its degeneration under Stalin. Yet the Cold War explanation of this trajectory, part of the dominant paradigm in Soviet studies since the 1950s, seemed to me both tendentious and incomplete. Foregrounding the concept of totalitarianism and focused on ideology and personality, it maintained that social groups mattered little in the analysis of Soviet politics or history. The country, ruled by a monolithic party, united from its inception by fixed, antidemocratic ideological precepts, wielded totalizing control over an atomized, terrorized, and passive citizenry. Soviet totalitarianism followed a ruthless logic: the soviets were supplanted by the party, and the party, in turn, was supplanted by Stalin, a single individual who ruled through violence, fear, and execution. Ordinary people, at the base of the pyramid of power, had no agency to resist, criticize, or even express their opinions. And if they had no impact on political decision making, why would their ideas, material conditions, or responses be worth researching?

For years, this Cold War narrative shaped the study of the Soviet Union, but with the impact of New Left social movements and Third World revolution, the practice of history began to change. Social history and its more politicized subfield, "history from below," captured the imaginations of a young cohort of historians who abandoned the study of elite men to embrace the history of peasants, workers, women, racial and sexual minorities, and resistance movements. Although not all practitioners of social history were on the left, its focus initially carried a political charge in both its choice of subjects and its commitment to a usable past. Its methodology infiltrated the highly politicized field of Soviet history more slowly than the American and European fields but with no less of an impact. New studies focused on workers, soldiers, and peasants uncovered broad support for the revolution, as well as sharp splits within what was once seen as a monolithic Bolshevik Party. Research on the 1920s and 1930s revealed multiple, competing visions of revolution, as well as social support for and resistance to Stalinist policies (Lewin 1975; Rabinowitch 1978; Fitzpatrick 1979; Koenker 1981; Filtzer 1987; Siegelbaum 1988; Stites 1989.) The party now appeared not as an iron monolith rolling inexorably along fixed ideological rails but as a small wooden craft desperately trying to steer its way through roiling and unpredictable social seas. If the great wave of revolution had lifted it to power, it was nearly capsized by the ensuing storms of famine, Civil War, peasant opposition, workers' discontent, poverty, and underdevelopment. The alleged monolith splintered and split. Lacking a tested navigational chart, its improvised policies often created new crises, and it turned to repression to counter resistance. Historians deemed the messy new paradigm, revisionism. Centered on social groups and political contingency, the rigid, old totalitarian model seemed to crumble beneath its findings.

The Terror and Social History

Yet no paradigm reigns supreme for long. The opening of the archives in the early 1990s had a mixed impact on Soviet historiography. Access to previously secret documents sparked new work on social groups, political culture, resistance, and local party organizations, among other subjects. At the same time, the most explosive documents gave fresh impetus to the older state-centered totalitarian model. Nowhere was this truer than in regard to Stalinism and the Terror. The revelation of the mass and national operations, successive decrees promulgated in 1937–38 for the arrest and execution of suspect social and national groups, convinced many historians of the top-down, state-controlled character of the Terror (Khlevniuk 2002, 2004, 140, 331; Gregory 2009). The decrees targeted former kulaks, White Guards, activist priests, and recidivist criminals, as well as Poles, Latvians, Koreans, and other Soviet national groups suspected of spying. Signed by the Politburo and sent to the People's Commissariat of Internal Affairs (NKVD) of every province and republic, the decrees also set quotas for the number of people to be imprisoned or executed. The mass and national operations, which were not made public until the early 1990s, were responsible for the largest share of people executed in 1937–38 (Khaustov, Naumov, and Plotnikova 2004, 273–81; Getty 2002; Hagenloh 2009, 227–87; Shearer 2009, 320–70; McLoughlin and McDermott 2003, 118–52; Vatlin 2004, 120–216). The decrees seemed to suggest that the social history of the Terror, which involved the study of mass support, the role of social groups and individuals in pursuing their interests, the impact of denunciations, the behavior of local party organizations, and the accompanying campaign for democracy, was largely irrelevant. These topics served merely as white noise for the targeted, controlled excisionary violence from above. Yet, like my earlier work on women, my research on the factories, the unions, industrialization, and local party organizations during the Terror suggested a different conclusion: actions from above and from below were intertwined in a propulsive dialectic that determined the beginning, the escalation, and the end of the Terror of the 1930s. Indeed, the orders from above could not be fully understood apart from the country's tumultuous social history.

I first began researching the social history of the Terror on a hunch that the archival records of the unions, workers, and local party and factory committees would yield a new perspective on the politics of the time. These holdings had not yet been used for this purpose, and like Aladdin in the cave, I quickly discovered that the archives were brimming with treasure (Goldman 2007, 2011). Those were tragic and heady days. As socialism collapsed and the archives opened, the new freedom of Western researchers was supported by Russian archivists who were barely surviving. Their salaries were in arrears, and their savings wiped out by hyperinflation and free market prices. In the canteen of the State Archive of the Russian Federation, the archivists were eating rice with ketchup. They paid for the rice; the ketchup was on the table. For a time, the Russian State Archive of Social and Political History lacked electricity and heat. In the winter, researchers worked in coats and gloves in the dim light of the windows. On the northern outskirts of Moscow, packs of starving dogs roamed around the branch of the Lenin Library that housed the factory newspapers. One archivist who lived in a *kommunalka* (communal apartment) told me that if not for her neighbors who shared food, she would have starved to death. Amid this unfolding human tragedy, my hunch that the social history of the Terror would add substantially to our knowledge proved truer than I predicted. The archival sources and factory newspapers told a new tale of reluctant local leaders soon overtaken by a whirlwind of mutual denunciations propelled by workers' resentments, simmering workplace differences, and complex personal histories. This mass phenomenon, which intersected with targeted repression from above, accelerated and spread the Terror through every institution and workplace.

Beginnings: Vacillation and Escalation

How did the Terror begin? The record showed that its origins fit poorly within the totalitarian model of a planned, unidirectional operation launched by a united leadership. As two leading historians demonstrated, "the road to terror" was long, winding, and marked by enigmatic stops and starts (Getty and Naumov 1999). In response to the assassination in December 1934 of Sergei M. Kirov, the head of Leningrad's party organization, party leaders charged N. I. Ezhov, deputy head of the Party Control Commission, with responsibility for the investigation. After the quick apprehension and execution of the assassin and a few alleged accomplices, and the arrests of a small group of former left oppositionists, Ezhov developed a narrative of a still-hidden, far-reaching conspiracy. His view, however, initially found little support among party leaders. The head of the NKVD himself, G. G. Iagoda, was skeptical that hidden enemies lurked within party, economic, and state institutions. The initial flurry of arrests subsided in the summer and fall of 1935, suggesting that top party leaders doubted and perhaps even opposed Ezhov's notion that a wider conspiracy needed to be uncovered and rooted out.

The escalation of the Terror proved to be a process of fitful starts and pauses, not a plan firmly set and executed in advance. Only a full year after the Kirov murder, in January 1936, did the pace of investigations and arrests accelerate. Coercive interrogations (and their transcripts) helped convince hesitant party leaders, and Stalin in particular, that the country was indeed under threat by hidden enemies with foreign connections. But doubts remained strong at the party's lower levels. Even after the first Moscow show trial in August 1936, central party leaders could not convince local party organizations to look for enemies among their members. Although local officials were stunned by the Kirov murder and the show trial, they refused to believe that remnants of antiparty groups existed in their organizations or that past opposition was an indication of present disloyalty. Local party activists maintained a tolerant, even protective view toward comrades who were previously involved in oppositional activity. As long as any member freely and honestly admitted such activities, they were not grounds for expulsion or arrest. As late as the summer of 1936, the director of Serp i molot, the country's premier iron and steel plant, flatly rejected the idea that the plant's problems were the result of intentional and conscious wrecking rather than negligence, technical shortcomings, and lack of work discipline. Workers were keenly interested in the show trial, but they believed the whole affair was a squall at the top. In Moscow, city party officials visited the factories to hector local activists to hunt for hidden enemies, but their audiences remained largely impervious to the pressure (Goldman 2007, 55–92).

Indeed, the escalation of the Terror was, in part, a response to this very lack of political motivation at the local level. The response from below—slow, halfhearted, complacent toward prior oppositionism—prompted a determined reaction from above. In the fall of 1936, party leaders recast a deadly explosion in the Kemerovo mines as an act of wrecking by a cabal of Trotskyists who deliberately aimed to kill workers. The intense publicity around the subsequent Kemerovo trial abruptly changed the atmosphere in industrial workplaces. According to the new public narrative, not only were party leaders like Kirov, Stalin, and Kaganovich under attack by terrorists but ordinary people as well. Within days of the Kemerovo mine explosion, Stalin replaced the more hesitant Iagoda with the far more aggressive Ezhov as head of the NKVD. The Commissariat of Justice instructed regional and local procurators to reexamine every explosion, accident, and fire as possible cases of intentional wrecking. By reframing workers as the target, the Kemerovo trial ignited the hunt for enemies on the local level, creating a frenzy of charges and countercharges of wrecking (Goldman 2007, 95–109). The social history of Soviet industrialization, with its attendant imbalances, high accident rates, and material difficulties, proved crucial in this process.

Spread: The Tensions of Rapid Industrialization and Capital Accumulation

After the Kemerovo explosion, workers, foremen, shop heads, engineers, and party activists operationalized the language of the Terror to shift blame for the technical problems and social tensions created by rapid industrialization. Dangerous working conditions, accidents, malfunctions, and shortages all became the fault of purported hidden wreckers. Repression widened through two channels: orders from above and mass participation from below. Wrecking charges were instrumental in the attack from above on leading economic officials and party members such as G. L. Piatakov, a former supporter of the left opposition and deputy commissar of industry. But they also fueled a firestorm of local accusations. Individuals and groups in every institution used the Terror to advance their interests. Workers quickly grasped the utility of political charges. In the absence of independent democratic unions, they frequently used the language of political denunciation to pursue their collective interests. In fact, workers, like most ordinary people at the time, did not view the arrests, the hunt for enemies, or the campaign against wrecking as a "terror." On the contrary, the newspapers framed the arrests as part of an "antiterrorist" campaign. The participation of workers, the most ideologically revered group in society, was particularly important to party leaders (Goldman 2007, 95–130; 2011, 81–139).

During the industrialization drive, party, union, and economic officials faced intense pressure to meet high production targets. They frequently ignored the complaints of workers about abusive foremen, safety and health issues, high accident rates, and poor living and working conditions. Yet after the Kemerovo trial in November 1936 and the second Moscow show trial in January 1937, which both focused on industry, workers realized that they could command attention and often redress through accusations of wrecking. Accident rates, which rose steadily from 1934 to 1936, dropped in 1937—the height of the Terror—as managers began remedying problems that might leave them vulnerable to charges of wrecking (Goldman 2007, 159, 225–36; 2011, 47–55). Throughout 1937 and 1938, squabbles between shop heads turned deadly. The factory newspapers carried banner headlines trumpeting the dismissal, party expulsion, and arrest of bosses. The newspapers were quick to cast work accidents, poor food in the canteens, and harsh living and working conditions as the result of intentional wrecking aimed at discrediting Soviet power. Workers viewed the latest bulletins about their fallen bosses on wall newspapers, and testified at huge, workplace-wide mock trials of managers, shop heads, and engineers. The union rank and file applauded the instructions from above to challenge authority and used them to criticize official power and privilege.

The upsurge of criticism and accusations from below intersected with policy at the highest level. Denunciations led to dismissals, expulsions from the party, and arrests. Stalin was hardly able to oversee all the anarchic and unpredictable meetings held in workplaces throughout the country. Ardent belief and creeping fear went hand in hand (Thurston 1996.) Some accusers genuinely believed they were purging hidden enemies; others made preemptive attacks to protect themselves. The Party Control Commission was forced to investigate charges workers made against managers and local officials, and its findings often resulted in dismissal, expulsion, and arrest. No one wanted to be accused of failing to unmask or overlooking an enemy. Long-standing rivalries between shop heads, technical design groups, and workers and bosses found new forms of expression in political accusations. These grievances alone would not have produced the Terror, but coupled with the efforts of party leaders to remove former oppositionists and their instructions to unmask enemies with party cards in their pockets, the Terror gave an amplified, albeit distorted, platform to workplace conflicts. As the hunt for enemies gained momentum among ordinary people, it transformed the culture of the workplace. Everyone began to understand that no one was immune to accusation and arrest. Millions of people were drawn into the process as victims, perpetrators, and sometimes both.

The Role of Denunciations

Many questions remain about the role of unsolicited denunciations from below in the widening of the Terror. Several historians believe these denunciations had little impact (Khlevniuk and Bekowsky 2021). Yet many archival sources, including the stenographic reports of local party meetings and records of the unions and the All-Union Central Council of Unions (VTsSPS), suggest an interplay between denunciations and arrests, as well as between confessions and new victims. Mass participation, regardless of whether it stemmed from support, fear, or coercion, was important. Party officials, for example, urged local party organizations to develop closer relationships with the NKVD and to turn over any information they received about suspected enemies. This information came from many sources, not the least of which was *zaiavleniia* (declarations.) The party required all its members to submit a *zaiavlenie* if they suspected someone of disloyalty, were aware of compromising information, or had contact with someone who was arrested. If a relative, close friend, or associate of a party member was arrested, and a member failed to submit a *zaiavlenie*, they could be charged with "failure to unmask an enemy" or "protecting an enemy," and expelled. If a party member did submit a *zaiavlenie*, they were subject to long interrogations by their shop committee, the party committee, or a factory-wide party meeting. These interrogations, which could involve between 15 and 500 people, could last for hours and stretch over weeks or even months. Although the NKVD could not arrest a local party member without permission from the first secretary of the city committee, attacks from fellow party members and workmates often revealed unexpected information, which was then forwarded by the party committee secretary to the NKVD and the district and city committees.

Politburo members, including Stalin, signed execution lists for people arrested in the mass and national operations, but at the same time, the center expected local party organizations, unions, and other institutions to purge their ranks. When a party member was accused by others, the local party organizations carefully considered the case and then voted to expel, reprimand, or acquit. The party committees held hearings, akin to court trials, in which other members presented information relating to the case. There were no rules governing the evidence that could be presented, which included hearsay, gossip, rumors, and opinions. Everyone with any knowledge of the accused was encouraged and even compelled to testify. The outcomes of these meetings were not predetermined, and the accused mounted vigorous defenses that were sometimes effective in persuading their comrades to retain them.

Once the Terror took off on the local level, arrests of officials and party activists were not solely the result of orders from above. Some victims were first dismissed from their posts, expelled from the party, and then arrested. Others were arrested and only then expelled and removed from their posts. When arrest preceded expulsion from the party, local organizations were strongly censured for overlooking the enemies in their midst. Although the NKVD needed permission to arrest party members, local party organizations frequently found themselves in the position of affirming the expulsion of members who had already been arrested. Clearly, they had received no warning from the city party committee if, in fact, the NKVD had even sought its approval. Given the tumult, turnover, and arrests decimating every level of party leadership, committees at various levels may not have been in any position to provide clearance to the NKVD. Arrests and expulsions also prompted the VTsSPS to launch its own investigations, which resulted in a raft of new victims tied to those who already had been arrested. In short, local officials and party members played an important role in the creation of victims (Goldman 2007, 179–91).

Associational ties, unrelated to orders from central party leaders, also played a role in arrests. Party members, for example, could be expelled and then arrested for recommending someone who was later "unmasked as an enemy" for a post or party membership. Family ties, which connected people from different national, social, and political backgrounds, proved another major risk factor. Party members who hid unsavory details of their biographies, such as a relative who was exposed as a kulak, a former oppositionist, or a member of an ethnic group targeted by the national operations, found themselves under fire. Once the mass and national operations began, party members who had successfully concealed suspect relatives were exposed when these family members were arrested. Local party meetings were soon almost entirely occupied with interrogating members whose relatives and spouses had been arrested. Orders from above thus affected not only the social and national groups targeted by the center but their relatives and acquaintances within the party as well (Goldman 2011, 140–98).

Mass participation in the Terror was a messy and ugly business. Stenographic reports of party committee meetings revealed that many people were both victims and perpetrators. Some people sent *zaiavleniia* about suspected comrades and workmates to their union organization, district or city party committees, the NKVD, and A. Ia. Vyshinskii, the prosecutor of the Moscow trials, but soon became victims themselves. Many who were victimized tried to save themselves by blaming others. As people became increasingly frightened about the possible exposure of their family and associational ties, they wrote preemptive or self-protective *zaiavleniia* to safeguard themselves from connections who were already in political trouble. These preemptive *zaiavleniia*, written to demonstrate their unimpeachable loyalty, worsened the plight of the victims by adding new suspicions to their files (Goldman 2011, 96, 98, 123–24, 128, 137, 138, 157, 161, 277, 296, 303).

Terror, Democracy, and the Mass Operations

The mass and national operations constituted the phase of the Terror that best fits the top-down model of centrally controlled and directed violence. Yet even these planned operations cannot be understood apart from the social history of the groups they targeted, the provincial party leaders who prompted them, and the actions of local NKVD organizations. The mass operations were initially modeled on the policing sweeps of the early 1930s of criminals, homeless, beggars, and the unemployed in the cities and the dekulakization campaign that accompanied collectivization in the countryside (Viola 1996). These sweeps targeted groups rather than individuals and subjected the victims to extrajudicial trials, exile, or imprisonment. They were reenacted with even greater violence in the mass operations of 1937–38 against similar target populations. Both the methods and the victim groups were closely tied to the social chaos and dispossession created by collectivization and industrialization (Shearer 2009, 320–70; Hagenloh 2009, 227–87; McLoughlin and McDermott 2003, 1–18.)

The mass operations, launched in the summer of 1937, were preceded by the February–March 1937 Central Committee Plenum, which set the stage for a new round of attacks on alleged enemies. The Plenum endorsed the purge of the former right oppositionists, and it also, paradoxically, launched a campaign for democracy. Amid the new wave of bloodletting, the campaign aimed to revitalize the party, the soviets, and the unions through multicandidate, secret ballot elections in place of appointments and rote voting by list. Officials would now be required to stand for competitive election, defend their records, and answer to their constituencies. Party leaders strongly encouraged criticism from below. Moreover, a newly adopted Constitution extended voting rights to previously disenfranchised groups, including former kulaks, priests, nobles, White Guards, and others, the very groups that would soon be targeted by the mass operations. Urban and rural votes were to be counted equally. Regional party leaders supported the democracy campaign and the planned elections, but they also voiced deep unease at the potential outcome. They feared the voting power of newly enfranchised groups in their regions and bemoaned the shortage of party educators. Many peasants were deeply embittered by collectivization, and the smaller towns and industrial settlements were swollen with migrants from the countryside.

The democracy campaign was quickly seized by various groups to pursue different aims and interests. Central party leaders sought to use democratic elections and popular criticism to break up the so-called family groups or circles of mutual protection. Reenergizing the rank and file was one way to remove former oppositionists in high positions who were protected by long-standing comrades. At the same time, workers seized on the democracy campaign to take back power from a newly privileged union bureaucracy. Not surprisingly, the electoral campaigns quickly became intertwined with political accusations. Workers actively sought to recapture their unions by using the language of the Terror to remove those in power, and entrenched officials countered their critics with matching accusations. In the end, democracy proved illusionary but the political mudslinging that ensued prompted new arrests and expulsions, which central Party leaders neither planned nor intended.

The upcoming elections for the soviets had even greater and harsher consequences. The fears of regional leaders, on ample display at the Plenum, encouraged the Politburo to launch the mass operations against the very groups most feared in the elections: those dispossessed and marginalized by collectivization and industrialization. With fascism ascendent in Germany, the mass and national operations were motivated by fear that embittered domestic groups and nationalities might collaborate in the event of a Nazi invasion. Nor were these fears entirely unjustified. Many groups that nursed grievances against soviet power did indeed collaborate with the Germans in the occupied areas. The turbulent social history of the 1930s thus proved pivotal to even the most centrally directed and controlled phase of the Terror.

Finally, mass participation in the Terror and the widespread political culture of denunciation also affected the implementation of the mass and national operations in the localities. After local and provincial NKVD organizations received their orders and target numbers for arrests for the mass and national operations, they rapidly exhausted their *kartoteki* (card files or indexes) of suspected or potential enemies. They needed new victims to meet the quotas imposed by the center. *Zaiavleniia*, denunciations, and information from individuals and local party organizations thickened the NKVD files, generating new investigations and fresh lists of suspects. In all likelihood, the NKVD in the republics, provinces, and districts used this information to replenish their exhausted index files of suspects. In Ukraine, NKVD records showed that an additional source of suspects came from the confessions of detainees, a practice that was likely common to all the republics (Viola 2017). Every victim had a network of relatives, friends, political comrades, and coworkers who were often dragged into an investigation through association. The information gained by the NKVD from denunciations and confessions undoubtedly affected its choice of victims in the mass and national operations. Events on the local level, which transpired with little to no control of Stalin or the Politburo, shaped the implementation of their orders. Indeed, it would have been impossible for Stalin and the Politburo to personally supervise and direct the arrest of over 1,500,000 individuals by the NKVD between 1937 and 1938.

The End of the Terror: Intended and Unintended Consequences

Many historians have argued that the best proof that the Terror remained firmly under central control was that it both began and ended from above. Yet just as its beginnings were tied to confusion, disagreement, and social issues, so too was its end. As a result of the Terror, work discipline in the factories collapsed and production suffered. Workers had little reason to respect or obey foremen or shop heads who might be arrested at any moment. In Dinamo, a leading electric locomotive and machine factory in Moscow, no less than four directors were arrested over three years. P. F. Stepanov, the wily director of Serp i molot, was occupied by endless political meetings in which he was forced to parry a stream of charges against him. By 1938, party leaders understood that the party and factory committees, the leading organizers of production in the industrial enterprises, could not devote all their energy and time to exposing their members as enemies. Hitler was on the march, and party members in the country's critical industrial sectors were busy tearing each other to pieces. The Terror was weakening production, defense, and the country.

While central party leaders initiated and encouraged mass participation in the Terror, they also set in motion unintended and damaging consequences out of their control. By 1938, the party was paralyzed; it could not enroll new members because its current members were terrified of endorsing someone who might subsequently be identified as an enemy. Current members could not be promoted to fill the positions of those lost to arrest and execution. The party committee of one large Moscow factory could not find a single member with a biography sufficiently unblemished to withstand the scrutiny necessary to serve as its representative to the district committee. The party, the country's leading body, was frozen in fear. Party members who were expelled and then reinstated after appeal found it impossible to regain employment. Managers, terrified of hiring someone who might be arrested, refused to restore exonerated victims to their jobs. No one in authority would put anything in writing. Many people had been fired or expelled because of testimony by those who were subsequently arrested. How were these cases to be resolved? Workplaces were in chaos. No one understood the rules, and everyone was terrified of aiding a potential enemy. The Terror had to stop, not because party leaders followed a planned script from beginning to end, but because its social, political, and economic consequences had gotten completely out of control.

Concluding Thoughts

It is impossible to understand the Terror, its beginning, escalation, and end, without taking into account the social history of the Soviet Union. In the final analysis, this history is important not only because it describes the lived experience of millions of people but because it motivated, shaped, and constrained state policy. The Terror's successive phases differed in their targets, but all were connected to the great social upheavals of the 1930s. The attack on former oppositionists who presented political and economic alternatives, the hunt for so-called wreckers in a rapidly developing economy, the grievances of workers, the exile of the alleged kulaks, and the disaffection within the party itself—were all consequences of Stalinist industrialization and collectivization. The forms of accommodation, resistance, and participation of various social groups in the great Stalinist project of capital accumulation and development set the parameters of state policy. Social reactions to state policies created unforeseen problems that, in turn, required new state responses. This dialectic conditioned the actions of the state, forcing it to respond, often violently, in new ways.

It is perhaps ironic that Stalinism, one of the most powerful state systems, and the Terror, its period of greatest violence, taught me to view history not as the story of a single dictator or an all-controlling state but rather as a dynamic and evolving interplay between state policies and social responses. The study of social history or history from below broadens our understanding of politics and ideology. It deepens the questions asked and the lessons learned. What motivated a class or social group to support a dictatorial regime? How did groups pursue their collective interests in the absence of political democracy? What strategies did ordinary people and officials use to maneuver, to "work around" shortages and to redress difficulties? And finally, what were the unintended consequences of Stalinist state policies, and how did these consequences, in turn, reshape societal and state responses? Even the most powerful state was forced to interact with social classes and groups, and in the end, these interactions proved the driver of the country's terrible and extraordinary history.

The great question that still draws me to the study of Stalinism is the same one that propelled me into graduate school so many years ago: How could the revolutionary ideals of 1917 have produced such a murderous, undemocratic regime? This question is essential for all leftwing movements to answer if we are to avoid the mistakes of the past. Whatever partial answers I have gleaned from a lifetime of study are rooted in the Soviet Union's social history. Party leaders faced immense difficulties in realizing their initial revolutionary vision in an undeveloped, impoverished society where the majority of the population—the peasantry—clung fiercely to petty household production and resisted state taxes, requisitions, and control. The pressure to accumulate capital for industrialization deeply shaped the system. It split the party, induced a disastrous rush toward forced collectivization, and resulted in a sharp drop in living standards. To paraphrase Alexander Pushkin's aphorism on the role of war in the reign of Peter the Great, "The Soviet Union was forced into shape by the drive to accumulate capital as metal is forged by the hammer." It is unlikely that the country could have industrialized as quickly as it did in a democratic society. Escalating violence and increasing centralization of power in the 1930s were, in part, a reaction to the political resistance, peasant uprisings, workers' dissatisfaction, and disaffection within the party. Despite Stalin's violence and brutality, many people fervently supported his policies. Commitment to the ideals of the revolution, pride in national achievement, and rapid social mobility created a strong social base. Ardent support persisted even during the Terror when fear and belief collided to create unresolvable personal conflicts for many people. Backing for the Stalinist regime was reinforced during the war years despite tremendous privations. The victory over fascism, unthinkable without the support of workers and massive defense production, became the basis for a powerful and enduring national myth.

When I first lived in the Soviet Union in 1984, the revolutionary past was present at almost every turn. It could be found in the modest plaques on otherwise nondescript buildings commemorating Bolshevik meetings or the lives of storied inhabitants, in the seats on the metro reserved for World War II invalids, and in the resounding absence of capitalist advertising. But most of all, it lived in the faces and histories of the people themselves, in the intense kitchen table conversations, the barely licit Soviet-American friendships, and the astounding family stories of ordinary people whose relatives had experienced the revolution, dekulakization, the Terror, and the war.

Many years later, a colleague invited me to visit Zorya Serebriakova, the elderly daughter of Leonid Serebriakov, an Old Bolshevik and close associate of Lenin, who supported the left opposition in the 1920s and was executed in 1937. Zorya was living with her extended family in a dilapidated nineteenth-century mansion, hidden by flowering bushes and vines, on the outskirts of Moscow. The house, once Serebriakov's dacha, was seized by Vyshinskii and not returned to the family until Serebriakov was rehabilitated by Mikhail Gorbachev fifty years later. Zorya and her children had suffered greatly through long years of exile, imprisonment, and dispossession. The walls of Zorya's room, with its narrow cot, desk, and floor-to-ceiling windows, were covered with photographs of her father, Lenin, Trotsky, and other famous revolutionaries. One showed two young men—Trotsky and Serebriakov—perched on an old-fashioned open jalopy, laughing with delight at who knows what: the car, the sunshine, the revolutionary victory?

As socialism collapsed in the 1990s, heartbreaking scenes played out at every turn: elderly World War II veterans, their medals pinned to worn suit jackets, begging on the streets, refugee families sleeping on blankets in the metro, and young girls flocking to nightclubs filled with businessmen flush with money and drink. I remember standing next to an older woman in the back of a crowded bus. Glancing with disgust at a picture of Sylvester Stallone's Rambo in one of the new tabloid newspapers, she told me she knew war; she had lived through the siege of Leningrad.

"The past," in Faulkner's famous phrase, "is never dead. It's not even past." And the Russian past, too, is still present. One hot summer afternoon, a Russian friend and I set off to find Butyrka, the notorious Moscow prison that once held people arrested during the Terror, and more recently, new political dissidents who expose oligarchical corruption and mass theft. After stumbling around, lost and confused, we suddenly realized the prison was right in front of us. Surrounded by back alleys, courtyards, and modest apartment buildings, it was hidden in plain sight. The door to its deserted, darkened reception room opened easily. As our eyes adjusted to the dim light, a strange chill passed over me despite the warm summer sunshine. The little recessed windows for handing over packages for prisoners were still there. But I could also see the ghostly lines of women, exhausted and afraid, desperate for information about loved ones who had disappeared in the Terror. The room was empty, but they were not gone.

So many of my colleagues over the years have shared my sense of the profound stakes of Soviet history. It is, after all, one of the greatest and most complex episodes in the long collective history of the left. I remember jogging with Kevin Murphy in Moscow one morning, passionately disputing the program of the left opposition as if we were still living in 1926; sitting on the polished floor in a museum exhibit on wartime Moscow with Don Filtzer, intently scribbling notes on ration amounts; slipping outside a conference with Lars Lih for a walk, oblivious to our surroundings and transported back to the great debates of another time. For me, no history has ever vibrated with so much meaning as that of the world's first socialist state; none has ever seemed so hopeful and so tragic, so intellectually and politically rich, and so filled with portent for the future of our burning, conflict-ridden world.

Works Cited

Filtzer, Donald A. *Soviet Workers and Stalinist Industrialization*. London: Pluto Press, 1987.

Fitzpatrick, Sheila. *Education and Social Mobility in the USSR, 1921–1934*. New York: Cambridge University Press, 1979.

Getty, J. Arch. "'Excesses Are Not Permitted': Mass Terror and Stalinist Governance in the Late 1930s." *Russian Review* 61 (January 2002): 113–38.

Getty, J. Arch, and Oleg V. Naumov. *The Road to Terror: Stalin and the Self-Destruction of the Bolsheviks*. New Haven: Yale University Press, 1999.

Goldman, Wendy Z. *Women, the State and Revolution: Soviet Family Policy and Social Life, 1917–1936*. New York: Cambridge University Press, 1993.

Goldman, Wendy Z. *Terror and Democracy in the Age of Stalin: The Social Dynamics of Repression*. New York: Cambridge University Press, 2007.

Goldman, Wendy Z. *Inventing the Enemy: Denunciation and Terror in Stalin's Russia*. New York: Cambridge University Press, 2011.

Gregory, Paul. *Terror by Quota. State Security from Lenin to Stalin*. New Haven: Yale University Press, 2009.

Hagenloh, Paul. *Stalin's Police: Public Order and Mass Repression in the USSR, 1926–1941*. Baltimore: Johns Hopkins University Press, 2009.

Khlevniuk, Oleg. "The Objectives of the Great Terror, 1937–1938." In *Stalinism. The Essential Readings*, ed. David Hoffman, 82–104. Malden, MA: Blackwell, 2002.

Khlevniuk, Oleg. *The History of the Gulag. From Collectivization to the Great Terror.* New Haven: Yale University Press, 2004.

Khlevniuk, Oleg V., and Bekowsky, Simon. "Archives of the Terror. Developments in the Historiography of Stalin's Purges." *Kritika: Explorations in Russian and Eurasian History* 22, no. 2 (Spring 2021): 367–85.

Koenker, Diane. *Moscow Workers and the 1917 Revolution.* Princeton: Princeton University Press, 1981.

Lewin, Moshe. *Russian Peasants and Soviet Power. A Study of Collectivization.* New York: W.W. Norton, 1975.

McLoughlin, Barry. "Mass Operations of the NKVD: A Survey." In *Stalin's Terror: High Politics and Mass Repression in the Soviet Union*, ed. McLoughlin and Kevin McDermott, 118–52. Hampshire: Palgrave, 2003.

McLoughlin, Barry, and McDermott, Kevin. "Rethinking Stalinist Terror." In *Stalin's Terror. High Politics and Mass Repression in the Soviet Union*, ed. McLoughlin and McDermott, 1–18. Hampshire: Palgrave, 2003.

Piercy, Marge. 1969. "The Grand Coolie Dam." The Feminist eZine. http://www.feministezine.com/feminist/modern/The-Grand-Coolie-Damn.html.

Rabinowitch, Alexander. *The Bolsheviks Come to Power. The Revolution of 1917 in Petrograd.* New York: W.W. Norton, 1978.

Shearer, David R. *Policing Stalin's Socialism: Repression and Social Order in the Soviet Union, 1924–1953.* New Haven: Yale University Press, 2009.

Siegelbaum, Lewis. *Stakhanovism and the Politics of Productivity in the USSR, 1935–1941.* Cambridge: Cambridge University Press, 1988.

Stites, Richard. *Revolutionary Dreams. Utopian Vision and Experimental Life in the Russian Revolution.* New York: Oxford University Press, 1989.

Thurston, Robert. *Life and Terror in Stalin's Russia, 1934–1941.* New Haven: Yale University Press, 1996.

Vatlin, A. Iu. *Terror raionnogo masshtaba: "Massovye operatsii" NKVD v Kuntsevskom Raione Moskovskoi Oblasti, 1937–8.* Moscow: ROSSPEN, 2004.

Viola, Lynne. *Peasant Rebels under Stalin. Collectivization and the Culture of Peasant Resistance.* New York: Oxford University Press, 1996.

Viola, Lynne. *Stalinist Perpetrators on Trial: Scenes from the Great Terror in Soviet Ukraine.* New York: Oxford University Press, 2017.

"Zapiska N.I. Frinovskogo v Politbiuro TsK VKP (b) s prilozheniem operativnogo prikaza NVKD SSSR No. 00447." In *Lubianka. Stalin i glavnoe upravlenie gosbezopasnosti NKVD, 1937–8. Dokumenty*, ed. V. N. Khaustov, V. P. Naumov, N. S. Plotnikova. Moscow: Izdatel'stvo "Materik," 2004.

Chapter 5

Lost and Found Revolutions
Between Emancipatory Dreams and Mass Terror in the Soviet Union

Gábor T. Rittersporn

The February Revolution of 1917 left hardly a trace in Soviet collective memory. The Petrograd uprising and the ensuing abdication of the tsar finished off a crumbling regime and replaced it with a stopgap successor that put off decisions until the enactment of a hypothetical constitution that was never going to appear on the horizon. Characteristically, few citizens of the USSR cherished the memory of February's sudden emergence of a wide variety of movements, groups, parties, factions, committees, and councils, which were rallying under different banners and eagerly debating the future in the name of different causes. And so it went with the multitude of attempts, even by bank clerks and diocesan employees, at creating bodies of collective management. Instead, people remembered the shortages of food and other necessary goods which started at the time.

The October Revolution was a different matter. The Bolshevization of the local and regional administrations left few recollections, but by the end of the 1920s most people had an idea of the Petrograd coup. The vision younger citizens formed of the event was increasingly influenced by the culture industry's relentlessly promoted imagery derived from John Reed's slightly censured book on the *Ten Days That Shook the World* and from the bowdlerized film Sergei Eisenstein made of it. The imagery did not conceal that for the new regime the Great October was about seizing the government in the capital. Things appeared simple: the coup d'état led to the supposedly happy life the

Soviet people would enjoy later. There was hardly any question of showing that the new regime had to struggle for years to find a solid social base and construct governmental structures at the price of moving away from the ideals which motivated many if not most revolutionaries of the first hour. By the early 1930s, the saga of the Civil War and industrialization eclipsed the old slogans calling for the creation of an egalitarian, self-governing and internationalist community in the future USSR and for the emancipation of the toilers of the world.

The Bolshevik narrative came to dominate the terms in which the world thinks about the Russian Revolutions of 1917 even today. One of these revolutions was largely absent from Soviet and Western mentalities and continues to be overlooked to this day. It deserves the name of April Revolution after the month when the momentous event of the revolutionary land seizures by large masses of the peasant population started (Ferro 1980, 113–36; Buldakov 2010, 179–220).

In a matter of weeks, the unbridled jacquerie transformed social and political relations in the countryside and beyond it. The new relations had little to do with the great designs of the other revolutions or with the progress they were supposed to stand for. Reviving the custom of the nineteenth century, peasant assemblies distributed the land among the families of the village according to the number of mouths to feed. In a departure from time-honored practice, women became full legal members of the communes in most places, above all because of the great number of husbands who were in the army or fell in the war. This was practically the only innovation.

For the rest, as in the past, the rural communes were anything but egalitarian collectives of revolutionary self-management. They were led by an elder and the richest farmers, and the rest of the population was expected to accept their decisions. The *obshchiny* concentrated on the solution to daily problems of the village without caring about the rest of the country and the world as long as the regime's policies did not touch them. They were not experimenting with new procedures for dealing with their affairs. Peasants were wary of the state, which they did not see as protecting their interests, and they mistrusted the soviets because they saw them (and not without reason) as meddlesome government organs. The Great Design of the April Revolution was embodied in individual farming, in the perpetuation of patterns of patriarchal authority, and in the conservative universe of the village commune.

Researchers exploring the new language of the village discovered in the mid-1920s that peasants were inclined to interpret the word "revolution" as *samovol'shchina*, "free, spontaneous and arbitrary action" (Selishchev 1928, 218). As a matter of fact, this was what they undertook after the collapse of the Old Regime, and this was the way they proceeded when it came to defending their revolutionary gains.

The villagers were busy distributing land in April 1917 when Lenin proposed to nationalize confiscated estates and organize model farms on them. By October he came to accept the new status quo. He had hardly any choice. There were about 20,000,000 peasant households in the country. Nearly 75 percent of the population were peasants, some 100,000,000 souls. If farmers had a future-oriented political project after a Civil War that the Bolsheviks won to a large extent because the peasants grudgingly sided with them, it consisted in the will to continue living as they had been doing since *their* revolution. The rural economy was archaic, the mechanization of the work processes was rudimentary at best, and around 20 percent of the households were hardly more than self-sufficient.

The peacetime version of the "free, spontaneous and arbitrary action" consisted in withholding produce instead of selling it for the prices fixed by the state, waiting for better terms of trade, and refusing the regime's interference with the affairs of the commune. Feeding the country was at stake. For the peasants, counterrevolution was the pressure of the regime that claimed to be revolutionary. For the regime, the village as such was the counterrevolution.

The social base of the April Revolution and its institutional arrangements were obvious from the beginning. They were the peasantry with old ways of taking decisions, no matter the conflicts between poor and rich farmers. This was not exactly the case with the October coup and its aftermath, and people were not impervious to Bolshevik propaganda. At the start, the public was not entirely immune to the received idea of the Bolsheviks about the historical mission of a self-conscious industrial proletariat and to their claim that October was a workers' revolution that opened new vistas for the whole world. Being able to claim the status of a worker valorized one in the new conditions. So much so that engineers, managers, employees, and sometimes writers, artists, or academics came to designate themselves as "white collar proletarians" or "toiling intellectuals."

But where were the much-praised workers? According to the 1926 census, in all economic branches taken together they numbered four and a half million. Lenin admitted shortly after the Civil War that, by and large, workers ceased to be proletarians in the political sense of the term, and a fellow Bolshevik had every reason to congratulate him on being the leader of a vanguard class that did not exist. By this time, masses of people were not convinced by the Bolshevik discourse about workers as the ruling class of the regime. For them, the functionaries of the administration were in command, officeholders who learned their trade in the ruthless struggle for the new regime's survival during the Civil War and in the merciless requisitioning of food in the countryside that went with it. Anti-Bolshevik insurgents, animated by the dreams of the idealistic militants of October and defining themselves as true revolutionaries, spoke of "commissarocracy" (Avrich 1970, 64, 112, 170, 173–75). Needless to say, their adversaries denounced them as counterrevolutionaries and dealt with them accordingly.

By far not all officials were veteran commissars or old hands of the Civil War. But one way or another, the regime's pitiless fight for its sheer existence was the political school of many of the new functionaries, even if they did not participate directly in military and policing operations. Cadres at all levels of the local and regional administration, they belonged to the victors and had some reason to claim that they were the revolution. Most of them learned that all expedients, including indiscriminate violence, were salutary if they could advance the cause of the Bolshevik Revolution. They seemed to confound a revolution with a putsch and a civil war, which was justified by the fact that October was about securing state power and not about the niceties of devising and running organs of proletarian self-emancipation.

The Bolshevik cadres claimed a monopoly on knowing how to lead the country and where it was heading, and they treated any interference with this monopoly as counterrevolutionary subversion. The faith in the project of redemption through an egalitarian and self-managing society gave way to a cult of the party that was presumably realizing it. This did not exclude tugs of war among the Bolsheviks, which led to the elimination of dissenters from prominent and not-so-prominent positions. Party members were obliged to carry out the decisions of the leading organs even if they had doubts about their merits. The overwhelming majority of the militants accepted this rule.

By the early 1920s the party ceased to be a political organization competing with similar groups for influence among the citizens and for participation in government. It had no rivals. At the local and regional levels, it became an administrative apparatus implementing policies and controlling the work of structures such as the local executive authorities (the soviets), the army, the police, the justice, or the agencies managing the economy. At the highest levels it was a body deciding policies. Lower-level organizations formed an institution of political socialization, which prepared members for agitation among the masses and constituted a pool for the selection of future cadres.

Linguists found that the word "commissar" was understood as "the chief under the present power" in the provinces (Selishchev 1928, 215). The villagers did not forget the revolver-waiving commanders of the food requisition detachments of the Civil War. The new chiefs were tired of the grain crises of the 1920s and of their uphill struggle to dominate the countryside and enthusiastically endorsed the policy of expropriating the peasantry and forcing it into collective farms, which was launched at the end of the decade. Stalin asserted and enshrined in the canonic history of the party that the violent exercise was nothing less than a second revolution. To be sure, the first for him was the October takeover. Stalin acted and reasoned in the spirit of the putsch and like his troops, he did not see the difference between a coup d'état, an internecine war, and a revolution. The victors of April had good reason to see themselves as victims of a brutal counterrevolution.

According to Bolshevik wisdom, the social base of the revolutionary (or counterrevolutionary) regime quickly enlarged with the ambitious program of creating a new industry. Millions of people poured into the industrial areas, and many of them came to be employed on the construction sites and in the factories, the transport system, and in the mines. The apparatus expanded; it recruited masses of newcomers, especially in the local and regional officialdom and in economic management. But this did not change the fact that the right to take decisions of local importance continued to be a privilege of leading cadres of the administration while the monopoly of far-reaching decisions about political strategies and their implementation remained in the hands of a small group of leaders and of a supreme leader who listened or did not listen to the opinion of his associates. Characteristically, as Stalin admitted in private, this group was part of the hypothetically topmost organ of the party, the Politburo, which meant that the prerogatives of the latter were usurped by a clique that had no legitimate status in the system.

Stalin hated the habit of notables forming similar coteries in the territorial and specialized apparatuses. In 1934 he condemned leading functionaries from the rostrum of a party congress as "petty appanage princes" with "well-known merits in the past" who were convinced that "party and soviet laws were not written for them but for fools" (*XVII S'ezd* 1934, 34). The reference to feudal hierarchy and past merits was quite to the point. The bigwigs earned their status through their prominent contribution to the Bolshevik cause, belonged to a stratified order of ranks, enjoyed large executive privileges on this basis, an immunity from censure by their underlings and, thanks to their old boy networks, even by top agencies. Little prevented them from proving their allegedly successful work by terrorizing the population and their subordinates or by doctoring their books and their reports. Their overbearing ways provoked tensions within the administration and conflicts between the latter and the rest of society.

But they played a key role in keeping the population in check and in the construction of new factories, railway lines, canals, and cities. Their portraits decorated offices, workplaces, and classrooms in their bailiwicks, where their wise sayings were respectfully quoted. The public was invited to praise them as worthy leaders of their district, region, enterprise, or agency and also as the best pupils of the Supreme Guide. They were not above financing a lavish lifestyle for themselves from the budgets at their disposal, which also served to entertain their retainers and win the loyalty of potentially useful people.

Rank-and-file citizens who filed complaints about their conflicts with higher-ups and institutions did not need Stalin's sapience to suspect official abuse everywhere and to compare their corrupt powers to aristocrats, landlords, and their gendarmes, that is to the losers of the 1917 revolutions and their henchmen. As a matter of fact, they scarcely ever quoted Stalin's speeches. People spontaneously resorted to the analogy with the ancien régime because this was their only way to make sense of their place in the new one. Even though they did not articulate their insight, it came close to suggesting that the shady deals, the arrogance of the new elite, and ultimately the elite itself were the genuine fruits of the Bolshevik Revolution. A few fundamentalists from the old guard and a small number of people sharing their views were ready to spell out this lesson and accuse the elite of betraying October. They were likely to pay a heavy price for it.

Peasants did not exaggerate much when they complained about Bolshevik serfdom. The victors of the Second Revolution degraded them into second-class citizens. In theory they could not leave their village without the authorization of the local soviet. Certain goods were sold for specific prices in the countryside if they were available at all. The villagers were obliged to do unpaid work to repair roads. The collection of taxes and obligatory deliveries of products sometimes resembled punitive expeditions. There was hardly a detail of the sowing, harvesting, and procurement operations or of animal husbandry, which escaped the vigilance of the police and the judiciary. In the late 1930s for a year's labor, on average, the collective farmer received one and a half times the mean monthly pay in other walks of life and 124 kilograms of grain, 50 kilograms of potatoes, and practically no meat.

In 1930, the hardest year of collectivization, the police counted more than 3,000,000 participants in nearly 14,000 riots. The next year it found about 34,000 collective farms where sabotage took place and more than 9,000 where this happened at least three times. The numbers look impressive. But they relate to a rural population of about 127,000,000 with 220,000 collective farms. Typically, peasant refusal to enter the collective farm (kolkhoz) system did not lead to open confrontation. Villagers invented strategies to limit individual and collective deliveries to the state, which ranged from increasing the weight of delivered grain by moistening it or mixing it with refuse to infect the crop with ticks. The trifling income they received from the kolkhoz forced them to slip away and earn some money elsewhere and concentrate their efforts on cultivating their household plots. On the eve of the war, 17 percent of the kolkhoz population worked exclusively in the household economy but benefited from tax reductions because they had a family member who was toiling on the collective farm. It turned out that at the same time the peasants illegally enlarged more than 45 percent of the household plots. This was the case with some 9,000,000 families, half of all kolkhoz homes, which were forced to relinquish the occupied land. No wonder the agriculture remained the Achilles heel of the Soviet system up to its last days.

The memory of the revolutionary land seizure vanished from popular memory. Usually only the silver samovars recalled it in the peasant huts, along with other valuables the insurgents looted from the estates of the Old Regime's masters. But the memory of the supreme gain of the April Revolution, the disposal of the land and its fruits and ultimately the right to decide how to live did not vanish. For decades, the 1920s remained the golden age in popular memory of the village. The imagery of a purportedly rich life and of the *volia*, the "arbitrary will and freedom" peasants supposedly enjoyed at the time regularly appeared in letters, petitions, and diary notes, even of people who were children or not even born in the post-revolutionary decade. Did the authors of bitter complaints who claimed that Lenin gave them the land resort only to a rhetorical device? Not necessarily. Recurrent rumors that the party-state was about to dissolve the kolkhozes indicate that the peasants came to rely on the regime instead of preparing to resort to their *volia*. The rumor spread all over the country in 1936, on the eve of the promulgation of a new constitution. It speaks volumes that the political police found it counterrevolutionary.

Younger kolkhozniki were not inevitably unresponsive to the siren songs of the regime. But they rarely felt that they could enjoy the promises of the propaganda in the countryside. Even activists whom the authorities wanted to train as tractor drivers and technicians of agricultural machines did not see their future in the village. The authorities had to replace their contingent nearly every year. Once in the city, the young rurals joined the mythical working class, became proud or eventually disillusioned builders of the new system and potentially also beneficiaries of social mobility. Most of the upwardly mobile workers conquered only the heights of the shopfloor hierarchy or those of the factory. But overall, the life conditions of the workers improved, even if they dwelt in crowded dormitories or communal apartments. Their cultural horizon had good chances to enlarge. Many of them turned into movie and theatergoers and readers of Russian, Soviet, and foreign classics (though often also of prerevolutionary pulp shockers and tear-jerkers). The courses of political education may have bored the worker public, but they brought them closer to patterns of rational reasoning than the poor elementary schools or the drinking companies and the church.

Workers quickly discovered the advantages of belonging to the alleged ruling class. This is evident from the petitions they addressed to the authorities, in which they referred, at times ironically or aggressively, to their social status as a particular merit. The Soviet proletariat did not try to influence the regime's policies through massive participation in the activities of the party. Worker representation in the ranks fell from nearly 37 percent of the membership in 1933 to a little more than 18 percent on the eve of the war. The promotion of workers to other positions accounted only for a small proportion of the change because the arrival of new toilers in the industries offset the number of the promotees. Apparently, the working masses did not believe that they had their place in the revolutionary vanguard.

They resorted to traditional ploys to improve their working conditions. They slowed down operations to hinder the rise of output norms and gradually transformed norm-setting with sophisticated bargaining on the shop floor. There was no question of open negotiations in most cases. The management simply reacted to the behavior of the personnel. At times but not often workers wrecked machines and, somewhat more frequently, intimidated norm busters. Industrial action was rare after a large-scale strike in Ivanovo in 1932. There were only three strikes with a few dozen participants in 1937, and they were triggered by norm increases and food shortages. The events were so remarkable that they were specially reported to the Central Committee.

Workers were far more convinced by the propaganda of the importance of diligent toil for a happy Soviet future than the kolkhozniki. Nevertheless, they were not necessarily loyal to their enterprises. At the start of the 1930s, while breaking work records, the builders who left the legendary construction site of the Magnitogorsk steelworks represented twelve times the number of the yearly average contingent of the personnel. For most of the 1930s, the number of toilers entering and leaving jobs exceeded the total industrial workforce. The bright future the regime promised and better wages and working conditions were two different things, but both could inspire people at the same time. The high leadership did not meditate on the problem and ended up criminalizing unauthorized quitting and absenteeism, which led to 17,000,000 criminal prosecutions between 1940 and 1953, including almost 4,000,000 to prison terms of up to ten years. The actual number of culprits was higher because managers often did not denounce erring personnel to retain much-needed manpower. Authors of letters complaining about the labor laws and statements the police attributed to citizens regularly evoked the putative workers' revolution and the opinion that it had not changed industrial relations.

Initially, the regime hardly trusted the white-collar proletarians. Specialists with prerevolutionary tenure were particularly suspected of hostility toward the new regime that equated them with remnants of the former ruling classes. They were ideal scapegoats for failures, but they could be prosecuted and even shot simply as suspicious leftovers of the Old Regime. Nevertheless, veterans of the scientific and industrial establishments were usually as enthusiastic about the Bolsheviks' modernizing projects as their colleagues who earned their diplomas after 1917. Specialists did not need to be unconditional admirers of Bolshevik policies to appreciate the breathtaking (though not entirely successful) attempt to transform a miserable country into a stronghold of the most advanced science and technology. Also, they could have serious reservations about certain policies and still see themselves as standard bearers of the Second Revolution in the struggle for what was seen at the time as the nec plus ultra of progress. Engineers and technicians were inclined to accept the somewhat unfriendly treatment of labor by the regime because, for many of them, the opponents of supposedly scientifically elaborated work processes and output norms and the factory nomads were ignorant Luddites.

Managerial and technical cadres were well integrated into the industrial establishment. So much so that they quickly learned how to get along with their assigned tasks, which were often unrealistic. They did what they could to minimize the plan higher authorities imposed on their enterprises through concealing production capacities and coped with them by turning out substandard or defective goods, producing excessively heavy commodities, refusing to produce light ones if their targets were defined in weight, or not fabricating cheap wares if their performance was measured in financial terms. The modest price of spare parts for lorries immobilized one-third of the country's trucks in 1937, a year of bumper harvest of fruits and vegetables, which could not be canned because tin was too light and less convenient to smelt than heavier metals. Because work safety was not part of plan indicators, cadres hardly cared about it to such an extent that foreign experts were horrified by the conditions they observed in Soviet plants and mines. Official statements like the one a speaker made at a party congress to the effect that sometimes methods of coercion were necessary to inculcate technical discipline in the workers encouraged managers and engineers to treat members of the putative ruling class more severely than the latter expected. If specialists were taken to task for work-related offenses, the old guard was sitting target of punitive measures, which included prosecution.

Needless to say, there was no specific project behind the coping tactics of the masses or the specialists. They were survival schemes, attempts to improve working conditions, expedients to secure careers and at times inevitable because of the thousand impediments the economic system produced and reproduced. There was also no plan behind the stratagems of the dignitaries of all ranks. In a way they were survival intrigues: strategies to survive as officials in profitable positions. Stalin stressed that collectivization and industrialization had increased the "strength and authority" of the party and state apparatus "to an unprecedented degree" and that "everything or almost everything" depended, therefore, on how officeholders fulfilled their "decisive [and] exceptional" role (XVII S'ezd 1934, 34.) In other words, the beneficiaries of the Second Revolution were responsible for running the country, even though the overwhelming majority of them managed only local and regional affairs or those of specific agencies and enterprises. For the rest, they had to submit to the decisions of superordinate authorities and ultimately to those of the topmost leadership. They hardly decided anything beyond the limits of their immediate sphere of authority; they had no legitimate say in determining the regime's policies. Still, the ways they implemented decisions influenced policies and, to a large extent, shaped them. Not only the top leaders' and the supreme leader's decisions were politics, but so were the modi operandi of the apparatus and, to hardly a lesser extent, the little tactics of the masses.

Stalin's speech at the 1934 Party Congress amounted to a declaration of war, although this was not quite clear for the audience. The delegates approved a resolution which manifestly bore the imprint of the supreme leader's strictures: "the Central Committee of the Party and the leading bodies of the soviets will remove from whatever post, demote to more junior positions and make strictly answerable, without consideration of person, any official who violates party and state discipline" (*KPSS v rezoliutsiiakh* 1971, 152–53). The most illustrious apanage princes were delegates ex officio. Perhaps most of them voted for the decision in the conviction that it was "not written for them but for fools." For a while, their optimism seemed justified. There was no large-scale campaign against bigwigs for two years, although a small number of erring princelings were taken to task in the provinces. Their cases received publicity, but they did not entail more than harmless disciplinary measures.

Things changed by early 1937 when somewhat surprisingly the Central Committee started to encourage the criticism of leading cadres by rank-and-file militants and petty officials, denounced potentates who persecuted troublesome critics and authorized local organizations to hold assemblies whose participants were invited to censure higher-ups "irrespective of person." The propaganda highlighted the authoritarian ways, arrogance, incompetence, cliques, and local cults of famous regional leaders, accused them of "political corruption," which should be "got rid of . . . quickly, determinedly and ruthlessly" ("Bol'shevistskaia samokritika" 1937, 1) The bigwigs and their associates had large powers at their disposal to silence rebellious activists or simply to prevent lower organizations from holding meetings. They had good reasons to worry. The assemblies which did take place were quite stormy and sometimes finished by deposing cadres, even those whose appointment was the prerogative of the Central Committee.

Part of the accusations pertained to alleged wrecking in the economic establishment and to the purported lack of vigilance of the officials who proved unable to discover it. Here and there the denunciations stopped short of suggesting that prominent cadres were sheltering wreckers or that they were even involved in subversive activities. The topic was closely related to the ongoing campaign to search for deliberate sabotage, especially in industry, the transport system and mining that was behind the failure of economic policies and increasingly frequent work accidents. The failures were inseparable from the regime's inability to administer the economy, although it also had to do with the ways managing and engineering cadres tried to show off successful job performance. Little stratagems other than producing work records by individual norm busters became current in the wake of the Stakhanovist drive.

The cadres were obliged to guarantee the fulfillment of excessive norms through technical and organizational expedients, which was utopian given the chronic shortage of raw materials, energy, spare parts, and the incoherent coordination of the operation of the enterprises and of the economic branches. Instead of trying the impossible, the cadres encouraged spectacular work records, which depleted resources, disorganized production, and damaged equipment. The speed-up led to conflicts among workers as well as between them and the cadres. Deteriorated equipment led to accidents. In the first nine months of 1936 the number of accidental deaths increased by 27.5 percent in coal mining, and by 43.3 percent in transportation compared to 1935. An average of 36 workers for every 100,000 perished on the job, but the figure rose to 79 on the railways and to 163 in the mines (GARF 5451/43/74/8–9). The theme of wrecking was high on the agenda of agitated meetings in the enterprises, the administrations, and at show trials. Workers often compared higher-ups to the exploiters of the past and did not shy away from calling for their prosecution and even for sentencing them to death.

To complicate things, the 1936 harvest was worse than the one in 1932 when a severe famine afflicted the country. The police noted bitter statements by people vainly queuing at bread shops, many of which sound credible. People blamed the 1932 famine on collectivization and asserted that the loudly propagandized workers' and peasants' state did nothing to help starving citizens, especially in the countryside. In many places the procurement campaign resembled police raids. The regime mobilized food reserves and in an exceptional gesture of magnanimity it wrote off the arrears of the villages. Understandably, the rurals greeted local show trials of responsible officials and sometimes applauded death sentences, which were warrants for judicial murder.

It was in this atmosphere that in March 1937 Moscow ordered the reelection of all officeholders of the party, including grandees who were members of the Central Committee. In a notable departure from past practice, it instituted secret ballots as well as the right to criticize and challenge any candidacy and to remove officials who had been imposed in the past by the highest authorities. The stakes were high for all incumbents because the losers had a good chance of being denounced as enemies of the people or their protectors. The first meetings were turbulent and as a rule ended with the deposal of the secretaries and their right-hand men. Understandably, local powers that be did everything to transfer unpopular cadres to other positions, intimidate protesters, refuse to hold secret ballots, or falsify their results.

Grassroots militants and low-level officials constantly suffered from the despotism of dignitaries of all ranks. They could not protest even when they were obliged to fulfill manifestly illegal orders, and they served as whipping boys for the mistakes their superiors committed. Many of them realized that their faith in the Bolshevik cause implied fealty to gangs of derelict bosses, and they started to wonder what exactly the Bolshevik cause happened to be. Now the top leadership authorized them to do away with official corruption and, along the way, to take revenge. For many militants the term bolshevism regained its idealistic interpretation as a synonym of equality and social justice, and they believed that the election campaign instituted revolutionary self-management even though it never really counted on the party's agenda. They were going to lose their illusions in less than three weeks.

Election meetings quickly became arenas of open conflict between the leaders and the led. Their main themes surfaced in conflicts between management and labor. Workers started to refuse to obey cadres under the pretext that they could turn out to be saboteurs. In short order the Central Committee reestablished the control over the elections by the bigwigs and their associates whom it had censured for interfering with the vote a couple of weeks earlier (Rittersporn 1991, 118–34). The schemes of officialdom had to be tolerated because their services were badly needed to curb the unruliness of the masses. Radical critics faced retaliation. For all that, one way or another, thousands of local and regional officials fell. After finishing with the uncontrolled meetings, the highest authorities put pressure on leading bodies to denounce their chiefs, who ended up being arrested as enemies, prosecuted, and usually shot. At times the police simply arrested dignitaries without regard for the intricacies of the party statutes. By the end of 1937, 24 percent of the members of local leading bodies and 50 percent of those at the regional level were fired, some 23,000 cadres (RGASPI 17/88/536/20). All apanage princes and their retainers were ousted by mid-1938, and most of them perished before firing squads. The economic apparatus and the industrial establishment also suffered heavy losses.

The drive against the princes was in full swing when in July 1937, suddenly, Stalin launched an unprecedented wave of mass murder. First, he requested data from the localities about the number of formerly deported kulaks and ex-convicts in the districts. Then he issued a secret instruction about sentencing to death and to terms in concentration camps people supposedly belonging to a large array of categories ranging from erstwhile White Guards to non-Bolshevik political activists from before and after October, nationalists, gendarmes, and officials of tsarist Russia, returned émigrés, participants in allegedly anti-Soviet organizations, as well as churchmen and sectarians, claiming that the figures were based on the reports he received. Manifestly, the list was drawn up in haste because new categories surfaced in the following months. Thus, Mensheviks and anarchists were remembered only in February 1938. A parallel action targeted members of ethnic minorities suspected of subversion. Initially only Poles were especially singled out, but the list expanded. Latvians appeared on it in late November because a regional police chief mentioned them to Nikolai Ezhov, the commissar of internal affairs, and the formal orders to arrest Finns, Estonians, Romanians, Bulgarians, Chinese, Iranians, Afghans, Macedonians, and Germans came only in February 1938. Stalin's decision came so unexpectedly that the apparatus discovered the need to mobilize the necessary troops, prison wardens, and railway cars and to organize additional camps for the new inmates only when the campaign started and, in some cases, even weeks later.

The orders concerning new purge targets sanctioned the status quo because the police were already busy arresting and sentencing people from the relevant categories for weeks or months. Local initiative played an important role in the progression, escalation, and disorganization of the campaign. The regions received quotas of people to execute and deport, which were originally fixed as threshold figures. Officials had the right to lower them but could not raise them without Moscow's permission. The figures soon became plan indicators. Stalin and Ezhov accepted practically all requests for new quotas. Many of the new figures surfaced because the police were instructed to discover the supposedly criminal connections of the arrestees. It had simply listed as enemies any unfortunates whom those in custody had mentioned, often under torture, as accomplices or people somehow related to them, or anyone else they considered worth apprehending. It also happened that officials asked authorization for new arrests to provide retroactive cover for arrests they had already made.

Quite a few requests for new quotas surfaced on Stalin's desk because officials felt well advised to boast of successes through proving their eagerness to fulfill and overfulfill the plans in view of the ongoing purge in the apparatus. Their stratagems resembled those of the economic administration with the exception that in this case human lives were at stake. It was easy to manipulate the plan indicators. In the Sverdlovsk region only 390 of the 4,218 people arrested as Polish subversives were of Polish origin, and only 12 ethnic Latvians landed in detention out of 237 people caught during the action against the Latvian minority. Individuals originally arrested as kulaks were reported as Germans and Romanians. There were places where police chiefs clamped down on unlucky people who had foreign-sounding names while their Ashkhabad colleague arrested all Greek residents of the town. To comply with the order concerning religious activists, he caught purported mullahs through rounding up all bearded men at the bazaar (Rittersporn 2014, 73–80, 254–59).

Initially, the purge was supposed to be over in four months. It lasted more than fourteen months. At the start, 75,950 people were slated for execution and 193,000 for imprisonment. By the end 681,692 individuals were executed, and 663,261 persons received terms of up to twenty-five years of hard labor (Vert and Mironenko 2004, 609). Nothing perhaps shows better that the purge got out of hand than the fact that shootings continued for a couple of weeks after Stalin stopped the drive in November 1938. Leaders explained the terror with the need to cleanse potentially hostile elements before a coming election to the Supreme Soviet and especially in view of the looming war. The claim was somewhat extravagant since it turned out that when the massacre was already underway, there were no reliable records of purportedly dangerous elements in most places. Thus, it would be an exaggeration to suppose that Stalin and his cronies conducted anything like purposeful social engineering. After all, engineers typically know from the start the nuts and bolts of their projects, the way they are going to realize them and manage to keep the work process under control. The terror was blind and indiscriminate.

Stalin was a powerful dictator. But the outcomes of his actions were by far not always the same as his original designs. He could not boast of any success as far as the terror wave was concerned. Another 1,260,300 suspected enemies were on the new rolls in early 1941, only 84,653 fewer than the 1,344,953 victims of his purge, and they belonged to the same categories the campaign supposedly neutralized (Rittersporn 2014, 79, 259, 371). Stalin could shoot thousands of peasants, kolkhoz chairmen, and officials and do his utmost to multiply livestock, but meat production did not increase sufficiently because the losers of the Second Revolution had slaughtered cattle instead of delivering them to the collective farms.

He could order the execution of the leading officials of the country, but it turned out shortly after that the new leaders formed their own cliques and resorted to the stratagems of their ill-fated predecessors. They did not need much originality because most of them came from the lower levels of the purged hierarchy. Managing and engineering cadres and officials in other walks of life also continued on the track of the enemies of the people. Still, it was impossible to get rid of them without destroying the party, the state, and the economic apparatus. The clans and the machinations were inseparable from the daily universe of the regime because officials and specialists could not pursue and advance their careers and sometimes just cope with their duties, without resorting to them. They were the regime's best allies in social conflicts, which they often provoked themselves. The regime could not function without the schemes of officialdom, no matter how dysfunctional they happened to be. No demiurge could do more about them than try to curb their most ruinous manifestations and bitterly close his eyes for the rest if he did not want to do away with the system as such (Rittersporn 1978, 29–30, Rittersporn, 1979: 859–61). When all is said and done, Stalin was the almighty head of an inherently confused and inefficient dictatorship.

* * *

The top leaders filled out the forms of the 1939 census (RGAE 1562/329/416/52-66). They indicated as their professions "people's commissar," "secretary of the Central Committee," or "chairman" or "deputy chairman" of this or that organization: ordinary occupations in a high administration far removed from the headquarters of a revolution, a counterrevolution, or a coup d'état. To the question about the social group to which they belonged, all grandees answered "employee," a typically Soviet statistical category that lumped together all nonmanual occupations from the salesclerk to the most illustrious jobs in the apparatus. Stalin gave "secretary of the Central Committee" as his profession. As for his social position, he indicated "professional revolutionary" and added "employee" in brackets. The supreme employee of the Soviet Union apparently saw no difference between the revolution, humdrum office work, and his other pursuits such as the direction of the mass terror.

Works Cited

XVII S'ezd Vsesoiuznoi kommunisticheskoi partii (b). Moscow: Stenograficheskii otchet Partizdat, 1934.

Avrich, Paul. *Kronstadt 1921*. Princeton, NJ: Princeton University Press, 1970.

"Bol'shevistskaia samokritika—osnova deistviia." *Pravda*, February 8, 1937, p. 1.
Buldakov, Vladimir P. *Krasnaia smuta: Priroda i posledstviia revoliutsionnogo nasiliia.* Moscow: ROSSPEN, 2010.
Ferro, Marc. *The Bolshevik Revolution: A Social History of the Russian Revolution* London: Routledge and Kegan Paul, 1980.
GARF, State Archive of the Russian Federation.
KPSS v rezoliutsiiakh i resheniiakh s"ezdov, konferentsii i plenumov TsK, vol. V, Moscow: Izdatel'stvo politicheskoi literatury, 1971.
RGAE, the Russian State Archive of the Economy.
RGASPI, the Russian State Archive of Social and Political History.
Rittersporn, Gábor T. "L'État en lutte contre lui-même. Tensions sociales et conflits politiques en U.R.S.S." *Libre* no. 4 (1978): 3–38.
Rittersporn, Gábor T. "Société et appareil d'État soviétiques (1936–1938): Contradictions et interferences." *Annales* 34, no. 4 (1979): 843–67.
Rittersporn, Gábor T. *Stalinist Simplifications and Soviet Complications.* Chur: Harwood Academic Publishers, 1991.
Rittersporn, Gábor T. *Anguish, Anger and Folkways in Soviet Russia.* Pittsburgh: University of Pittsburgh Press, 2014.
Selishchev, Afanasii M. *Iazyk revoluitsionnoi epokhi: iz nabliudenii nad russkim iazykom poslednikh let (1917–1926).* Moscow: Rabotnik prosveshcheniia, 1928.
Vert, Nikola [Werth, Nicolas], and Sergei V. Mironenko, eds. *Massovye repressii v SSSR*, vol. 1 of *Istoriia stalinskogo Gulaga*. Moscow: ROSSPEN, 2004.

CHAPTER 6

Wrestling with Aspects of Interwar Stalinism

WILLIAM J. CHASE

Writing about one's views on Stalinism after fifty years of study and rumination is an alluring but daunting challenge. Trying to do so briefly only complicates the task. Given that my research focuses on the interwar years rather than reflecting on changing interpretations of Stalinism over time, this chapter offers some perspectives on specific aspects of political repression during the interwar period. It confines itself to questioning the labels used to define the mass repression of 1936–38 and how archival materials declassified since 2020 challenge some of our assumptions and interpretations. To illustrate the latter point, it focuses on two defendants in the August 1936 Moscow trial: Ivan Smirnov and Valentin Olberg. Declassified materials force us to reassess whether that trial was simply political theater. Many Europeans wondered why Stalin chose to hold a political trial when the fascist threat was mounting, and the new Soviet Constitution suggested that the USSR might become more democratic. The new evidence suggests that he did so because he feared the threats were real.

Let us begin with the labels used to define the repression of the 1930s. Whether one dates mass repression from collectivization or Sergei Kirov's murder or the August 1936 trial or mid-1937, all agree that it reached its violent zenith in 1937–38. But researchers and authors disagree on the most appropriate label to describe the repression of that decade. The most common label is Great Terror, the title of Robert Conquest's 1968 book, in which he argues that Stalin's personality and paranoia led him to destroy past and potential rivals. Even some researchers who disagree profoundly with his interpretation use that label. Because it reflects and reinforces the anticommunist assumptions in the Western world, it is a powerful label. Others use the term Great Purges. Some use *Ezhovshchina* because when Nikolai Ezhov headed the NKVD the number of people arrested and executed reached inhumane heights. One occasionally encounters the term *Stalinshchina*. I have problems with each of these labels.

The label Great Terror is unsatisfactory because it stresses victimization above all and implies that most people living in the USSR were at risk or lived in fear of being victims. But save for Stalin's personal animus and alleged paranoia, it offers limited insight into the dynamics of repression, that is who became victims, why, and how. We now know that ordinary Soviet citizens participated in the same way that some ordinary US citizens participated in the anticommunist repression of the so-called McCarthy Era. They denounced or urged the investigation of comrades, coworkers, or neighbors either for political or personal reasons, or in response to Stalin's call to unmask enemies, or because of peer pressure. By denouncing others, they validated and fueled the repression. Let us not assume that by so doing they knew that they were often sentencing a person to the Gulag or death nor that vigilance protected them. It did not; some were later arrested. Because of its lack of precision, the label Great Terror offers little insight into such complexities. The term Great Purges muddies the distinction between the Bolshevik practice of a purge (*chistka*) of the party's rolls and repression. Maintaining that distinction is of analytical importance as the two were linked, yet distinct, during this period. Bolsheviks never confused those terms. The terms *Ezhovshchina* or *Stalinshchina* identify key figures behind the mass repression, but they, too, mask more complex dynamics, just as McCarthyism masks the complex forces of that period of US history.

Until we agree on a common label, I prefer Stalinist mass repression (or simply mass repression) because it permits us to acknowledge the scale and political group that implemented the repression, while leaving it open to exploration and debate issues about its dynamics, actors, and intentions. The power to label is the power to define; scholars must wield that power responsibly. In that vein, we must recognize that the labels used by Stalinists to justify repression—double-dealer, Trotskyist, enemy agent, and others—had meaning to them, although those labels proved ambiguous enough to be misused, as they often were.

Stalin's precise role in the mass repression continues to be a contentious issue. There is universal agreement that he was politically and morally responsible for unleashing repression, be it during collectivization or in 1936–38, during which more than 681,000 people were executed, or later. While the scale of lives ended or broken is difficult to comprehend, of Stalin's overall responsibility there is no doubt. That should not obscure the issue of whether he controlled or directed it all. What role Stalin's personality played, I leave to others.

My research of late centers on small group political behavior among party members and oppositionists, in particular Trotskyists, in an effort to appreciate some of the dynamics of the political struggles and repression during the interwar years, and why some Stalinists believed that Trotskyists posed real political threats. Although they accounted for a distinct minority of those arrested, Trotskyists were disproportionally victims of repression and execution. Focusing as it does on Trotskyists, this chapter does not address the reasons for the scale of the mass repression or what justified political mass repression. While most people arrested in the 1930s were charged with what any state might consider criminal activities (such as crimes against people or property, corruption, official misconduct), Trotskyists were convicted of political crimes. To those raised in liberal democracies, the very concept of political crimes is unsettling. But that need not deter us from interpreting the past based on the available evidence.

Among the issues that divide researchers is who were the repression's victims. Many have singled out Old Bolsheviks. But various studies make clear that they were not the primary victims. Rather, where Bolshevik party members worked on the eve of arrest is a more reliable indicator. Party officials and economic administrators at many levels suffered heavily, as did their political networks or family circles. Among the elite, many victims served on the Central Committee (CC), which experienced a dramatic turnover of members between 1934 and 1939. But their CC status was often a function of their position in the party or state apparatus. The political and economic realities of the 1930s, not Stalin's past, not Leninism, provide better explanations for why Old Bolsheviks, members of the elite, and their networks or clans were arrested. Those at greatest risk for arrest were former oppositionists—Trotskyists, Zinovievites, and others. By mid-1936, Stalin and his allies viewed them as real dangers. Recently declassified archival documents enable us to continue to explore why they did so. Because the Old Bolsheviks who became defendants in the 1936 trial had been in exile or prison for several years, one cannot explain their fate based on where they worked. Rather, it was because they were accused of being double-dealers and their political plans that landed them in the docket.

My research on the political activities of Trotskyist networks in the 1920s and 1930s offers some insight into why Stalin and his allies considered them to be such a serious threat that they routinely arrested them, organized the major

Moscow trials of 1936–38, and executed most of the defendants. I have argued elsewhere that those trials were carefully crafted. What I did not appreciate then was the evidence upon which Stalin decided to include certain defendants. This chapter focuses only on the 1936 trial, specifically on Smirnov and Olberg, both of whom were Trotskyists. Based on investigations from early 1936, NKVD head Iagoda sent Stalin regular reports accompanied by portions of the two men's interrogation records (*protokoly doprosov*). Iagoda also sent comparable materials for other detainees. Those materials proved sufficient to convince Stalin, state prosecutor A. Ia. Vyshinskii, and other leaders that the defendants in the August 1936 trial were guilty as charged and hence necessitated a public trial.

Following years of political battles, in October 1927, the Politburo expelled Trotsky, Zinoviev, Kamenev, and other supporters of the United Opposition for their chronic defiance of the party's rules of democratic centralism. During the 1927 celebration of the October Revolution, their supporters organized counterdemonstrations. Those efforts came to naught but brought to light many of their supporters, whom the party expelled. Those who recanted their activities and views were, as a rule, readmitted to the party and returned to work in state or party offices. Those who refused to do so—they numbered in the hundreds, most of whom were Trotskyists—were sent into political exile, where they chafed at being removed from political work. Starting in late 1929, some agreed to recant, to capitulate, so as to rejoin the party and return to political work, which often also meant returning to Oppositional activities.[1]

Consider the case of Ivan N. Smirnov, arguably the leading Trotskyist in the USSR and a defendant in the 1936 trial. After capitulating in late 1929, he rejoined the party and held responsible positions. Soon after his readmission, he urged others to sign the recantation statement that he wrote and to rejoin the party. Smirnov viewed his capitulation as a tactical "maneuver" that enabled him to return to the party to engage in Oppositional activities. Following his example, many of his supporters, between 200 and 400 people, "capitulated" (Broué 1988, 639; Mozokhin 2013, 32). Most were readmitted to the party and resumed clandestine Oppositional activities. They viewed staying in the party as essential to helping them to revive it or to create a new party. In the party's eyes, doing so made them double-dealers.

Back in Moscow, Smirnov regularly organized clandestine meetings of Trotskyists, at times in his apartment, where they debated and decided upon political activities and tactics and organized a small operational center. In 1931, he was allowed to travel to Berlin, which suggests that party leaders believed that he had broken with the Trotskyists. He had not. There he met with Sedov, Trotsky's son, with whom he discussed the Opposition's activities and his views on Soviet state policies and rising popular dissatisfaction. In 1932,

Smirnov's comrade, Goltsman, also visited Sedov, from whom he received Trotsky's approval to form a "bloc" with other oppositionists, including the Zinovievites, and to use various methods, including terrorist methods, to remove Stalin. Sedov served as Trotsky's proxy; doing so provided his father with plausible deniability against any charges. Trotsky always denied approving the bloc, but evidence from his own archive makes clear that he did so (Broué 1980; Getty 1986). Not until early 1936 did the NKVD and Stalin learn of the bloc and its intentions.

On January 1, 1933, Smirnov and sixty-eight other Trotskyists were arrested. In his January 15 report to Stalin, Iagoda reported that OGPU (*Ob"edinennoe gosudarstvennoe politicheskoe upravlenie*, Joint State Political Administration) officers had confiscated directives that Trotsky sent from "abroad (known to us)" as well as Smirnov's correspondence with comrades about maintaining contact after being readmitted to the party. Smirnov was sentenced to five years of imprisonment (Khaustov 2003, 388–89; Mozokhin 2013, 19–176 passim). Only following Smirnov's arrest did Iagoda conclude that his recantation "contains a number of 'rubbery' formulations in which the Trotskyist double-dealer easily accommodates his disagreements with the party" and that others who had signed statements like Smirnov's continued to engage in clandestine activities (Mozokhin 2013, 32). When discovered, they were again exiled. According to Iagoda, even in political exile, Smirnov and others continued their clandestine activities.

The term double-dealer deserves attention in this context because it conveys that a comrade had lied to the party, the community that had forgiven Smirnov and others and restored them to its ranks. To Bolshevik leaders, double-dealers were a serious threat: "double-dealing is the evil that alone can support and cover up the existence of antiparty elements within the party. The challenge is to eradicate this evil without a trace. A double-dealer is not only a deceiver of the party. At the same time, a double-dealer is also a scout of forces hostile to us, their wrecker, their provocateur, who has penetrated the party by deception and is trying to undermine the foundations of our party— hence, the foundations of our state" (*Izvestiia TsK KPSS*). In their eyes, not only had Smirnov and his supporters betrayed the party, but they also had not disarmed themselves, that is laid down their weapons of political struggle as promised. Of the defendants in the August 1936 trial of the Trotskyite-Zinovievite Terrorist Center, eleven were former oppositionists; five were German Trotskyists who had moved to the USSR.[2] Because the Soviet defendants, like Smirnov, had been in political exile or prison, some writers argue that the trial was the first step in Stalin's plan to eliminate Old Bolsheviks. Today, there is reason to question this view. For their part, Trotsky and Sedov denied the accusations against the key defendants (Smirnov, Goltsman, and Valentin Olberg). Many Western writers have taken their denial at face value.

During the trial, state prosecutor Vyshinskii said that of all the defendants, "The most persistent in his denials is Smirnov." He repeatedly refused to admit to Vyshinskii's charges until confronted by the other defendants. He denied that the bloc acted on "Trotsky's instructions," referring to them instead as "Sedov's 'personal opinion'" (*Report of Court Proceedings*, 79–86, 153–60). Only on the eve of his execution did Smirnov confess to his daughter that he had lied in court:

> I want you to liquidate the remnants of Trotskyism in your mind, and . . . to go on with the party line. . . . I said this in my last words to all the vacillating Trotskyists. We must disarm decisively and quickly. . . . You must disarm in the next few days. Keep in mind that the Gestapo who figured in the trial were not dummy figures, but the most real [and] clever fascists. Whether TROTSKY wants it or not, his periphery has become intertwined with the Gestapo. . . . In one of the articles of the bulletin [*Bulletin of the Opposition*], he [Trotsky] did indeed write: "STALIN must be removed." What does it mean? To GOLTSMAN, he really gave instructions for me about the terrorist attack. It has reached a dead end, and our youth need to get out of it as soon as possible. (RGASPI 671/1/185, 20–24)

When Smirnov wrote of "the most real [and] clever fascists," he no doubt had in mind Valentin Olberg, whose confessions under interrogation contributed to Smirnov's and others' becoming defendants. The son of a prominent Menshevik and a family friend of Menshevik leader Rafael Abramovich, Olberg joined the German Communist Party (KPD) in 1928. In late 1929, he joined the Trotskyists, led by his friend and comrade Kurt Landau, Trotsky's authorized representative in Berlin. Soon after, Olberg began working closely with Trotsky. He played an active role in unifying Berlin's divided Trotskyists in 1930, served as Trotsky's translator on occasion, wrote for the *Bulletin of the Opposition*, and communicated Trotsky's and Sedov's views to supporters in the USSR. Trotsky shared with Olberg his letter to the Bolsheviks' 1930 Congress and reminded him that the "most important thing is not to waste time, to act quickly and try by all means to get the letter into the USSR" (RGASPI 495/205/8318, 243). In 1931, when Landau and his supporters were preparing to break from official Trotskyism, Sedov urged Olberg to "break with the Landau clique" (RGASPI 495/205/8318, 215).

In 1932, members of Olberg's KPD cell entered his apartment and removed documents revealing his ties to Trotsky and Sedov, including their lengthy correspondence from January 1930 to May 1932. The KPD sent those materials to the Comintern. From January 30 until April 27, 1930, Trotsky wrote at least fourteen letters to Olberg, each in response to letters from Olberg. Those letters make clear that Trotsky treated him as a trusted supporter (Trotsky 1975, 210–15; RGASPI, 495/205/8318, 243–46). The confiscated correspondence, which is now available, includes forty-three letters and postcards from Sedov to Olberg. The correspondence between them leaves no doubt that they had a close working relationship and were friends. Yet after the KPD sent those materials to Moscow, Olberg entered the USSR on three occasions. In 1935, he carried a Honduran passport and went to Gorky where he secured work.

Olberg's arrest on January 1, 1936 was not due to NKVD diligence. He was only arrested after an investigation in Ukraine led to information about a Trotskyist network in Gorky, where Sedov had recommended that he contact Trotskyists there. From the time Olberg arrived in Gorky, he called himself Trotsky's "emissary," who had come to the USSR to help revitalize the Trotskyist movement. His political network in the USSR came to include fellow Trotskyists who he had recruited in Berlin, some of whom had illegally entered the country, and local Oppositionists. During interrogations, Olberg, his wife, his brother, his former wife, and his German comrades independently (they were in solitary confinement) provided detailed information about their activities, intentions, and Olberg's ties to Trotsky and Sedov. During his interrogations and the August 1936 trial, Olberg stated that Sedov had approved the purchase of a Honduran passport, which he received in Berlin from a SS officer. He, his wife, and his brother testified that he had warned Sedov that he suspected that the passport would come from the Gestapo. Olberg's father-in-law was a Nazi in whose apartment Olberg openly lived before entering the USSR. These facts, among others, led his accusers to deem Olberg a Gestapo agent.

These and other revelations shocked me and my collaborator Olga Novikova-Monterde. We have found ample evidence that Trotsky, Sedov, and their supporters lied about Olberg and invented the allegation that he was an NKVD agent. His NKVD record makes clear that he was not. Details about his activities and political network come from his and his comrades' interrogation records and from other primary and secondary material. Some may argue that interrogation records cannot be trusted because interrogators tortured Olberg and others or invented the confessions. We cannot say whether they were tortured, but a careful analysis of his and his comrades' statements reinforce each other in many ways, which lends credence to their statements. These materials offer a different and plausible perspective. More importantly, the NKVD and Stalin believed them to be true.

These and other findings challenge our understanding of Olberg and the 1936 trial. But it is important to appreciate that it was Trotsky, Sedov, and Max Shachtman, an ardent Trotskyist, who crafted the image of Olberg that we have inherited. Sedov's and Shachtman's 1936 books, on which they collaborated, significantly influenced the Dewey Commission and the French Commission Rogatoire, both of which concluded that Trotsky was not guilty of the charges against him at the 1936 trial. Those verdicts validated Trotsky's and Sedov's testimony, which came to be widely accepted. The available evidence makes clear that father and son lied about their relationships with Olberg and withheld evidence from those commissions (Broué 1980).

Olberg's trial testimony shocked Trotsky and Sedov, who scrambled to undercut it. Although Trotsky dismissed his contact with Olberg as "an absolutely insignificant episode," it fell to Sedov and Shachtman to undermine his testimony. Because Sedov had to do so within certain constraints, he proposed that they label Olberg an "agent of the GPU" (*Gosudarstvennoe politicheskoe upravlenie*, State Political Administration) from perhaps as early as 1931 (Broué 1993, 136–37). Trotsky quickly accepted the suggestion. Just as quickly, Landau denied it and defended Olberg, forcing father and son to retreat, and leading Trotsky to ask his and Landau's friend Alfred Rosmer "Could you do a little 'judicial' investigation on that [Landau's argument] dear friend?" (Rosmer 1982, 187). But after Landau went to Spain and it was decided that the investigation into the charges against Trotsky in Moscow would take place in the United States and Mexico, the allegation that Olberg was an "agent of the GPU" became central to Trotsky's defense. What was at stake was not truth but who would win the hearts and minds of more people. In that sense, Trotsky's and Stalin's interests were similar.

From Olberg's and his Berlin comrades' interrogations, the NKVD learned about the activities of Landau, about whom it had previously known little. Upon arriving in Barcelona in November 1936, Landau committed himself to the POUM (Partido Obrero de Unificación Marxista), which opposed the Popular Front, the Spanish Republic, and Stalin. In September 1937, Alexander Orlov carried out Moscow's orders to assassinate Landau.

Whatever problems Olberg's testimony created for Trotsky and Sedov, they paled in comparison to the consequences for Smirnov, Goltsman, and other defendants. Everyone agreed that Olberg had never met Trotsky or any of the Soviet defendants. But the evidence at the disposal of the NKVD, Vyshinskii, and the court—Olberg's and his Berlin comrades' confessions, the materials from Berlin—made clear that Olberg and Sedov had worked together closely in Berlin, that he had helped Trotsky and Sedov to communicate with their supporters in the USSR, and went there at Sedov's request. What appears to have convinced Stalin to include Olberg among the defendants was that he confessed that Sedov told him about the 1931 meeting with Smirnov, the 1932 meeting with Goltsman, and Trotsky's agreeing to form a bloc and approving the use of terrorist methods. Because interrogators checked on some of Olberg's and other defendants' statements, the NKVD and Stalin were convinced that Olberg, Smirnov, and other Trotskyists were guilty. In a March 25 letter, Iagoda informed Stalin that, based on the "recent arrests" of Trotskyists in a dozen cities and facts established "during the investigation of the Olberg case," their confessions were true. He offered Stalin proposals that he believed would "entirely destroy the Trotskyist cadres." On May 20, 1936, the Politburo recommended resentencing 611 convicted Trotskyists (Mozokhin 2013, 285; RGASPI 17/171/224, 130).

Other defendants admitted in court to knowing of the 1932 bloc and of plans to use terrorist methods, but only Olberg could testify to what Sedov told him about the birth of conspiracy. He testified that Trotsky had approved sending him to the USSR "with the aim of conducting Trotskyist counterrevolutionary work in the Soviet Union and organizing terrorist acts against Stalin . . . to start real preparations for organizing the assassination of Stalin." He stated that Sedov told him that "Lev Davidovich [Trotsky] is sure that you will carry out this assignment like all the previous assignments."[3] During the trial, Olberg challenged Smirnov about his and Sedov's meetings and conversations. That rare event undercut Smirnov.

Olberg also testified that Sedov told him about Smirnov's plan for organizing cadres and consolidating the Trotskyist movement in the USSR, creating conspiratorial organizations, urging Trotskyists who were party members to become double-dealers, and sending to the USSR, "mainly by illegal means," supporters who could "prepare terrorist acts" against party leaders (RGASPI 17/171/220, 147–48, 149–54, 155–71). Olberg's comrades from Berlin and Gorky also spoke of their plans and preparations to assassinate Stalin. Their statements implicated more than seventy people. On June 19, 1936, Iagoda sent Stalin a 174-page detailed memorandum on eighty-two people who he recommended be tried before the USSR's Military Collegium of the Supreme Court and that those convicted should be shot. For each person, he provided biographical and political information, their confessions, the allegations against them, and who testified against them. He organized them into five groups; he assigned twenty-five of them to the Olberg group and ten to the Smirnov group. His grouping of people illustrates the important role that political networks or clans played in identifying real or potential threats. Eighty-one of them were subsequently executed (RGASPI 671/1/193, 1–174).

The key point is that before the decision to hold the August trial, Iagoda, Stalin, and other leading party leaders believed these statements and threats to be true and acted on that belief. In their eyes, Trotskyist agents were not an imaginary enemy; they posed real threats. Of course, the number of real and alleged Trotskyists arrested and executed was much greater. This chapter does not discuss the scale of the mass repression or of all Trotskyist victims. The precise number of the latter remains to be determined. But on March 1, 1938 alone, 173 Trotskyists were executed in the Vorkuta labor camp (Chase and Novikova-Monterde, n.d.). It was not an exception.

Given the importance of Olberg's testimony, Stalin's decision to include him in the 1936 trial is understandable. He was a crucial defendant. The July 29, 1936 CC letter to party organizations announcing the August trial relied heavily on the testimony of Olberg and some of his Trotskyist comrades, men he had recruited, from Berlin.[4] The fact that his trial testimony adhered closely to his available interrogation records validated Stalin's decision. The trial conveyed to the public the importance of political vigilance against domestic and foreign threats.

That NKVD interrogators checked on aspects of statements made by Olberg and the German defendants during interrogation stands in stark contrast to the brutal methods used under Ezhov, Iagoda's replacement, and is documented in recent works based on archival materials (Viola 2017; Vatlin 2004). It seems that, in the case of the foreign defendants in the 1936 trial, the NKVD double-checked some of the prisoners' statements because they sought to validate them so as to gain reliable operational intelligence about the domestic and international Trotskyist organizations, about which they had understood little prior to Olberg's arrest. While in this case, the NKVD sought to enhance that agency's operational intelligence, under Ezhov extracting so-called confessions of one's ties to foreign agencies or networks was of primary importance. Toward that end, interrogators used torture and often wrote a prisoner's "confession."

One example of the operational intelligence derived from the NKVD's 1936 investigations was what it described as the tactics of the Trotskyist Opposition: the creation of conspiratorial groups of double-dealers within both the Bolsheviks and German Communist Party; the unification of the Trotskyists and Zinovievites into a bloc, a prototype of a new party; efforts to link oppositional groups in political exile; and in some cases, planning terrorist acts with the Gestapo's assistance. The July 29, 1936, CC letter announcing the trial made these fears and views explicit.

The full interrogation records are not complete because the Russian Federal Security Service still considers them to be classified. What is available consists of portions of interrogation records that Iagoda sent to Stalin along with his cover letter. Their value lies in the insight that they offer into how Stalin and Vyshinskii understood the activities and intentions of Olberg, Smirnov, and the other defendants. It seems that rather than writing the trial's script, Stalin and Vyshinskii were responding to the investigation's revelations.

Olberg's and Smirnov's cases offer examples of how research into specific cases of repression using recently declassified archival documents challenges some of our assumptions. In an earlier article on show trials, I presumed that Olberg and the other German defendants were simply assigned the role of alleged agents of the alleged conspiracy (Chase 2005). If I were to write that essay today, I would present Olberg and the trial differently. Olberg would play a central role as he was arguably the crucial defendant. In early 1937, Ezhov told the CC Plenum that "the disclosure of the conspiracy" revealed in the 1936 trial began with Olberg's arrest. Although agreeing with Ezhov is most unsettling, we must be willing to reevaluate our own work and assumptions when the evidence warrants it.

Olberg's case poses another dilemma. Who was the real Valentin Olberg? Was he Trotsky's and the Gestapo's agent who sought to murder Stalin, as Vyshinskii charged, or was he the man portrayed by Sedov and Trotsky, an NKVD agent whose testimony was created by the NKVD, and for performing his role he was rewarded with execution? Put bluntly, do we take the word of Sedov and Trotsky, who we know lied about Olberg, or that of Iagoda, Vyshinskii, and Stalin, whose policies destroyed so many lives? It is a most uncomfortable position in which to find ourselves. How we answer that question is bound up with how we assess the value, reliability, and plausibility of interrogation records and other relevant primary sources, the insight they offer into how Iagoda, Vyshinskii, and Stalin viewed them, and how we cling to assumptions. While one might be quick to dismiss interrogation records, we are confronted with testimonies from various people, who were in solitary confinement or distant from each other, who described similar events or plans, and who named the same people. While researchers are wise to be skeptical, the available evidence, which though incomplete is quite extensive and consistent, cannot be ignored if for no other reason than that party leaders, the NKVD, and Soviet judiciary believed the confessions. Such is but one example of the intellectual and moral complexity that confronts those wrestling to understand the Stalinist mass repression. Another is that we must consider that even political show trials have elements of truth.

Other scholars will have to investigate in detail the 1936 trial's other defendants before we can ascertain whether Olberg's and Smirnov's cases were exceptions. Only then will we know if that trial was political theater staged by a cynical Stalin or an expression of his real fears of a threat that had long gone undiscovered. In September 1936, Stalin removed Iagoda from the NKVD because he was "four years behind." He arrived at that decision, in part and ironically, based on Iagoda's reports to him about the NKVD's investigations over more than nine months.

Olberg and the German defendants also exemplified a mounting anxiety about foreign threats. By early 1936, Bolshevik and Comintern leaders believed that enemy agents disguised as political émigrés had infiltrated the USSR in the service of foreign states or hostile political organizations. The allegation grew out of investigations dating to 1933, including the verification of émigrés, especially those from Germany and the border states, who were party members. Olberg and his German codefendants provided evidence to corroborate that fear. Because it blended the threats posed by domestic and foreign Trotskyists with the threat of foreign aggression, the 1936 trial set the stage for later trials, more repression, and the national operations of 1937–38 often directed against émigrés and people living in the borderlands.

Although the primary causes of the mass repression were domestic, one should not underestimate Moscow's fear of foreign intervention and a two-front war against Germany and Japan, which invaded Manchuria in late 1931. In that year, Stalin warned that "We are fifty or one hundred years behind the advanced countries. We must make good this distance in ten years. Either we do it or they will crush us." The Soviet press routinely fanned the fear of war, which fueled xenophobia and revived the anxieties of those who had lived through seven years of war and severe deprivation. Moscow's embracing collective security and its 1935 call for a Popular Front grew out of its fear of fascism. That party leaders were woefully late in adopting a strong antifascist policy need not diminish their sincerity as their commitment to the Spanish Republic's battle against the Nationalists and their fascist allies proved. While the USSR supported the Spanish Republic's battle, Britain, France, and other European states blocked the republic's right under international law to purchase weapons.

Some writers continue to cling to the view that the Spanish Communist Party and the republic's leaders were little more than vehicles for Moscow's policies and that the NKVD had free reign in Spain. The evidence available today shows how flawed such arguments are. Appreciating the role and limits of Soviet efforts in Spain helps one to understand the Kremlin's increasing anxieties about Britain's and France's anemic response to Hitler's militarism and signing the Munich Accords, which confirmed Stalin's distrust of them and contributed to his agreeing to the 1939 Non-Aggression Pact, which exemplifies his willingness to use Realpolitik in defense of socialism in one country.

Researchers are prisoners of the available sources. Since the opening of Soviet-era archives, we have used previously classified documents to examine how and why Stalin and Soviet leaders behaved as they did. Such materials have also provided insight into how Soviet citizens understood their world and behaved in Stalin's time. As new types of sources, such as interrogation records, become available, we must be willing to scrutinize them carefully to ascertain their reliability and, if appropriate, rethink our interpretations and assumptions. Challenging, let alone unlearning, assumptions is difficult. It requires humility and patience. This need not be a solitary effort. We depend on others' research to develop a fuller understanding of Stalinism. Collaboration plays an important role in this process because it forces us to explain and justify our views, debate the nature and quality of evidence, and agree on how to craft our arguments.

The arrests and convictions of Smirnov, Olberg, and their associates arose from investigations conducted over time by various NKVD offices. The available materials about those men's cases suggest that investigators pieced together the evidence against them and their comrades rather than simply rounding up the usual suspects. They do not appear to have worked according to a script or directive. On the contrary, Iagoda frequently communicated the findings of ongoing investigations to Stalin, Vyshinskii, and the Politburo. Based on those reports, Stalin decided to organize the August 1936 trial and press for further investigations. He entrusted the latter task to Ezhov, who removed many of Iagoda's associates, investigators, and interrogators. The contrast between the available materials related to the cases of Olberg and Smirnov, and those prosecuted during Ezhov's tenure as the head of the NKVD is stark.

Stalin initiated and approved many policies, but it fell to others to implement them. He periodically used populist appeals to mobilize support for and to implement policies, ranging from unleashing worker discontent in 1928–32, to calling for "25,000ers" to enact collectivization, to launching a public discussion of the draft of the 1936 Constitution, to urging citizens to speak their minds in 1937–38. But populism and local implementation of policies are not the same. Whether Iagoda or Ezhov headed the NKVD, they had to follow their superiors' orders, but they also depended on their subordinates to enact them. How and why they did so, and the orders they received, is essential to enhancing our understanding of Stalinism.

Consider NKVD Order 00447, which transformed political vigilance into a frenzy of violent repression during Ezhov's tenure. The NKVD sent a draft of that order to Stalin and the Politburo on July 30, 1937; he approved it in the name of the CC. Of his role, there is no doubt. That order aimed to remove from society the "chief instigators of every kind of anti-Soviet crimes and sabotage" and defined which "anti-Soviet elements" the NKVD could arrest. It divided the alleged enemies into two groups (those to be executed and those to be sentenced to forced labor). For each group, it assigned the numbers (limits) of arrests in each republic, ASSR, and region. The order made clear that the "entire operation is to be completed within a period of 4 months" (Getty and Naumov 2000, 473–80). It is a chilling document for many reasons, not the least of which are its scale, perhaps a quarter of a million people, and the palpable sense of fear that it conveys. But the order left it to regional officials to identify who to arrest and who to assign to which category. While Stalin approved the order and Ezhov issued the guidelines, local influence over its fulfillment is obvious.

Many aspects of the investigations into what became of the August 1936 trial suggest that they evolved in response to the investigations' findings, which offers a stark contrast to the formulation and enactment of Order 00447. In both cases, Stalin and party leaders responded to recommendations from NKVD leaders, but the contrasts and resulting consequences are shocking. Under Ezhov, interrogators used brutal methods to extract from detainees so-called confessions. Interrogators often wrote the confessions. The available materials related to the interrogations of Olberg and his Berlin comrades are of a different quality in that they often sought operational intelligence about domestic and foreign threats, which led to the identification of culprits, which led to their arrest. In examining the NKVD's investigation of perceived hostile elements from 1933, Order 00447 was exceptional. Iagoda's recommendations that the Politburo resentence Trotskyists, who numbered 611, and send the cases of 83 people to the Supreme Court pale in comparison to the scale of Order 00447. The differences beg for attention.

After a half century of trying to define Stalinism to my satisfaction, in some respects, that goal remains somewhat elusive. There are several reasons, among them being that during his reign numerous subperiods existed, which had distinct dynamics, and much remains uncertain as the recently declassified materials discussed here suggest. The uncertainty that arises from new evidence strikes me as a proper response. One must always be willing to challenge one's views when the evidence warrants doing so. Fortunately, the Bolsheviks insisted that state and party officials maintain written records, although it leaves us wondering why Stalin insisted on doing so in certain cases unless he viewed his policies as valid. Accessing and interpreting those documents will take time. As that process unfolds, we must not be constrained by models or assumptions that limit our critical judgment.

Notes

1. Olga Novikova-Monterde and I discuss these and various related issues at length in our manuscript, tentatively titled "The Many Faces of Antifascism."

2. Given the vagaries of Russian archival access, it is fortunate that RGASPI had made many documents available online. For materials related to the 1936, 1937, and 1938 trials, see http://www.showtrials.ru/home/pervyj-process/dokumenty-sledstvia/zapiska-agody-o-trockistah. See also https://istmat.org/, https://www.memo.ru/en-us/ and https://shop.alexanderyakovlev.org/db-docs.

3. The quote is from Olberg's February 13, 1936 interrogation and appears in Ezhov's unpublished manuscript, titled "Ot fraktsionnosti k otkrytoi kontrrevoliutsii," RGASPI 671-1-284, 143–51.

4. For the July 29, 1936 CC letter to party organizations, see RGASPI 17-171-230, 72–78ob, and *Izvestiia TsK KPSS*. For an English translation, see Getty and Naumov (2000: 250–55).

Works Cited

Broué, Pierre. "Trotsky et le bloc des oppositions de 1932." *Cahiers Léon Trotsky*, no. 5 (January–March 1980): 5–38.
Broué, Pierre. *Trotsky*. Paris: Fayard, 1988.
Broué, Pierre. *Léon Sedov, fils de Trotsky, victime de Staline*. Paris: Editions Ouvrières, 1993.
Chase, William J. *Enemies within the Gates? The Comintern and the Stalinist Repression, 1934–1939*. New Haven: Yale University Press, 2001.
Chase, William J. "Stalin as Producer: The Moscow Show Trials and the Construction of Mortal Threats." in *Stalin: A New History*, ed. Sarah Davies and James Harris, 226–48. Cambridge: Cambridge University Press, 2005.
Chase, William J.. and Olga Novikova-Monterde. "The Many Faces of Antifascism." n.d. Unpublished manuscript.
Getty, J. Arch. "Trotsky in Exile: The Founding of the Fourth International." *Soviet Studies* 38, no. 1 (January 1986): 24–35.
Getty, J. Arch, and Oleg V. Naumov. *The Road to Terror: Stalin and the Self-Destruction of the Bolsheviks, 1932–1939*. New Haven: Yale University Press, 2000.
Izvestiia TsK KPSS, 1989, no. 8, 78–95.
Khaustov, Vladimir N., ed. *Lubianka: Stalin i VChK-GPU-OGPU-NKVD. Ianvar' 1922–dekabr' 1936*. Moscow: Mezhdunarodnyi fond "Demokratiia," 2003.
Mozokhin, O. B., ed. *Politburo i Lev Trotskii: Sbornik dokumentov, 1923–1940gg*. Bk. II. Prague: Sociosfera-CZ, 2013.
Report of Court Proceedings. The Case of the Trotskyite-Zinovievite Terrorist Centre. Moscow: People's Commissariat of Justice of the U.S.S.R., 1936.
RGASPI, Rossiiskii gosudarstvenyi arkhiv sotsial'no-politicheskoi istorii.
Rittersporn, Gabor T. "The Omnipresent Conspiracy: On Soviet Imagery of Politics and Social Relations in the 1930s." In *Stalinist Terror: New Perspectives*, ed. J. Arch Getty and Roberta T. Manning, 99–115. New York: Cambridge University Press, 1993.
Rosmer, Alfred, Marguerite Rosmer, and Leon Trotsky. *Correspondance 1929–1939*. Paris: Gallimard, Collection Témoins, 1982.
Schafranek, Hans. "Kurt Landau." *Cahiers Leon Trotsky*, no. 5 (January–March 1980): 71–96.

Sedov, Lev. *Livre rouge sur le procès de Moscou documents recueillis et rédigés.* Paris: Éditions populaires, Parti ouvrier internationalist, 1936.
Shachtman, Max. *Behind the Moscow Trial.* New York: Pioneer Publishers, 1936.
Trotsky, Leon. *Writings of Leon Trotsky [1930].* New York: Pathfinder Press, 1975.
Vatlin, Alexander. *Agents of Terror: Ordinary Men and Extraordinary Violence in Stalin's Secret Police,* trans. Seth Bernstein. Madison: University of Wisconsin Press, 2016.
Vatlin, Alexander. *Terror raionnogo masshtaba: "Massovye operatsii" NKVD v Kuntsevkom raione Moskovskoi oblasti.* Moscow: ROSSPEN, 2004.
Viola, Lynne. *Stalinist Perpetuators on Trial: Scenes from the Great Terror in Soviet Ukraine* New York: Oxford University Press, 2017.
Zhuravlev, S. V. "Sudebno-sledstvennaia i tiuremno-lagernaia dokumentatsiia." In *Istochnikovedenie noveishei istorii Rossii: Teoriia, metodologiia, i praktika,* ed. A. K. Sokolov, 148–98. Moscow: ROSSPEN, 2005.

Part Three

Beliefs and Emotions

CHAPTER 7

Affective Dispositions, Bolshevism and Stalinism
The Rational Actor in His Emotional Environment

RONALD GRIGOR SUNY

Stalin was at the center of the "riddle, wrapped in a mystery, inside an enigma" that Winston Churchill said constituted the problem of trying to understand the Soviet Union. "I cannot forecast to you the action of Russia," he admitted when he learned that the autocrat in the Kremlin had agreed to the Nazi-Soviet Pact. Less well-known is that he suggested that "perhaps there is a key. That key is Russian national interest" (Churchill 1939). For a ruthless strategic realist like the British prime minister, the rationality of acting in the national interest was a sufficient explanation for the perverse act of the greatest antifascist power allying opportunistically with Hitler's expansionist, racist empire. But national interest should not be understood as something objective, eternal, or transhistorical but rather the subjective understanding of state leaders of the way of the world, how they calculate the threats to the state's existence and well-being as well as the opportunities offered to the state. To get beyond the mystery of the choices made by Stalin in domestic and foreign policy in the 1930s, simple economic calculations of programs to advance socialism as he understood it, or personal insecurities and the desire to hold on to power, or deductions from Marxism-Leninism as it was being formulated are inadequate. The rationalities of development and the self-interest in remaining in power were conceived in a cognitive and emotional environment, an affective disposition, which sutured those ends of political power, and building socialism to the choice of means to achieve them. The

119

greatest mystery of all—as long ago my colleague and comrade Lewis H. Siegelbaum lamented after we emerged from watching the Argentinian film *The Official Story* in Austin, Texas—was: Why did they have to kill them? Or, more generally, why so much violence? Indeed, violence linked to Stalin fatally doomed the socialist experiment. As my good Soviet communist friend, Vahan Mkrtchian, sadly remarked—"Begho isportil delo" ("The man with the mustache [rendered in Armenian] ruined the project"). But explanations of the use of violence need to go beyond rational or strategic choices. They were embedded in and nourished by the affective disposition of the Russian revolutionary movement, its extraordinary ambitions, and the vulnerabilities that Bolsheviks experienced before and after October 1917.

Affective dispositions are associated only at a microlevel with individual persons. A disposition is better understood as an emotional environment, a regime in which certain emotions and responses become more habitual and familiar, and in which other emotions are marginalized, excluded, and delegitimized. In a book in which I attempted to understand why the Young Turks in the late Ottoman Empire decided to carry out a genocide of their Armenian subjects, I defined affective disposition as "the emotional world" that contains "certain proclivities to belief, perception, and behavior, the context in which certain actions are likely to occur and other choices are not made. Conceptually affective disposition bridges the space between structural and environmental influences and human action. Rather than structures, environmental conditions, or experience determining motivation for action, it is within the affective disposition that particular meanings are created, and it is on the basis of those understandings that people are propelled to act on their feelings and convictions" (Suny 2015, 134).

Language reflects the availability and intensity of these emotions, and the historian must rely on expression in letters, diaries, artistic representations, and even police reports to capture the elements that make up this environment and influence people to act in certain ways and not in others. In autocratic regimes with limited access to alternatives deviating from the limited sources of information and the dominant discourses, the role of certain authoritative figures is unusually influential. In the Ottoman realm it was the sultan, Abdülhamid II, and the genocidaire Talat Paşa. In the Soviet 1930s, Stalin was the principal generator of the affective disposition of 1930s Stalinism. But as influential as the views and sensibilities of Stalin and his entourage might have been, the affective disposition was more encompassing than individual psychologies. Methodologically, a distinction must be made between the expressions of emotion of individuals and the affective disposition in which such emotions and accompanying cognitive understandings are generated and maintained.

Exploring Stalin's emotional and ideological evolution in my biography of the young Stalin and his *Passage to Revolution*, I concluded the exploration of the first thirty-nine years of his life by arguing that his years as a revolutionary outlaw, many of them spent in the underground and in prison and exile, had resulted in an erosion of empathy. "Revolution was his profession, and through his work in the party underground and with workers in Baku and Saint Petersburg, hardened by the violence of 1905–1907 and his suffering in prison and exile, he arrived in 1917 a man who had preserved his own ideals and was prepared as a pragmatic Marxist to use the means necessary to further the Bolshevik cause. Sentimentality had largely been suppressed. Empathy had eroded. In their place was a Machiavellian calculus—discipline, toughness, violence, even cruelty were requirements in this bitter political battle" (Suny 2021, 689–90). The young Stalin displayed ambition, "self-confidence that passed beyond the boundary into arrogance," and disdain and condescension toward his party elders (except for Lenin). "Whether it was resentment, jealousy, or disgust, he was unable to subordinate his affective disposition toward such people to what might better serve the movement. He did not appreciate refinement or gentility but preferred a rougher manner, affecting what he took to be a proletarian toughness." "Like Lenin he could be contemptuous of intellectuals, even though in the scheme of things he was an intelligent. His intellectual interests, however, were directed toward confirmation rather than questioning. He was not introspective like [his fellow Bolshevik Iakov] Sverdlov. He appreciated the plainness of ordinary people. His nature was narrow, not as open and generous as Lenin's." Once he made up his mind, he was usually inflexible, which led to dogmatism. Yet, when necessary, "he was able for practical reasons to shift quickly and decisively" (Suny 2021, 691).

Over time the humane sensibilities of the romantic poet [that he had been as a teenager] gave way to hard strategic choices. Feelings for others were displaced or suspended and were trumped by personal and political interests. What originated as empathy for the plight of one's people (the Georgians), a social class (the proletariat), or humanity more broadly was converted to a rational choice of instruments to reach a preferred end. Empathy was replaced by an instrumental cruelty. Once in power those earlier emotions and ideals were subordinated to the desire to hold on to the power so arduously and painfully acquired. Power became a key motivator as the imperatives of the precarious new conditions in which Bolsheviks found themselves forced them to make unanticipated choices. "Possession of power," wrote Immanuel Kant, "debases the free judgment of reason." "But power was seldom simply about personal aggrandizement or advancement. Based on convictions derived from experience, history, and Marxism, power also served the commitment to a certain vision of the future. (Suny 2021, 691)

Both as an underground revolutionary and later as the most powerful leader of the largest country in the world, Stalin was involved in what he conceived of as an epic historic and heroic struggle. Erik van Ree argues that the self-heroization of revolutionaries like Stalin, Mao, Che Guevara, and others was a way of coping with the travails of the outlaw life. Their "ambitious, high-risk and not self-serving lifestyle" was bearable because they imagined themselves as historical heroes. They were class warriors defined by their choice to sacrifice for the cause. "In adopting an epic consciousness and imagining themselves to be protagonists in real-time heroic myths, they reassure and emotionally charge themselves to continue a fight that carries a far from sure outcome" (Van Ree 2022, 284–85). That sense of heroic struggle was heightened by the colossal efforts at social and economic transformations of the 1930s, combined as they were with the bitter, bloody political purging that accompanied them.

Politics as War

The experience of vicious infighting within the Bolshevik wing of the Russian Social Democratic Workers' Party (RSDRP) was both a school for learning about politics as well as a substitute for real politics that would have consequences for ordinary people outside the narrow walls of the party. Leninist practices, with their highly accusatory rhetoric and propensity to divide and conquer, had lasting effects on postrevolutionary governing norms. Lenin, who studied Clausewitz on war diligently, would have subscribed to Foucault's inversion of the great military theorist's adage: "politics is the continuation of war by other means." War was a central metaphor for Marxists—class war, civil war—and particularly for more radical Marxists such as Lenin. As much as winning hearts and minds of the masses was desirable, revolution was, for Lenin, not an election campaign in which the goal is to garner majority support. It is not normal democratic politics with rules of engagement that included gracious retreat from the contest. Rather it is warfare, in which the consequence of losing could easily be death. Unlike elections and liberal democratic practices, war and revolution are about having sufficient forces, almost invariably armed men, at the right place at the right time. This was a concept equally well understood by Lenin's principal enemies, the White generals. Both sides understood that support can more easily be a product of revolutionary or military victory than a precondition, that hearts and minds could be conquered more easily by victors than by embattled contestants. For the Bolsheviks, the civil war was simply war, a matter of overwhelming the opposition militarily and subduing the population that supported the enemies of the old order. And war as politics became politics as war once victory in the civil war had been won.

The harsh lessons of the civil war, 1918–21, were formative for the Bolsheviks. Civil war was an armed struggle for sovereignty within what was left of the Russian Empire. An internal war between rival camps giving no quarter to the other. Victory and defeat were guaranteed only by violence and persuasion. In 1917 the concept and practice of *dvoevlastie* (dual power), the division of power between the soviets and the Provisional Government, already contained the seeds of civil war once neither side no longer recognized the right of the other to share in power. Already in mid-1917, society was divided between the *demokratiia* (revolutionary democracy, the lower classes) and *tsenzovoe obshchestvo* (propertied society and the liberal intelligentsia), with the lower classes overwhelmingly voting socialist and supporting the soviets. Those seeds of civil war grew into a thorny plant with the October Revolution when the Bolsheviks constituted a government but not yet a state. They held power but hardly a monopoly of legitimate violence, could not control vast areas in the country they claimed to rule, and were faced by numerous rival governments, each claiming their own sovereign authority, either over Russia as a whole or over national regions. For Reds as well as Whites, the Civil War was both a contest over supreme power and a process of trying to build a state. Over the next four years the Soviets managed that successfully, but the Whites failed to restore or build anew a counterrevolutionary state.

The Bolsheviks were certain that their struggle was about destroying or being destroyed, dedicating all efforts toward the preservation of Soviet power in Russia and working toward the international socialist revolution then on the horizon. As the Bolshevik defender of Cheka terror Martyn Latsis put it, "one must not only destroy the forces of the enemy but also demonstrate that whoever raises the sword against the existing order of class, will perish by the sword." Such harsh calculations were not based simply on necessary strategic choices and ideology. Here emotions, ubiquitous in wars, revolutions, and civil wars, motivate actors and mobilize groups, guide preferences and choices, heighten commitment, and provide heuristics for discriminating friend from foe, and danger from security. Yet it would be a mistake to make the easy Hobbesian deduction that violent emotions are so fundamental to universal human nature that the simple removal of restraints is a sufficient explanation for violence in these anarchic conditions. In conditions of great uncertainty and unpredictability, a dominant emotion is anxiety—fear without a clear and present object. When horrors befall loved ones or comrades, unfocused rage may explode. But more directed emotions, such as anger at what someone has done to you or yours, or hatred of a person or group that poses by their very presence an existential threat to you, or resentment at unfair distributions of wealth, power, or privilege, are also loose in the revolutionary land. Violence can be both the product of emotions and the cause of emotions.

Violence and the use of terror were ubiquitous in the years of the civil war. All sides, and most parties, used such means to gain advantages over others, to prevent desertion, and simply to win on the field of battle. Left Socialist Revolutionaries carried out assassinations, including the German ambassador to Soviet Russia; White forces steeped in images of Judeo bolshevism murdered more civilians than did the Reds. Some Bolsheviks like Uritskii urged restraint, but Lenin and Trotsky adopted the example of the bourgeois revolutionaries of the French Revolution and called for mass terror. When Lenin heard of Petrograd's mild reaction to the killing of the popular commissar V. Volodarskii (Moisei Goldshtein), he angrily cabled:

> We are compromising ourselves: we threatened, even in the resolutions of the Soviet of Deputies, mass terror, and when it comes to that we hold back the revolutionary initiative of the masses, which is completely in the right.
>
> This is in-tol-er-able!
>
> The terrorists will consider us rags. The time is one of extreme warfare [*arkhivoennoe*]. It is essential to encourage this energy and the massive quality of the terror against the counterrevolutionaries, especially in Piter, which sets a decisive example. (Lenin to Zinoviev, June 26, 1918)

The Bolsheviks won the civil war because they effectively used raw armed power and violence to eliminate their opponents, and consequentially, any democratic alternative to Bolshevik dictatorship. They did not play fair. Up to October 1917, they had advocated the expansion of bourgeois democracy as the best environment to accelerate the development of an organized, conscious working class. (That is a central argument of my biography of the young Stalin.) But once they took power, they no longer respected the very rules of democratic politics that they had defended up to October. Lenin told his comrades to be merciless and recommended that to carry out this program they had to "Find some truly hard people" (Pipes 1996, 50).

The harsh lesson was that terror could establish the preliminary conditions after which loyalty would follow, and with loyalty would come acceptance, acquiescence to the state's authority and legitimacy rather than raw force. Politics was an extension of warfare. That was the political environment in which Stalinism developed. Politics was about coercion, not persuasion or negotiation. The casualness with which Stalin would suggest murder as an effective practice of governance is illustrated in his letter to Molotov in the summer of 1930: "A whole group of wreckers in the meat industry must definitely be shot and their names published in the press" (Lih et al. 1995, 200).

Yet, the 1920s, the decade of NEP, was a period not of war, revolution, and civil war as the preceding and succeeding decades would be but of one of relative stability, of reduced intervention by the police, and of slow recovery from the ravages of war. "Having defeated the White armies," Orlando Figes quips, "the Bolsheviks surrendered to the peasantry" (Figes 2007, 6). Roles and identities developed in the revolution and civil war underwent changes in the 1920s, and once again, in a different way, in the tumult of the 1930s. A revolutionary rejection of material comforts and possessions gave way to an acceptance of goods that a decade earlier would have been regarded as bourgeois—or worse, petty bourgeois. Stability was replaced by instability and unpredictability, of greater vulnerability and danger, personal, political, social, and international.

Fear and Vulnerability

The eggs were broken, and the omelet was made. And the Soviet Union was fatally formed as an authoritarian party dictatorship that eventually devolved into a personalist autocracy under Stalin by the early 1930s. The 1920s had been marked by concessions from the communists to the peasantry and the non-Russian peoples, limited degrees of autonomy, and control of their own resources. Rough stability prevailed until the grain supply crisis at the end of the decade, when the moderate Stalin turned radical and reverted to the use of political coercion characteristic of the civil war struggles.

The affective disposition that dominated the 1930s was heavily weighted with fear of encirclement by hostile capitalist powers, domestic opposition and disunity that reached the highest levels of the state and party, and smoldering discontent and potential resistance of the peasantry and others. Soviet leaders and their supporters felt their vulnerability living in a relatively weak state with only fragile connections with the great mass of the people. For ordinary Soviet people Marxism in its Leninist form soon became the required, enforced scientific tool to understand history, reality, and the future. But for the leadership including Stalin, it was at one and the same time a frame through which they understood the dynamics of the political and social world, a cold logic with which to estimate possible trajectories, as well as an emotional inspiration that propelled them to undertake mammoth efforts of social engineering and accept the harsh political costs that such efforts entailed. The turmoil of the period—mass, violent collectivization of agriculture and the brutal dekulakization campaigns; the Holodomor and other state-induced famines; the Great Terror and massive purges of party members, the Special Operations, and the killing of hundreds of thousands of people—and its resultant trauma were accompanied with highly emotional language from state authorities that both stimulated and justified violence. The newspapers of the 1930s printed screaming headlines that combined wild accusations of betrayal with warnings that hidden, disguised enemies were everywhere. Lurking dangers, claims that sabotage and wrecking were rampant, raised anxiety to high levels and encouraged calls for revenge.

My sense is that the headlines and the sense of danger were the public expression that reflected Stalin's mind once what he had experienced earlier in the prerevolutionary underground and in the power struggles with other communists in the 1920s turned at the beginning of the 1930s into bitter bouts of false accusations, the use of the OGPU and NKVD to supply materials to discredit (even kill) those targeted by the General Secretary, and consequently the political destruction of a whole generation of important Bolsheviks. While Stalin had had serious policy differences beginning in 1928 with Nikolai Bukharin, they had been friends until Stalin began to suspect Bukharin of conspiring with Zinoviev and Kamenev (after the famous meeting in the cave). Once he began to distrust Bukharin, those suspicions of being betrayed dissolved the filaments of friendship that had existed for over a decade. Bukharin was stunned, confused by the depth of Stalin's viciousness, even though he must have seen signs of it earlier. The secret police conjured up cases of terrorist organizations made up of rightists—the Peasant-Labor Party, the Industrial Party, the Kondratiev-Sukhanov-Bukharin Party—and Bukharin tried to have a heart-to-heart talk with Stalin after an accusatory phone call. Stalin refused. Bukharin then resorted to a letter on October 14, 1930, continuing to address him, as he would to the end of his life, with Stalin's favorite revolutionary klichka: "Koba. After our telephone conversation I immediately left work in a state of despair. Not because you had 'scared' me—you will not scare me and you will not intimidate me. But because those monstrous accusations that you threw at me are clear evidence of the existence of some sort of devilish, vile, and low provocation, that you believe, on which you are building your policy, and that will lead to no good, even if you were to destroy me physically as thoroughly as you are destroying me politically" (Iz pis'ma N.I. Bukharina I.V. Stalinu s protestom protiv presledovanii. 14 oktiabria 1930 g.; https://istmat.org

/node/31786). Within months, with the attack on the Syrtsov-Lominadze organization and the removal of Rykov as head of government and his replacement by Stalin's choice, Molotov, the Stalinization of the Politburo and the political destruction of Bukharin and the Right had been completed, and the will—and emotional perceptions—of a single individual incubated the affective disposition of a country and an era.

Many of the elements of what would become a widespread emotional environment were revealed in a speech by Stalin to the Central Committee in January 1933. He spoke darkly about "former people" who "wormed their way into our plants and factories, into our government offices and trading organizations, into our railway and water transport enterprises, and, principally, into our collective and state farms." He declared menacingly that "certain professors" were injecting cattle with plague and anthrax and that hidden enemies lurked, consumed with enmity and hatred of "the forms of economy, life, and culture" (Khlevniuk 2009, 19). An atmosphere of menace coexisted with hopefulness and optimism about the future pictured in Soviet posters, novels, films, and festivals. The present was full of danger, while the future would see the fulfillment of the humanistic values and the material abundance promised by official ideology. Those values were taken seriously by many, and the evident failure to realize them elicited complaints and discontents expressed in the rhetoric of Soviet ideals. As Jochen Hellbeck argues in his study of Soviet subjectivity under Stalin, "personal narratives were so filled with the values and categories of the Soviet revolution that they seemed to obliterate any distinction between a private and a public domain. Many Stalin-era diarists were preoccupied with finding out who they were in essence and how they could transform themselves" (Hellbeck 2006, 5).

Soviet individuals maneuvered within a society rapidly transforming itself and portraying itself as the vanguard of history, the future in the present, and a modernity beyond and superior to capitalism. "The Soviet ethos," writes Amir Weiner, "was ingrained in the politics that shaped the modern era where states sought the transformation of societies with the help of scientific models and a myriad of institutions charged with managing all social spheres" (Weiner 2001, 7). Among elements borrowed from American and other Western societies like machines and speed-ups, Soviet socialism emphasized the collective over the individual, unity and social harmony (even as it touted class struggle), and the exclusion of alien elements, foreign, traditional, and inimical. All societies are built on exclusions as well as inclusions, and Stalinism practiced purging of deviants and undesirables in a desperate search for unbreakable unity and permanent security.

There were enough contradictions in Soviet goals and methods to allow for choices to be made in what to adopt and model oneself on and what to reject. This was a far cry from the monolithic totalitarian fantasy of Western theorists and Sovietologists. Soviet citizens had to reconcile their enthusiasms and convictions with the evident shortfalls and repression of everyday Stalinism. As with the succor provided by the American Dream, always a future hope and always out of reach, so in the Soviet Union the future was a source of relief, a real presence, even a present. In the 1930s the Soviet vision of the future rivaled and competed with the future visions of the fascists and the liberal West. In his project to study the Space Age in both the USSR and the United States, Renny Hahamovitch notes, "Industrial labor like shoveling coal—as party posters, slogans, and speeches everywhere reminded workers—was building socialism, the central symbolic act around which Soviet civilization rested. To pick up a shovel was to do politics, to throw coal in the fire was to intervene in the future" (Hahamovitch 2022, 19). Soviet officialdom expressed great confidence in the building of the future by heroic efforts at the present time to overcome all obstacles. "There are no fortresses that Bolsheviks cannot storm." This might have been an illusion, but disillusionment was not permitted.

The belief in the communist future, scholars have noted, was particularly sincere in children and teenagers, who clung to that faith even when their own parents suffered from arrest and they were forced to live in special children's homes (Holmes 1999, 77, 97–98; Slezkine 2017, 656, 887). "Soviet schoolchildren," writes Irina V. Volkova, "assimilated the Communist ideology aimed at them quite selectively, depending on their social, age-related, and individual needs, and that some aspects of this process were beyond the authorities' control. Vulnerable and underprivileged teenagers found the Communist myth appealing due to its axiological perspective, which partially compensated for the feelings of anxiety they experienced in real life. Progressive young people, on the other hand, were attracted by the possibility of transforming human existence through innovation, a project in which they could invest their efforts and skills" (Volkova 2020, 204). In her research Volkova found that Soviet children "assimilated the priority of the spiritual over the material, of the public over the personal, and of one's enthusiasm over career aspirations—all values, in fact, inculcated by their Soviet upbringing" (Volkova 2020, 215). But in sharp contrast to the future envisioned by National Socialism in Germany, where the privilege of belonging to the Aryan race benefitted or disadvantaged a person, "the Soviet Communist project [was] oriented toward universal equality and fraternity [and] did not impose any a priori restrictions" (Volkova 2020, 221). There was no decline in revolutionary zeal in the 1930s, and whatever personal material advantages people might seek, their goals often reflected the widespread desires to be useful and serve the common good—

most markedly among urban, upwardly mobile youth. "The difficult living conditions in the countryside during the 1930s," Volkova explains, "were not conducive to the consolidation of Communist beliefs, nor to inspiring dreams of highly creative achievement" (Volkova 2020, 223). A profound chasm divided the village from the city. But not only between peasants and workers but also with the *intelligenty* and *bol'shie shiski* ("big shots"). The aspirations and achievements of the upwardly striving created new hierarchies and social distances between those that benefitted more from the affirmative action policies of the Soviet project and those left behind. Whoever through hard work, intelligence, ambition, or patronage rose higher protected their newfound status and condescendingly looked down on the very people whom the Soviet system purported to promote.

In her study of popular opinion Sarah Davies uses police reports (*svodki*) to learn about the dissenting views of ordinary Soviet citizens and how they framed them in Soviet speech. There was much grumbling and alienation, but along with complaints about the lack of bread there remained a faith in the revolution, even socialism, and a sense that the egalitarian promise of 1917 had been violated. Class resentment and suspicion of those in power marched along with patriotism and a sense of social entitlement. People employed the official rhetoric of Bolshevism even though their meanings did not always conform with those in charge. Rather than fitting a widespread image often found in the West of Soviet people as loving, strong, authoritarian leaders, there is an impression of a people who had imbibed values more often identified with democracy and socialism, egalitarianism, shared burdens, and a government that cares for and acts in the interest of the people.

But the constant shortages were not patiently borne. One party worker summed up the attitude of Soviet consumers: "Soviet power! The power has changed but there are no galoshes. That's how good Soviet power is!" (Davies 1997, 38). There was a sense that the "gains of the revolution had been squandered, that the rights in the Constitution were being violated, that the country was regressing to capitalism, fascism, or even a 'second serfdom'" (Davies 1997, 46). Precisely the striving for equality produced envy and resentment. Workers favored the affirmative action measures during the First Five-Year Plan that gave workers and their families privileged access to education and were dismayed at the conservative "Great Retreat" of the mid-1930s. "In 1936 we won't recognise the USSR. They've started Christmas trees. now they're burying the social past. They're wearing epaulettes. Soon we'll get the 'tsar-batiushka'" (Davies 1997, 69). The discontent of workers intensified on the eve of the war, especially after the draconian labor decrees of December 1938 and June 1940 that criminalized absenteeism and lateness, but it remained inchoate, unorganized, and ineffectual. A sense of betrayal and treachery combined with resentment at those more privileged in what was supposed to be an egalitarian social order.

At the same time the generalized notion of "us," the people, against "them," those in power, who were leaders without the people (*vozhdi bez naroda*), was expressed in public expressions of enthusiasm for the Great Terror, which was a "clearly popular" quenching of "popular thirst for violent retribution against the verkhi [higher ups]." "One peasant commented: 'All the leaders in power and Stalin should be shot'" (Davies 1997, 131, 132). Russians turned their resentments against Jews, linking them with the despised political and intellectual elites, as well as Caucasians, who seemed as tricky and self-serving as the Jews. The government was seen as made up of foreign elements, and it was felt that the authorities did not have the large and broad soul and infinite patience of the Russian people.

Soviet subjectivity, Hellbeck demonstrates, at least in the 1930s, was directed not toward forging an individual identity in a liberal mode but toward remaking themselves into politically conscious citizens who fused with the cause of the revolution and the building of socialism. Individual autonomy and private values, signs of a bourgeois consciousness that needed to be eradicated, were not prized. Living in an environment structured by an authoritarian regime with enforcement of ideological conceptualizations that constrained them to operate and think within a thick web of discursive constructions not of their own making, Hellbeck's diarists searched, not for a liberal subjectivity but for a distinct, authentic Soviet subjectivity. Whether they were the norm or the exception is difficult to estimate. In Stalin's USSR there were still people who had come of age before Bolshevism; there were religious believers of many stripes; millions who were untouched or only slightly affected by the urban-based, thinly stretched regime; criminals, dissenters, ornery outsiders, principled opponents, and the self-interested rational actors like Ostap Bender, about whom Sheila Fitzpatrick writes (Fitzpatrick 2005, 265–81). Standing at the other end of the grocery store queue from Stepan Podlubny was thirteen-year-old Nina Lugovskaya, the unreconstructed daughter of a Socialist Revolutionary father. The last entry in her diary before she was arrested and the diary confiscated and read carefully by the NKVD in 1937 expresses quite ordinary but intense emotions, ones that may be both Soviet and universal: "When I drink a few glasses of wine, the first sensation is one of companionship with the people around me, all the barriers come down. I feel close to people. Who hasn't felt that pleasant, dizzy excitement from shaking a man's firm hand or suddenly felt someone take you gently by the shoulders, or stood alone with someone in the room and said something, gazing into a handsome, exciting face? Perhaps it is drunken excitement, but it is beautiful and innocent" (Lugovskaya 2000, 253).

Such experiences of everyday beauty and innocence went along with the quotidian annoyances and cruelties of Soviet life. But shaping the affective disposition of Stalinism was a socialist romantic, rather than realist, approach to apprehending what life was about—or at least supposed to be about. "Starting in the early 1930s, the party leadership endorsed a momentous shift toward a romantic sensibility," writes Hellbeck (2006, 21). A new heroic self-reliant individualism, epitomized in Stakhanovism, was promoted, a revival on steroids of the positive heroes of the nineteenth-century realist novels. "The qualities ascribed to the new men and women of the Stalinist age were Romantic to the core. They were rich personalities who expressed themselves in fantastic feats and whose artistic creativity helped shape the beautiful new socialist world" (Hellbeck 2006, 31). The new individualism extended beyond heroes to impure villains who sought to thwart the successes of socialism. "In exterminating all individuals deemed harmful to the new, socialist order, the terror was the flip side of the Stalinist humanist program of creating a social body defined in terms of absolute purity of spirit" (Hellbeck 2006, 35).

History was dynamic, purposeful, moving in a progressive direction, and individuals had to swim with or drown in its torrential flow. One revolution, that of October, had been revived in another, that from above, and identification with that revolution was intoxicating, particularly for the intelligentsia (Mandelstam 1971, 126). A simple soul like Podlubny was tormented by his kulak background and admired "people with a strong will" able to overcome the limitations of their class and through struggle reforge themselves as a new man (Hellbeck 2006, 71, 101, 165–221). Hellbeck's diarists repeatedly wrote about merging their personal lives with the "'general stream of life' of the Soviet collective," which was the "ultimate destination of Soviet self-realization" (Hellbeck 2006, 97). Anxiety about separation from the collective body of the Soviet people, loneliness and angst about their failure to achieve that merger mixed with pride and happiness when they got close. The lonely Zinaida Densevskaya experienced a euphoric moment of self-realization when in 1931 she joined the parade of Voronezh teachers and students (Hellbeck 2006, 161). Even a historian like Orlando Figes, who doubts Hellbeck's claim that the driving ambition of many, if not most, Soviets was to merge with the great aims of Stalin and the party, and believes that becoming a Soviet activist "was a common survival strategy" for the children of the repressed, not a desire to recreate oneself as a "new Soviet man" or woman, presents stories that confirm Hellbeck's view that acceptance by the party and the collective was something sincerely desired. A kulak child, Dmitrii Streletskii, "despite all his suffering at the hands of the Soviet regime," remained a Soviet patriot, "believed fervently in the justice of the Party's cause, and wanted desperately to become part of it." "To be recognized as an equal human being," he said, "that is all I wanted from the Party" (Figes 2007, 355).

Stalinism was both inspiring and punitive. Punishment for wrongdoing, inadequate commitment to the cause, accidental missteps, or serious deviation from acceptable behavior or thought was always present. It was easy to break the shifting laws and find oneself on the wrong side. Innocents were punished as easily as the guilty. Crimes were fabricated by the NKVD and Stalin, and criminals were tortured out of good Bolsheviks. Which brings us to the Siegelbaum question: Why did they have to kill them? What was the extraordinarily punitive affective disposition of the 1930s in the USSR that led to hundreds of thousands murdered by the state and millions condemned to exile, imprisonment, forced labor, starvation, and stunted lives?

Pervasive in the emotional environment of Stalinism was a toxic mix of hardness, distrust, and fear. Hardness was a positive trait in the Bolshevik morality, and nowhere was it better expressed than in the often-quoted passage from Lev Kopelev, who observed the suffering of the peasants as he and his comrades took their grain: "It was excruciating to see and hear all this. And worse to take part in it. No, it was worse without taking part when you tried to persuade someone, to explain something. . . . And I persuaded myself, explained to myself. I mustn't give in to debilitating pity. We were realizing historical necessity. We were performing our revolutionary duty. We were obtaining grain for the socialist fatherland. For the five-year plan" (Kopelev 1980, 235).

Distrust was pervasive. The writer Mikhail Prishvin confided in his diary in October 1937, "People have completely stopped trusting each other. They devote themselves to work and do not even whisper to one another. There is a huge mass of people raised up from poor social backgrounds who have nothing to whisper about: they just think 'That's how it should be' Others isolate themselves to whisper, or study the art of silence. Yet others have simply learned to keep quiet. . . . Gas masks are no use! What we need to protect ourselves against is psychological infection, the mask of gloom and silence" (cited in Hosking 2014, 15). Vigilance, one of the most frequently deployed words by the authorities, was the duty of Bolsheviks. Enemies were everywhere, and they were masked. Their masks had to be torn off, for, as Elena Bonner's younger brother spit out when his father (who was an old Armenian Bolshevik, by the way), "Look at what these enemies of the people are like. Some of them even pretend to be fathers" (Bonner 1992, 317). Uncertainty about whom to trust made friendship dangerous. Neighbors and relatives avoided those tainted by the arrest of family members, while some bravely risked associating with and aiding them. Friendship or kinship was not supposed to get in the way of one's obligation to the security and success of the system. In this respect, Stalin was exemplary.

Fear was both produced and propagated by the regime and a consequence of the general turmoil and tumult of the pell-mell drives to collective agriculture and rapidly industrialize the economy. While diagnosing Stalin as clinically paranoid is beyond what historians can achieve, the threats from the capitalist and fascist West and imperial Japan, as well as the signs of domestic discontent and resistance from the peasants, fed into his suspicious nature to produce a cascade of false accusations that resulted in a flood of executions. Informers were everywhere, and political opportunism and rivalries encouraged denunciations. Speaking the truth could be fatal. When the Old Bolshevik Osip Piatnitskii courageously spoke out at a party plenum of the Central Committee in June 1937 and accused the NKVD of fabricating evidence against enemies of the people, he committed not only political but physical suicide as well. Ready "to sacrifice his life and, if necessary, to trample on the corpses of his children and his wife" for "the unity and moral purity of the Party," he told his wife that he simply could not bear the innocents "forced to live under constant psychological stress" and warned his son "not to fight against Stalin" (Figes 2007, 227–37).

The Effects of Affect: Losing Your Way

If Marxism has an affect, it might be a cool reasonableness. But those who set out on the revolutionary road in Russia did not do so from a purely rational calculation or, usually, because they thought there would be personal gain if they became outlaws. Analysis of the way of the world was combined with a myriad of emotions, from anger, resentment, and a sense that the autocracy and nascent capitalism were unjust to hatred of the oppressors, resentment at the privileged, and rage at the repression of the masses. Once in power those revolutionaries made strategic calculations to stay in power and to realize their political and social goals. Both in the underground and in the halls of government they were usually aware of the precariousness of their position, and that sense of precarity governed many of their calculations. Vulnerability, a feeling perhaps that their new position was illegitimate, influenced and amplified the suspicions they harbored toward others and the outside world. Revolution itself is an illegitimate act, and the search for legitimation by revolutionaries begins with violence, with a seizure of power, and only later tries to turn coercion into persuasion, the grab for power into accepted authority. But for the

Soviets, enemies were indeed everywhere. Within and without there were opponents working to take away the victory they had won on the barricades. Capitalist encirclement was real and constant. It was a palpable, relentless threat that, ultimately, helped to bring down the regime. Ironically, however, the counterrevolution that they feared did not come primarily from abroad but from within, from the regime itself, which in its effort to reform committed suicide. While some late Soviet leaders were anxious to continue as usual, others were desperate to overcome the stagnation and inefficiencies that Stalinism and its successors' improvised and limited reforms had failed to eradicate. The intrepid, incompetent reformers were inspired by beliefs in the viability of Leninism, but in the end, they forfeited one of the key lessons of Lenin: that without the exercise of force, even violence, revolutionaries do not have a chance.

Works Cited

Bonner, Elena. *Mothers and Daughters*. New York: A. Knopf, 1992.
Churchill, Winston. "The Russian Enigma." BBC Broadcast. October 1, 1939.
Davies, Sarah. *Popular Opinion in Stalin's Russia: Terror, Propaganda and Dissent, 1934–1941*. Cambridge: Cambridge University Press, 1997.
Figes, Orlando. *The Whisperers: Private Life in Stalin's Russia*. New York: Metropolitan Books, 2007.
Fitzpatrick, Sheila. *Tear Off the Masks! Identity and Imposture in Twentieth-Century Russia*. Princeton: Princeton University Press, 2005.
Hahamovitch, Renny. "The Space Age." PhD diss. proposal, University of Michigan, 2022.
Hellbeck, Jochen. *Revolution on my Mind: Writing a Diary under Stalin*. Cambridge, MA: Harvard University Press, 2006.
Holmes, Larry E. *Stalin's School: Moscow's Model School No. 25, 1931–1937*. Pittsburgh: University of Pittsburgh Press, 1999.
Hosking, Geoffrey, *Trust: A History*. Oxford: Oxford University Press, 2014.
"Iz pis'ma N.I. Bukharina I.V. Stalinu s protestom protiv presledovanii. 14 oktiabria 1930 g." Istoricheskie materialy. https://istmat.org/node/31786.
Khlevniuk, Oleg V. *Master of the House: Stalin and His Inner Circle*. New Haven: Yale University Press, 2009.
Kopelev, Lev. *The Education of a True Believer*, trans. Gary Kern. New York: Harper & Row, 1980.
Lih, Lars T., Oleg V. Naumov, and Oleg V. Khlevniuk, eds. *Stalin's Letters to Molotov, 1925–1936*. New Haven: Yale University Press, 1995.
Lugovskaya, Nina. *The Diary of a Soviet Schoolgirl, 1932–1937*. Moscow: Glas, 2000.
Mandelstam, Nadezhda. *Hope against Hope: A Memoir*. New York: Atheneum, 1971.
Pipes, Richard, ed. *The Unknown Lenin: From the Secret Archive*. New Haven: Yale University Press, 1996.
Slezkine, Yuri. *The House of Government: A Saga of the Russian Revolution*. Princeton: Princeton University Press, 2017.

Suny, Ronald Grigor. *"They Can Live in the Desert but Nowhere Else": A History of the Armenian Genocide*. Princeton: Princeton University Press, 2015.
Suny, Ronald Grigor. *Stalin: Passage to Revolution*. Princeton: Princeton University Press, 2021.
Van Ree, Erik. "'The Day the Dragon Licks Its Flank, You'll Find Us at Your Side': Self-Heroization and Revolutionary Organization." *Politics, Religion & Ideology* 23, no. 3 (July 2022): 265–86.
Volkova, Irina V. "The Future as Perceived by Soviet Schoolchildren of the 1930s." *Russian Review* 79, no. 2 (April 2020): 204–26.
Weiner, Amir. *Making Sense of War: The Second World War and the Fate of the Bolshevik Revolution*. Princeton: Princeton University Press, 2001.

Chapter 8

Fear, Belief, and Stalinism

J. Arch Getty

As a high school student in the Midwest, my education about communism came from the books by J. Edgar Hoover and George Orwell that were assigned in civics class. I was taught that the Soviet state was a formidable, well-organized totalitarian leviathan that crushed a helpless, atomized population. Except for the crushing part, the Soviets projected a similar image of rational hierarchical efficiency. I wondered how people could stand to live in an Orwellian nightmare. By the time 1984 came around, Merle Fainsod's study of Smolensk had solved the puzzle for me, pulling back the curtain to expose complicated social and political lives that did not much resemble Orwell's *1984*.

Interacting with Russians confirmed that view. A Moscow taxi driver routinely sped through red traffic lights but could not understand my question about it. He told me, "But there aren't any police around!" An elderly archivist in a small Volga town remembered how sometimes men in leather jackets on motorcycles would appear, issue some orders from Moscow, then leave. When they left, life continued as before. Moscow was far away.

In the 1980s, I also began to wonder about brave, confident Bolsheviks. Robert McNeal had pointed out to me that Leningrad party boss Sergei Kirov's jackets on display at his apartment-museum had inside pockets to hold a pistol. (Kirov was right to be worried; he was shot to death outside his office.) By the 1990s, I came to doubt that Big Brother Stalin and his cronies were as fearless as they wanted us to believe. The top leaders carried guns and fortified their homes and workplaces. The First Department of the secret police was devoted to physical protection of party officials. What were these totalitarians afraid of?

Fear

The Politburo's command documents were meant to inspire fear and awe. But as I sat in the party archives in Moscow paging through these assertive texts, I wondered if they betrayed the opposite of what was intended. These documents were written by heavily guarded men who looked over their shoulders as they wrote. Behind the confident language, I detected the bully who tries to frighten others because of his own hidden fears.

George Kennan noted years ago that from tsar to commissar Russian foreign policy makers felt threatened and hid their vulnerability with bluster and bullying. Stalin's archive showed that he feared a wily and sophisticated British *intellidzhens servis*, which he suspected of fomenting the 1927 war scare and of providing disinformation in 1941 about Hitler's plans to attack the USSR. His attitude resembled one I remembered from my native Oklahoma, where rural folk (some of them related to me) were wary of clever city slickers trying to trick them.

From the beginning, all Bolshevik leaders were insecure. Although they loudly claimed to be the will of history, they knew that their small party had been catapulted to power in a wartime crisis. It could easily go the other way at any moment, and they were pleasantly surprised when their precarious new regime lasted longer than the two months of the Paris Commune in 1871. As time passed, they realized that they were not the vanguard of an immediate world revolution. Before long, they also recognized the overwhelming challenge of building socialism in an isolated, backward peasant country whose population was by no means uniformly on their side. Throughout the 1920s, Politburo members regularly read top-secret police summaries of the mood of the population. These read like a catalog of frightening anti-Soviet opinions and actions from around the country. I still wonder if Bolsheviks did not think in their Marxist hearts that they might have taken power too soon. Whether they did or not, they could not give up power and had no choice but to push on. Given the always threatening international situation, the backwardness of the economy, and their own tenuous hold on power, the anxious party majority first led and then dominated by Stalin felt that it had a narrow range of choices. Lenin's last writings on overcoming the challenges of governing and Stalin's cheerleading about building socialism in one country were theoretical attempts to reassure.

Huddled together, surrounded by a sea of private property-loving peasants with a recent proclivity to violence, the Bolsheviks were afraid to make public their weakness or any of their internal disagreements. Even hinting at dissent within the party gave aid and comfort to enemies domestic and foreign. So it was a rare admission of the leadership's fragility when Aleksei Rykov told an American journalist about the haunting fear of an intraparty fight turning into a civil war (Wynn 2022, 292). Lev Trotsky committed two unforgivable sins when he attacked the party leadership at a particularly dangerous time in 1924, and took the inner party struggle public in 1927. At both times, the regime felt itself hanging by a thread while not admitting it.

Among the Stalinists' main internal fears were the military, religion, and ethnic conflict. After all, next to the party, the army was the other organization with strong discipline and a chain of command. And unlike the party, they were armed. From the time of the Civil War, the Stalin group never completely trusted army officers. Over the years, the Bolsheviks tried to protect themselves from a potentially rebellious army by installing party political watchdogs beside regular officers, and they worked hard at political education in the ranks. Just in case, they also formed separate police military units under party control.

Another abiding fear was religion. Just as the army was the other organization with a chain of command, the Orthodox Church was the competing organization with a millenarian belief system. Despite relentless persecution of the Church since 1918, twenty years later more than half of the adult population bravely told census-takers in 1937 that they were religious. Religious believers outnumbered communist believers by a factor of roughly 5:1, far more in rural areas. Party leaders saw religion not only as a competing belief system but as a likely ideological support for peasant uprisings. Central and regional party officials constantly expressed apprehension about religion at closed-door meetings, and their concern grew in 1937. The bloody mass operations of 1937–38 would take a heavy toll among priests.

Separatist tendencies based on nationality and ethnicity also worried the Bolsheviks. They were a small elite trying to control a huge area populated by many non-Russian nationalities. Stalin was the party's specialist on the national question, and he knew full well that conflict between nationalities could easily bring the regime down (as it would in the 1980s.) Even though they believed in the eventual disappearance of nationalism, Bolsheviks celebrated the friendship of peoples while crushing any political assertion of nationalism. As early as 1925, Bolsheviks feared that Volga Germans were involved in information-gathering, and that in wartime they would be saboteurs behind the lines. In 1937, a staggering 1.4 percent of the entire Volga German population would be shot or sent to camps (Junge 2008, 562).

Stalin had additional fears. Even though he and his allies had marginalized Trotsky in the early 1920s, Stalin always feared that some future crisis could bring him back. In 1929 he voted to execute a police official who had merely contacted Trotsky in exile. Stalin was so worried about Trotskyists that he authorized the mass shootings of those already in prison camps in 1936. In 1940, even after his complete triumph, he had Trotsky hunted down and killed. Similarly, when in 1941 German troops approached the Orel prison, Stalin ordered the execution of any remaining imprisoned Trotskyists, along with poor old Socialist Revolutionaries like Maria Spiridonova, who had been in exile or prison since 1923. As with the tsar in 1918, who knew what could happen if the enemy liberated them?

Stalin and his Politburo knew that if they were removed in a war, a military coup, a revolt of senior party members in the Central Committee, or a peasant uprising, they would be assassinated. No successful revolt could afford to leave them alive. In addition to defending their correct policies, they feared for their lives.

Angry dissidents were everywhere. There were numerous reports of Zinovievists, Trotskyists, tsarist officers, dispossessed kulaks, and political emigrants who had military experience in the Civil War on different sides of the fronts and in peasant uprisings. They had weapons and knew how to handle them. Vyacheslav Molotov's grandson, himself an eminent historian, reports that Stalin and Molotov had little reason to doubt the validity of these conclusions. By the mid-1930s, the Romanian prime minister, the Polish minister of internal affairs, the Bavarian premier, King Alexander of Yugoslavia, the Austrian chancellor, and dozens of prominent German politicians were shot dead by fascist insurrectionists. The assassinations had come close to home with the assassination of Kirov in December 1934, and Stalin and his team thought they might be next. The cadets, soldiers, and honor guards who accompanied Kirov's funeral procession in Leningrad were each checked by the NKVD that their guns were not loaded in Stalin's presence (Akhmedov, n.d.). Molotov was aware of at least a dozen attempts to kill Stalin (Nikonov 2016, 229, 249, 264).

It would be a mistake to be taken in by triumphant claims, congresses of victors, or other performances of strength. James Harris has aptly called this time "The Great Fear" (Harris 2016). Behind their bravado, Stalinist anxiety reached new heights in the 1930s. Ridiculous reports that should have died at lower levels were put on Politburo agendas. Silly student meetings in a forest were dangerous counterrevolutionary organizations, and citizens applying for tourist travel abroad were obviously trying to connect with White Guard-Fascist organizations in Germany. Stamp collectors and students of Esperanto were just as obviously foreign agents. Even birds were dangerous. Bird watchers in Leningrad were suspected of using homing pigeons to spy on military installations, and in 1937, the deputy commissar of state security reported to Stalin that crows with German leg bands were spies flying over the Soviet motherland (Khaustov 2004, 251). How they would report back was not explained.

Censors and Politburo members scrutinized the written word for any signs of deviation and in later years, even songs and orchestral music could sound subversive. Speakers at Central Committee meetings reminded their fellow Bolsheviks how they had used jokes before 1917 to weaken the tsar's regime. This consciousness of fragility plagues all dictators with rags to riches histories. Jokes could get you killed in Hitler's Berlin as easily as in Stalin's Moscow.

Socialist Realists blurred time in the 1930s; they looked at the present but saw a positive future. Enthusiasts looked at a messy construction site but saw the finished building. Stalin had a negative version: He looked at present doubters and saw future traitors. Small threats were embryonic beginnings of fatal ones. Those who might betray have already betrayed. Stalin's bloody 1937 attack on the elite was fueled by fear and what Khrushchev called sickly suspicion. We will never know the nods, winks, frowns, and gossip among the cliques that gathered in the buffets at party plena and congresses, but in the corridors and meeting rooms, everybody knew who was on what side, so it took little to earn Stalin's distrust. Officials who had never expressed any criticism could be shot if there was the slightest fear of possible disloyalty. When asked about such innocent victims, Molotov admitted that many of those shot were innocent, but such people were undependable and might easily turn on Stalin in times of crisis (Chuev 1991, 389–91).

Stalin's suspicions could be triggered by a comrade's single incautious word. He and his cronies thought that it was better to arrest too many than too few, that it was justified to shoot nine innocents to get one guilty person. As far back as 1928, Stalin had said that even if criticism is only 5–10 percent true, it was worth serious attention (Wynn 2022, 274). In 1937, after the arrest and execution of the Soviet high command, he told a meeting of military leaders that even if only 5 percent of all denunciations were true, that was enough [*eto uzhe khleb*, literally "it's already bread"] (Tarkhova 2008, 140). Molotov tells us that Stalin "correctly" wanted to be doubly sure of loyalty (Chuev 1991, 416).

The Politburo's chronic fear was shared throughout the party elite from Stalin and Molotov brooding about the Red Army down to local party officials in the countryside worrying about being murdered by peasants with shotguns. It had been only fifteen years since the Civil War threatened the regime, and more recently the Stalinists had provoked another civil war—collectivization—

to achieve something like control over the majority rural population. There was a lot of bitterness out there to worry about and plenty of firearms in circulation.

One of the symptoms of clinical anxiety is the inability to tell small dangers from large ones. Anxiety-induced aggression has been widely studied by modern psychologists, and there is a large literature about how emotions can lead to fear-induced preemptive aggression when uncertainty and fear of vulnerability imply preemptive strikes. Long before modern psychology, Thomas Hobbes wrote under the heading of "distrust" that the most reasonable way for one to feel safe is to strike first, particularly when one doubts one's own abilities at self-defense. Killing anyone who might oppose the regime is a textbook case of fear-induced aggression.

Fear as a precondition to violence helps contextualize Stalin's trigger of mass violence and explains why it resonated with others who were prepared to believe in all kinds of dangers and conspiracies. That Stalin (and many others in and outside official positions) feared so much in no way justifies his bloody reaction. Rather the point is that this was not a case of clinical paranoia at the top or mass hypnosis at the base. Their fears were not entirely baseless.

A Plan?

Decades ago, when I began to study the violence of the 1930s, the books I read characterized it as a single planned event, a rising crescendo from 1934 to 1939. As I began my research, I defaced the wall of my apartment with a timeline on which I recorded the events of that period. I saw that there were zigs and zags, periods of intense repression alternating with quiet times, and an overlapping series of initiatives with confusing cross-purposes and contradictions in official statements. There were too many anomalies, too many contradictions. There still are, and I continue to believe that Stalin's violence was not the result of long-term intentional planning.

For one thing, if Stalin had a long-term master plan, he would have got his story straight at the beginning. Instead, the official version of events changed constantly. Stalin's official explanations for the discrete phases of the violence were "chaotic, reactive, and dizzyingly erratic" (Brandenberger 2013, 157). Whenever a group came under suspicion, official propaganda had to reformulate the definition of the enemy. In 1937, NKVD chief Nikolai Ezhov was writing a book about anti-Stalin conspiracies. His manuscript shows that he went through draft after draft, constantly posing new and improved final lessons that contradicted the previous ones.

The prescribed lessons about vigilance made it difficult to keep track of who was a hero and who was a traitor. Officials were promoted and publicly lauded, only to be executed as traitors a short time later. On Stalin's motion, M. E. Mikhailov was promoted to full membership of the Central Committee at its October plenum in 1937, only to be expelled and arrested three weeks later. Nestor Lakoba, a famous Georgian Bolshevik and friend of Stalin, died of natural causes and had a state funeral. But soon thereafter, his body was exhumed, branded as a traitor, and burned. In just a few months' time, Ezhov himself would go from being the best Bolshevik and Stalin's best pupil to an enemy.

Stalin also changed his mind several times about Bukharin, who had been his coleader in the 1920s. Between September 1936 and March 1937, he twice cleared Bukharin of charges. Finally in February 1937, when others wanted to shoot Bukharin out of hand, Stalin suggested merely exiling him to a distant territory without arrest or imprisonment. In the second draft of the minutes, Stalin's moderate proposal was crossed out and replaced with the decision to arrest (and therefore condemn) Bukharin. It also took Stalin a while to make up his mind about Avel Enukidze, his old comrade from Georgia. Arrested in February 1937, he immediately confessed to being part of a conspiracy to overthrow the government. Yet five months later, in a list of officials to be shot, Stalin crossed his name off and penciled in, "let's wait for now." Perhaps this is what Central Committee secretary A. A. Andreev meant when he referred to Stalin's "angelic patience" with oppositionists? Stalin would also hesitate to arrest N. A. Voznesenskii in 1949, even when presented with a damning indictment for treason prepared by Malenkov and Beria. All these documents remained secret for decades. Being human, even dictators can be indecisive, but nobody should know about it (Brandenberger and Pivovarov 2023).

These anomalies raise the question of what caused the 1937–38 violence. With the documents we now have, we can discard some old explanations. Some thought that Stalin launched the violence to cement his personal power and terrorize the population into obedience. But by 1937 he seemed to have no competition for the top spot, and the population already worshipped his every word. Much of the terror was kept secret.

We used to think that because of Stalin's inferiority (or superiority) complex, he sought to destroy his fellow Old Bolsheviks. But statistical analysis of victims shows that Old Bolshevik status was not the major determinant of risk of being killed; instead, high office and personal connections were (Chase and Getty 1993). Perhaps Stalin sought to destroy the current ruling generation to reengineer the elite with new younger officials who had grown up idolizing him? Although many old timers fell victim to the slaughter, so did their young Bolshevik replacements, and often their replacements. Stalin killed the best and brightest of the new person golden generation he had promoted.

Some saw preparation for war as Stalin's main motive in 1937; he was preempting a future fifth column behind the lines in case of attack (Khlevniuk 1995). The Bolsheviks had always been afraid of impending war. There were war scares in 1923, 1926, and 1927. In 1932 Stalin warned that the capitalists were preparing to invade "in the next year or two." To worry about foreign invasion was to worry about internal uprising because like their French Jacobin predecessors, the Bolsheviks always saw internal uprisings and foreign invasion as two sides of the same coin. Although the term fifth column originated in the Spanish Civil War, the Stalinists had long assumed that internal enemies were waiting for an invasion to rise up and coordinate with foreign attackers, as had been the case in the Civil War. From the mid-1920s the Stalinists had warned of the national security threats posed by internal oppositionists who were said to constitute a united front from Trotsky to Clemenceau. Worry about war and fifth columns was constant from 1918 to 1953, and was used to justify all kinds of policies, but as I will suggest, long-term context and immediate precipitants are separate factors.

I still wonder how Stalin could have imagined how suddenly killing the top military command staff (and executing the entire foreign and domestic spy networks) could contribute to war preparedness. The 31,000 death sentences he confirmed with his signature in 1937–38 constituted the top leadership of provincial and central party and state bodies, so if war broke out key Soviet leaders would have been inexperienced. The special folders of the Politburo also show that in the early 1930s, the leadership was worried about being able to fill the annual military conscription quotas because of low birth rates during the Civil War. Those available to be drafted in 1937 would have been born in the terrible civil war, hunger, and disease year 1919 when the birthrate had plummeted. Stalin's slaughter or imprisonment of a million and a half potential soldiers in 1937–38 would compound this problem. If Stalin were preparing for a longer-term war threat, it would have been far less disruptive to quietly marginalize officers he distrusted, to pick them off one at a time and promote others in a smoother transition. Instead, his sudden urgent purge of the military left the USSR weaker and less able to defend itself. This was Hitler's opinion at the time.

We often read that it was the Spanish Civil War that touched off Stalin's terror. But in the spring of 1936 before the Spanish Civil War even began, Stalin had already moved against the leftist opposition and prepared the script for the first show trial of Trotskyists. Although Spain was closely covered in the Soviet press, it is hard to imagine that events in a minor country 2,000 miles from Moscow would by themselves make Stalin suddenly destroy his military and intelligence capabilities. Stalin's coup against the military was an anxious response to a perfect storm of domestic as well as foreign threats to an already fearful and insecure regime. It triggered several simultaneous bloodbaths in the summer of 1937.

The trajectories of prewar international crises and what would become the terror do not match up well and often show an inverse correlation. The terror built up momentum during a relatively calm time on the international front, and it was being wound down as foreign tensions grew. Without the benefit of hindsight, when the terror exploded in mid-1937 it was by no means clear at the time that Hitler would make further territorial demands leading directly to war. Hitler's annexation of Austria was eight months in the future and coincided with Stalin's first moves to stop the terror by purging the purgers. The Munich Agreement that made war likely was more than a year ahead, at precisely the time that Ezhov's lieutenants were being arrested. A few weeks after Munich, as international temperatures began to rise, Ezhov himself was fired from the NKVD and the murderous troikas and mass arrests were abolished. When Hitler seized the rest of Czechoslovakia in March 1939, sharply ratcheting up international tensions, Ezhov had been arrested, and the terror was over.

Rather than part of a prewar plan, recent research shows that Stalin's decision to launch the military purge seems ad hoc and aimed at forestalling a palace coup (Whitewood 2015). Molotov tells us that the situation was dangerous because military leaders were preparing to seize power in 1937: Tukhachevskii was "a very dangerous military conspirator who was only caught at the last moment. . . . There is no doubt about it." (Chuev 1991, 390, 418). Comintern leader Georgi Dmitrov observed in his diary how the leadership feared a coup in the summer of 1937 (Banac 2003, 70). Decades later, Kaganovich recalled, "So many [shadow] governments were at liberty. . . . They were organizing an uprising against Soviet power and would lead it. We knew that they organized a strong group. . . . such opponents who could carry out terror, murder, anything. Coups are real. Today we see various coups in all kinds of countries" (Chuev 2001, 187–89).

A military plot against Stalin was believable. One Moscow historian told me that given the disaster of collectivization, Stalin's amateurish meddling in military affairs, and his support for his second-rate friend Marshal Voroshilov, it would be surprising if professionally competent and patriotic generals were not plotting to do something. As we shall see below, the same might be said of senior party leaders, who had their own grievances about Stalin.

Whether or not there was a real military coup, Stalin and Molotov believed there was and acted urgently. Four days before the arrests, the watchdog political commissars that had been abolished ten years before were reestablished. Passes to the Kremlin were suddenly revoked, the Kremlin garrison was put on high alert, and there were NKVD troop movements in the suburbs. The officers were mostly arrested en route, away from their commands and levers of power. At the 1937 May Day parade, Marshal Voroshilov (reputed to be the best pistol shot in the country) stood on Lenin's Mausoleum next to Stalin displaying his revolver. In the midst of his countercoup, Stalin did not attend his mother's funeral. He thought the situation too dangerous to leave Moscow for even a few days (Nikonov 2016, 258–59).

After the execution of Tukhachevskii and the top military leaders, Stalin was still worried, and at a hastily called meeting of 120 members of the Military Council, he tried to convince his senior military audience that the conspiracy was real. (In an unprecedented security measure for a Military Council meeting, the officers had their weapons confiscated at the door.) Afterward, Voroshilov and Ezhov issued an unusual statement to all army officers, offering them immunity from prosecution if they told about their own or others' conspiracies (Tarkhova 2008, 463–64).

With the military purge in the summer of 1937, a different cataclysm began. The major strands of violence—arrests of heretofore loyal members of the party apparatus, troika-based executions of class-alien anti-Soviet elements in the countryside, and executions of members of suspect ethnic populations—all began shortly after the execution of the generals.

Although they had supported Stalin in his struggles with oppositionists in the 1920s, by the 1930s many senior Bolshevik revolutionaries felt bypassed by Stalin, whom they considered only first among equals. Themselves members of the Central Committee, they claimed a more significant role in running the country. They felt displaced because they knew more than the young loyalists Stalin promoted, and they wanted a more active role. "Members of the Central Committee could not keep their mouths shut" about this, and some of them openly suggested that the defeated oppositionists from the 1920s had been right about Stalin (Khaustov 2009, 141–45).

Regional party secretaries had created their own personality cults and family circles, and many of these circles were guilty of massive financial corruption. They routinely lied to Moscow about their activities, even doing so in person when summoned to Moscow. They defied the Central Committee (meaning Stalin) in various ways, including illegally making personnel appointments without Moscow's approval, suppressing *Pravda* editorials that criticized them, and complaining about Stalin to their underlings. They coopted local NKVD chiefs, control commission inspectors, and various plenipotentiaries sent from Moscow (Harris 2000; Getty 2013). Some of them had suspicious connections to the arrested generals. Stalin knew all this. Beginning in the summer of 1937, he decided to smash the corrupt and disobedient satraps; nearly all the regional party first secretaries and their staff (and their staff) were arrested. 1937 arrest patterns and interrogation transcripts show that his goal was crushing and uprooting their family circle networks.

Numerically, the largest number of victims was claimed by the so-called mass troika operations that also began suddenly in Summer 1937.[1] Just four years earlier, in 1933 Stalin had banned further mass operations, complaining that even after collectivization local agencies were constantly asking for the right to repress large numbers. In the interactions between Stalin and regional officials in the twenty years before 1937, it was almost always panicked locals who asked for mass repression. During that time, the number of occasions Stalin put firm limitations on such requests was greater than when he had to press to increase violence (Getty 2020). As recently as the spring of 1937, Ezhov had also banned future mass operations. But that Summer, Stalin suddenly reversed course and unleashed this largest mass killing in Soviet history. It showed little long-term planning. No logistical or budget provisions had been made, and only after the operation began did the Politburo transfer 75,000,000 rubles from the state budget to fund suddenly overburdened police, transport, and prison camp agencies.

From early 1937, local NKVD chiefs had worried that kulaks, priests, Baptists, and even pretenders claiming to be lost members of the former royal family were urging peasants to resist the regime. Party and police leaders worried that these anti-Soviet elements were using the new contested elections to the Supreme Soviet to organize (Danilov 2004, 79–91; Bakulin 2020; Getty 2002). At Central Committee plena throughout the year, regional party leaders also warned constantly about a rise in religion among peasants. Despite five years of the passport regime to fix residency, population movements of kulaks, criminals, and others were out of control. Previously deported kulaks were returning to their homes, and 600,000 of them were missing from their special settlements. Local NKVD officials talked about insurrectionary organizations in the countryside.

The resulting NKVD Order No. 00447 called for troikas to execute or imprison class-alien kulaks, priests, former White Army officers, and others, who were "the chief instigators of all sorts of anti-Soviet crimes." These were the same categories of enemies as in the 1918–21 Civil War, dekulakization and collectivization, and now it was time for "finally putting an end, once and for all, to their vile undermining of the foundations of the Soviet state." The mass operations were the end of an incomplete twenty-year civil war "with all its political, social, and ethnic cleavages" that Stalin sought to finally eliminate the old class enemy (Viola 2017, 24).

The use of extra-judicial troikas empowered to impose immediate death sentences on the spot with no trial or appeal suggests how the regime viewed the situation in 1937. From 1918, lethal troikas had been used only in emergencies when the regime was confronted with serious threats to its control when things seemed too urgent to use the regular court system. They were authorized everywhere during the Civil War, dekulakization and collectivization, and on a case-by-case basis at various other times against armed bandit groups. In addition to worrying about a future war, in 1937 anxious Stalinists were worried in the short term about losing control of the countryside. Their use of troikas in the mass operations has all the hallmarks of an urgent, emergency reaction.

Stalin triggered mass violence in Summer 1937 and would stop it in late 1938, but his control of these levers does not mean the processes were orderly. Important initiatives were entrusted to groups that were themselves being exterminated. Party secretaries responsible for fulfilling economic plans, purging their ranks of suspicious Trotskyists, and organizing Stalin's showy new elections were themselves (and their successors) arrested as conspirators even as they were serving on troikas ordering mass shootings of others. Most regional leaderships and ministries were replaced at least three times in succession in 1937–38.

On July 13, 1937, the Politburo confirmed Cheliabinsk NKVD chief I. M. Blat as chair of the regional troika. Two days later, before the troika could even begin its work, Blat was arrested in his office. He would later be shot. Of the members of the infamous troikas originally confirmed by the Politburo and charged with the mass killing operations of 1937–38, nearly all were themselves arrested and shot within a few months. The NKVD was tasked with arresting and killing enemies while Stalin simultaneously encouraged NKVD clans under Iagoda, then Ezhov, then Beria to annihilate each other. Ezhov killed his own men before Beria could arrest and interrogate them to testify against him. Ezhov killed Iagoda's men and Beria killed Ezhov's men, often at the same time. Stalin killed the killers while they were killing others.

Belief

The several drafts of Ezhov's book manuscript finally posited a composite "Right-Trotskyist Gang of German and Japanese Agents" consisting of traitorous party officials, former oppositionists, military men, NKVD officers, economic officials, foreigners, monarchists, former White officers, kulaks and priests. Bizarre and oxymoronic as it seems, it was plausible at the time.

This brings us to the question of belief. We used to think that Stalin projected his paranoia about enemies onto his followers and the public at large, that some kind of mass hypnosis befell a passive population. But no single person, however powerful, could convince millions of people of something they were not prepared to believe. Although he shared it and used it for his own purposes, Stalin did not invent the belief in conspiracy. It haunted all levels of society. From peasants' superstition to sneaky two-faced Trotskyists, hidden dark forces were everywhere. People are inclined to believe in conspiracies in light of their own experiences, especially when more rational explanations are unavailable.

For a long time, I could not understand what went through their heads as Politburo members signed death warrants (shooting lists) of friends and comrades they had known and worked with for years. On a single day, August 10, 1937, they condemned 987 senior leaders to death by list (RGASPI, 17/171/409/2). Those who left memoirs do not seem to have signed because they were afraid of Stalin. They were "Team Stalin" and Stalin was the coach they admired (Wheatcroft 2004). They trusted Stalin and a heroic police to unmask the guilty. Khrushchev remembered how he admired Stalin for being unafraid to purge the party of enemies everywhere.

Another reason for going along with killing was suspicion of their peers. The party Central Committee was made up of former professional revolutionaries whose early lives had been about secret circles, political spies, and infiltrators, and about hiding their subversive activities. One might think that this shared experience would bond them together, but the contrary was true. Trust among them was in short supply. Overthrowing governments was what they had always done; it was the only thing on their resumes. Party leaders in the 1930s all came from the same kitchen, to use a Russian phrase, so it was easy for them to believe that their fellow revolutionaries were still conspiring. They did not trust each other because they would have done the same thing in their place.

When those under attack tried to defend themselves by claiming that meetings among themselves were innocent social occasions, they were ridiculed by their peers. Kaganovich described an incident in which former oppositionists Tomsky and Zinoviev met to pick out a dog for Zinoviev. Nobody in the audience could imagine that their fellow Old Bolsheviks could have a nonpolitical meeting. Stalin ridiculed the idea with sarcasm and comic relief: "What about this dog? he asked. Was it a hunting dog or a guard dog? Was it a good dog or a bad dog? Did they get a good dog? Does anybody know? [laughter in the hall]" (RGASPI, 17/2/575/159-167). Years later, when Molotov was asked if the massacre of Old Bolsheviks was unnecessary, he replied that only someone who was never a Bolshevik before the Revolution could ask this (Chuev 1991, 440). Even the accusation that traitors wanted to cede territory to German or Japanese enemies seemed plausible. After all, had not Lenin done the same thing in 1918 to preserve a regime that had overthrown a government in a coup months before?

Belief in enemies was strong. Aleksandr Shcherbakov, who would go on to become a Secretary of the Central Committee, sincerely believed that in his region the party and Soviet leadership was entirely in the hands of enemies. Pavel Postyshev thought the same when he disbanded most of the district (*raion*) party committees in the Kuibyshev region because they had been infiltrated by traitors. Moscow secretary Nikita Khrushchev told Stalin, "You can't believe how many enemies there are" (Chuev 1999, 439). Bolsheviks like Robert Eikhe, Vlas Chubar, and Ian Rudzutak all wrote to Stalin from prison about a "still unliquidated center" of enemies inside the NKVD who were skillfully fabricating cases and forcing innocent people to admit to crimes they did not commit. When Stalin decided to call a halt to the violence in 1938–39, he used conspiracy belief as a reliable discursive strategy: The Enemy was so crafty that he had infiltrated the NVKD and caused persecution of innocent people.

At the grassroots, belief in Stalin and the ubiquitous enemy had social and ideological support, a reality confirmed to me by Russian friends. My archivist friend Nadia was the third generation of a party family. Her mother had been a party activist. One day I saw Nadia spit at the new Louis Vuitton boutique across the street from the party archive, "say what you will but that obscenity would have been impossible in Stalin's time." Nadia's mother and her peers were not clever maneuverers trying to get ahead, nor were they passive or sullen victims who had to "speak Bolshevik." They were not victims of mass hypnosis or totalitarian atomization. They were collective-minded people who supported a socialist version of modernization. (It is worth remembering that in the 1918 elections to the Constituent Assembly, some 85 percent of the country had voted for some kind of socialism.) They were the opposite of atomized units. They knew and cared about their neighbors more than they looked for ways to report them to the police. Nadia remembers how apartment doors were left open more often than locked and residents lived collectively with those in neighboring flats. People took care of the common areas in their entryway (*pod"ezd*). They felt as if they lived in a socialist community rather than in some Orwellian *1984*.

Nadia's mother had told her that in the 1930s, the Revolution was still going on. "*We* had won in 1917 but that was only the beginning. *They* were still around doing everything they could to hold *us* back." Conspiracies were real and not only within the echelons of Soviet government. Nadia's parents had little sympathy for many of those arrested in the 1930s unless they knew them personally, and then they believed the arrest was a mistake. They thought the country was at war and they were on the right side. Many took a grim satisfaction at seeing the fall of bosses, bureaucrats, crooks, and go-slow nay-sayers. They saw the defendants at show trials in the same way as others would later see captured war criminals after the Great Patriotic War.

For adults in the 1930s, foreign invasions, conspiracies, betrayals, and peasant uprisings had been parts of their formative years, a continuous twenty-year civil war against class enemies and foreign threats. The comparatively peaceful six years of the NEP in the 1920s were merely a lull in the civil war, sandwiched between the violence of the 1918 Civil War and the storm of collectivization. For Nadia's parents, politics had always been about war, both internal and external, declared and undeclared, and everyone assumed that a foreign invasion would be coordinated with an internal uprising, just as it had been in 1918–20. They felt themselves part of a *we* fighting a good fight against *them*. We will never know how many agreed with Stalin that it was time to put an end to civil war enemies "once and for all," but as Anna Akhmatova wrote, there were two types of people then: those who were in prison and those who put them there.

In his study of the English Revolution of the seventeenth century, Lawrence Stone offered a three-part framework for the causality of major historical events (Stone 1972). *Preconditions* are long-term structural and environmental factors that make an event possible. *Precipitants* are shorter-term factors that make an explosion likely. Both preconditions and precipitants provide not only the background setting of the event but also help explain how it would unfold. *Triggers* are immediate catalytic events that set off the explosion. One of my California students aptly compared Stone's model to a forest fire, with drought being a precondition, dry forest tinder as precipitant, and someone lighting a match as the trigger. The drought and dry forest environment help explain why the spark spread so quickly.

Stone's method invites us to look at the violence of the 1930s as a phenomenon with a prehistory, setting, and tensions that together make up a comprehensive explanation of it. It allows us to avoid comparing causal apples and oranges by categorizing and classifying causes and backgrounds. It also can help put Stalin's role into a broader context.

Long-term preconditions would include a variety of factors stemming from the 1917 revolutions and their aftermath: a tradition of social and political violence, and constant fears about a coming war coinciding with internal uprisings. A legally unrestrained political police and a center/periphery tug of war were also structural preconditions for violence. Belief in Stalin was certainly another precondition that affected victims and perpetrators.

Among *shorter-term precipitants* one could include events of 1937: immediate fears of a military coup, plus perceptions of continued underground oppositional activity, the rise of religion and the return of kulaks and other class-aliens. The growing power of regional power centers with their local cults of personality and disobedience fueled Stalinist suspicion and increased the likelihood of a preemptive violent reaction.

The *trigger* was Stalin. I think there is no single answer to why Stalin launched the violence, nor could there be. Stalin had many motives: a need to scapegoat officials for industrial and agricultural failures, a belief that criticizing or disobeying him was betraying the Soviet state, a pathological suspicion of almost everyone, a real (to him) fear of spies and saboteurs, and worries about peasant discontent are examples. Fear of an upcoming war was part of the background, but it will not do as a single explanation because it cannot account for equally serious domestic fears that also precipitated the killings. Nor can purely domestic threats without their foreign context fully explain things. Although historians give different weights to foreign and domestic threats, there is general agreement that they are not mutually exclusive but rather coincide and work together (Khlevniuk 2021, 377; Getty 2002, 136).

But there was more to Soviet political history than Stalin. Since the late 1970s, social and political historians have described a complicated society and political system, and showed that it was possible to write Soviet history without constant reference to Stalin's violence. A lot of other history was happening. It is difficult to agree that it is impossible to fully comprehend any phenomenon of Soviet history in the Stalin period without the factor of terror, or that NKVD perpetrators and torturers were the most significant social base of the Stalinist state (Khlevniuk 2021, 369, 384).

Thomas Carlyle wrote in 1840 that all history is the "History of the Great Men" and the practical realization and embodiment of their thoughts. I always envied my colleagues in French, German, and Chinese studies as they moved beyond Great Man history. Using tools of social history, sociology, and anthropology, they situated Napoleon, Hitler, and Mao Zedong in broader historical contexts, as products of their eras as much as sole creators of them. Yet perhaps because of the awesome scale of Stalin's deeds, the political history of the period is often still written as Stalin's biography. His brutality, combined with the regime's grandiose self-assertions, have led us to think in terms of omniscience and omnipotence more than unintended consequences. Anomalies are explained with the deus ex machina of Stalin's cleverness: false starts, retreats, and indecision are things Stalin planned. Sudden course changes were just clever tricks to fool others. Scholarly works still draw on the huge genre of Stalin apocrypha.

Lacking a dependable bureaucracy, Stalin's governing apparatus was capable of responding to commands like START or STOP, but not precision or fine-tuning. Absent an efficient bureaucracy, he had to rule by storming fortresses. Whether it was to achieve collectivization, industrialization, or to inflict violence, implementation *was* mobilization; it began with Stalin announcing strategic goals, assigning tasks, and specifying deadlines. Then the campaign began, but it soon little resembled the original instructions as incompetent, self-interested, or overenthusiastic actors adapted the original orders to their particular situations. Enthusiasm soon sent things spinning out of control, and deadlines and limits were exceeded. After a time, Stalin ended the offensive, claimed that everything had gone according to plan, declared victory, and cleaned up by scapegoating his agents for excesses. Stalin's metaphor for this was that one had to grasp the main link that would pull in everything else in the chain. But it rarely did without broken links and high costs.

Implementation meant unleashing campaigns that guaranteed chaos and innocent victims. According to much of the scholarship, the mass operations of 1937–38 were planned and controlled by Stalin. Yet a mobilization that began suddenly, reversing recently stated policy, and with vague goals susceptible to various interpretations can be described as planned only with major reservations. And an operation in which many of the provinces and republics exceeded the victim limits ordered by the Politburo in more than three times the allotted timeframe can be called controlled only with similar reservations. Local police rounding up men with beards in bazaars and shooting them as mullahs also does not speak to central control. Zig-zags do not suggest planning, and chaos does not suggest control, at least in the usual understanding of those terms.

Stalin started the terror and stopped it. Nobody has said otherwise. The terror did not originate from below. Stalin was not a "weak dictator" but rather an active organizer of a vicious and cruel repression (Getty 1985, 2, 9, 203; 1993, 42, 60; 1999, 6; 2013, chs. 6–8). But does that exhaust the meaning of control? What took place between Stalin's start and stop signals was a vital part of the process and our understanding of it as a phenomenon. Knowing that Stalin started the killing and stopped it is not the end of research but rather the beginning. Stalin initiated the hunt for enemies, and Ezhov kept the pressure on NKVD officials who labeled all kinds of innocent people as disloyal enemies or kulaks and destroyed them.

But they were not the only ones looking for enemies. The terror licensed party members to speak out against their superiors. In the factories and party committees the terror brought existing conflicts and animosities to the surface. The same thing happened in the countryside, where victim selection was colored by existing conflicts and blame-shifting. In light of a poor 1936 harvest that threatened famine, party agriculture officials blamed their subordinates for quotas not being met. Collective farm chairmen and field brigadiers denounced helpless collective farmers as lazy, counterrevolutionary troublemakers and criminal violators of labor discipline. Everyone targeted priests. Passive and active participation from ordinary citizens was an important part of the violence. Studying that participation helps explain how the violence spread as it did and provides a window into the political sociology of the system in general.

Stalin's was not the only kind of control in the mass violence. Michel Foucault wrote that in any system, power in some measure exists everywhere, not only at the top. While "working toward the Leader" and his presumed wishes (to use Ian Kershaw's apt description of the Nazi bureaucracy) everyone had some measure of control and some field to deploy it. "Stalin opened a floodgate of repression, and it is within this flood that the NKVD operated, allowing it immense institutional and individual agency" (Viola 2017, 18). Party and police were where the population met the regime, so for the average citizen the decision about whether she or he lived or died was a local one. For millions of people it was the only kind of control that mattered.

Neither Stalinist bravado nor widespread violence are signs of a confident regime sure of its control of the country. These were frightened, anxious men who were armed to the teeth. Bolshevik anxiety predated Stalin's rule and outlived it. Before Stalin, a sense of weakness and mortal threat had led Lenin to launch a red terror, and after Stalin, decades later Soviet leaders panicked and invaded Hungary and Czechoslovakia. Khrushchev and Brezhnev were as afraid of bibles, transistor radios, and rock and roll as they were of US missiles. Right up into the 1980s, they persecuted individual dissidents whose small protest demonstrations on Red Square were neutralized within minutes.

Russia is not the Soviet Union and Vladimir Putin is not Stalin, but at this writing Russia is ruled by veterans of the Soviet political police whose insecure mindset was forged in Lenin's day and whose cult continued as a constant thread through Stalin and across changes in war and peace, communist and anticommunist leaderships (Fedor 2011). Lenin and Stalin would have understood Putin's fear that an encroaching foreign encirclement aims to cancel Russia by, among other things, sending signals to stir up color revolution fifth columns behind the lines. It is easy to dismiss these seemingly exaggerated fears of the Soviet and post-Soviet elites as groundless paranoia. But whether their fears were justified the fact is that rulers acted on them.

We sometimes read that Stalin was a master gardener, accurately identifying and pulling troublesome human weeds while cultivating others to shape a modern state. Although much of his terror was aimed at excising present or future enemies, efficiently pruning and sculpting the country was beyond his reach. Instead, he lurched from policy to policy, constantly changing plans while staying in power. Stalin's political cultivation was a premodern subsistence slash and burn type, a fearful struggle for survival against uncontrollable bad weather and dangerous pests.

The idea that weak and insecure regimes are the ones that resort to terror and violence is not new. Hannah Arendt, Moshe Lewin, and others have noted that strong, confident regimes do not need terror, that the strength of a regime and the level of violence it deploys are inversely proportional. This rather obvious and logical observation was drowned out over the years by the simplistic white noise of totalitarian theory and Great Man history.

It still is. Over the years, I asked my students to apply a real-life test to historical events. Without a priori assumptions, what seemed plausible in the real world? One of my seminar students started a discussion of historical methodology when he wondered whether Orwell's *1984* helped shape our views of the USSR more than it reflected Soviet reality. It seems that preconceived assumptions about Stalinism, more than primary sources, allowed scholars to posit a political system unlike any other, a special case where the accepted forms of power and politics are suspended, a different analytical world where common sense does not apply. Only there could a dictator prepare for war by massacring the entire military leadership. Only there could one imagine the ability of one man to hypnotize a huge population, successfully realizing his dreams across the largest country on earth with a primitive apparatus composed of people with goals ranging from communism to personal power to theft. Only there could one define unintended consequences as actual intentions or equate outcomes with plans. An older student who had lived in a USSR where real-life avoidance strategies were routine could not recognize the high-tech Soviet political controls described in the books she read. Yet sixty-five years after Fainsod's study of ramshackle Soviet Smolensk, the idea of a modern total Stalinist state lives on.

Theodore Von Laue wrote that Westerners should not inflict their own sensibilities and judgments on people whose history and beliefs were so different from theirs (Von Laue 1981). To demean the beliefs of the Stalin-era population as delusions imprinted from above on tabulae rasae, or to expect Russians today to come to grips with their violent history as Westerners think they should, are forms of patronizing Orientalist othering. The hardest part of the historian's job is to step inside the shoes of people with vastly different cultures, lives, and beliefs than ours.

As I became older, the passing of friends and family made me more emotionally conscious of tragic death and of the almost incomprehensible horror of the 1930s Stalinist violence. But with that horror came a need to apply the tools of the historian to understand it. Some felt that in light of the mass killing of innocents, an analytical approach that rejected simple answers normalized the violence, excused Stalin, or denigrated the suffering of so many. I continue to believe that it does not and that beyond commemoration historians have an obligation to explain. That was the approach of the Moscow Memorial Society that sought to understand horror by documenting and analyzing it before it was liquidated by politicians for whom it was not useful to remember or understand. It is also the approach of laboratory scientists who study the horrors of cancer, AIDS, or Alzheimer's. I saw archives as laboratories, and like my colleagues with their test tubes, I still feel the need to try and explain the unimaginable.

Note

1. Sometimes called "kulak operations" these killings also targeted criminals, priests, members of former political parties and others in both rural and urban areas. Additionally, there were mass national operations against suspect ethnic groups.

Works Cited

Akhmedov, Ismail. *Memoir. Semeinye istorii.* http://www.famhist.ru/famhist/ahmedov/0006182d.htm.

Bakulin, Vladimir I. "Biuro Kirovskogo obkoma VKP(b) i problema politicheskikh repressii v 1937g." *Istoriia i arkhivy* 2 (2020): 12–37.

Banac, Ivo, ed. *The Diary of Georgi Dimitrov, 1933–1949.* New Haven: Yale University Press, 2003.

Brandenberger, David. "Ideological Zig-Zag: Official Explanations for the Great Terror, 1936–1938." In *The Anatomy of Terror: Political Violence Under Stalin*, ed. James Harris, 143–60. Oxford: Oxford University Press, 2013.

Brandenberger, David, and Nikita Pivovarov. "What Caused the Fall of Nikolai A. Voznesenskii? The Gosplan Affair, the Leningrad Affair, and Political Infighting in Stalin's Inner Circle, 1949-1950." *Slavic Review* 82, no. 1 (2023): 90–111.

Chase, William J., and J. Arch Getty. "Patterns of Repression among the Soviet Elite in the Late 1930s: A Biographical Approach." In *Stalinist Terror: New Perspectives*, ed. Getty, J. Arch and Roberta Thompson Manning, 225–46. Cambridge: Cambridge University Press, 1993.

Chuev, Feliks Ivanovich. *Sto sorok besed s Molotovym.* Moscow: Terra, 1991.

Chuev, Feliks Ivanovich. *Tak govoril Kaganovich: Ispoved' stalinskogo apostola.* Moscow: Olma Press, 2001.

Danilov, V., Roberta Manning, and Lynne Viola, eds. *Tragediia sovetskoi derevni. Kollektivizatsiia i raskulachivanie. Dokumenty i materialy v 5 tomakh, 1927–1939.* Vol. 5, bk. 1. Moscow: ROSSPEN, 2004.

Fedor, Julie. *Russia and the Cult of State Security: The Chekist Tradition from Lenin to Putin.* New York: Routledge, 2011.

Getty, J. Arch. *Origins of the Great Purges: the Soviet Communist Party Reconsidered, 1933–1938.* Cambridge, New York: Cambridge University Press, 1985.

Getty, J. Arch, and Roberta Thompson Manning, eds. *Stalinist Terror: New Perspectives.* Cambridge: Cambridge University Press, 1993.

Getty, J. Arch, and Oleg V. Naumov. *The Road to Terror: Stalin and the Self-Destruction of the Bolsheviks, 1932–1939.* New Haven: Yale University Press, 1999.

Getty, J. Arch. "'Excesses Are Not Permitted': Mass Terror and Stalinist Governance in the Late 1930s." *Russian Review* 61, no. 1 (2002): 113–38.

Getty, J. Arch. *Practicing Stalinism: Bolsheviks, Boyars, and the Persistence of Tradition.* New Haven: Yale University Press, 2013.

Getty, J. Arch. "Democracy and Violence, 1917–37." In *The Fate of the Bolshevik Revolution: Illiberal Liberation, 1917–41,* ed. Lara Douds, James R. Harris, and Peter Whitewood, 127–39. Library of Modern Russia. London: Bloomsbury Academic, 2020.

Harris, James. "The Purging of Local Cliques in the Urals Region, 1936–37." In *Stalinism: New Directions,* ed. S. Fitzpatrick, 263–85. New York: Routledge, 2000.

Harris, James. *The Great Fear: Stalin's Terror of the 1930s.* Oxford: Oxford University Press, 2016.

Junge, M., G. A. Bordiugov, and R. Binner. *Vertikal' bol'shogo terrora. Istoriia operatsii po prikazu NKVD No. 00447.* Moscow: Novyi Khronograf, 2008.

Khaustov, V. N., V. P. Naumov, and N. S. Plotnikov, eds. *Lubianka. Stalin i Glavnoe Upravlenie Gosbezopasnosti NKVD, 1937–1938.* Moscow: Fond "Demokratiia," 2004.

Khaustov, V. N., and Lennart Samuelson. *Stalin, NKVD i repressii. 1936–1938 gg.* Moscow: ROSSPEN, 2009.

Khlevniuk, O. V. "The Objectives of the Great Terror, 1937–1938." In *Soviet History, 1917–53: Essays in Honour of R. W. Davies,* eds. Julian Cooper, Maureen Perrie, and E. A. Rees, 158–76. London: Macmillan, 1995.

Khlevniuk, Oleg V. "Archives of the Terror: Developments in the Historiography of Stalin's Purges." *Kritika* 22, no. 2 (Spring 2021): 367–86.

Nikonov, Viacheslav A. *Nashe delo pravoe.* Bk. 1. Moscow: Izdatel'stvo AO Molodaia gvardiia, 2016.

RGASPI, Russian State Archive of Socio-Political History, Moscow.

Stone, Lawrence. *The Causes of the English Revolution, 1529–1642.* New York: Harper & Row, 1972.

Tarkhova, N. S., et al. *Voennyii sovet pri narodnom komissare oborony SSSR, 1–4 iiuniia 1937 g.: Dokumenty i materialy.* Moscow: ROSSPEN, 2008.

Viola, Lynne. *Stalinist Perpetrators on Trial: Scenes from the Great Terror in Soviet Ukraine.* New York: Oxford University Press, 2017.

Von Laue, Theodore. "Stalin among the Moral and Political Imperatives, or How to Judge Stalin." *Soviet Union* 8, no. 1 (1981): 1–17.

Wheatcroft, Stephen. "From Team Stalin to Degenerate Tyranny." In *The Nature of Stalin's Dictatorship. The Politburo*, ed. E. A. Rees, 79–107. London: Palgrave Macmillan, 2004.

Whitewood, Peter. *The Red Army and the Great Terror: Stalin's Purge of the Soviet Military*. Lawrence: University Press of Kansas, 2015.

Wynn, Charters. *The Moderate Bolshevik: Mikhail Tomsky from the Factory to the Kremlin, 1880–1936*. Leiden: Brill, 2022.

Part Four

The Ideological

Chapter 9

Stalin as Historian and Legalist

Alfred J. Rieber

Stalin as a historian hardly surprises; as a legalist perhaps more so. Stalin was a historical materialist who believed in law governed processes operating dialectically. The course of history was determined to the extent that social change and political institutions were founded on economic foundations. To that extent he fit the classic mold of Marxism. However, he embraced a theoretical innovation first introduced by Georgi Plekhanov and adopted by Lenin, that the political superstructure enjoyed a degree of autonomy in its capacity to intervene in the substructure, depending on historical circumstances, thus accelerating the trajectory toward socialism. He followed Lenin's path, but not always in his footsteps. Stalin considerably enlarged the autonomy of the superstructure, rather than accepting Trotsky's view on skipping stages of historical development. Once having taken power, Stalin endowed state institutions, especially the army and security services, with performance and ideological functions equal and occasionally superior to those of the party. Gradually, he assigned them a more prominent place in his pursuit of socialist societies at home and especially abroad than the class struggle, without abandoning the classic foundations of Marx's revolutionary scenario. This modification was necessary if the backward agrarian tsarist empire was to be transformed within his lifetime to become the most advanced form of society and polity as well as the driving force of the international revolutionary movement. This view underlaid his policies of forced industrialization and collectivization of agriculture as the foundations of socialism in one country. It further implied that the international perspective of the Comintern would be subordinated to the national interests of the Soviet Union as embodied in the leading role of the Russian people.

From his first major publication on Marxism and the national question he asserted that the nation was "a historically constituted community of people" (Stalin 1946–1952, 2:304). But by the 1930s he recorded a significant change in his thinking to emphasize that the nation possessed a primordial quality. In other words, there was a fundamental continuity of the essence of a nation over time. In effect this meant moving the nation out of the superstructure and de-emphasizing the role of class in its formation. In giving examples, he recovered the importance of premodern poetry in defining the essence of a nation. Examples were drawn from the work of Taras Shevchenko in Ukraine, and one of Stalin's most admired Georgian poets, Shota Rustaveli. The search for others turned up folklorist poets of Dagestan and the Kirghiz people. The propaganda apparatus picked up the idea, as was often the case with his pronouncements, and began a massive investment in research institutes on national cultures. As part of the new campaign Stalin also shifted the use of the term *smychka* (alliance, union, or harmony) from its original meaning to describe the merging of the peasantry and proletariat to the relations between nations under socialism, although retaining a class element to identify and condemn counterrevolutionary nationalists. He personally embellished this approach in a much-publicized 1935 meeting with Turkmen and Tadzhik leaders, even going so far as to donning their national costumes for the event. He took the occasion to enlist history by contrasting the Soviet with the tsarist period. He contrasted the "friendship of peoples" in the former with the "savage wolf-like policy" of the latter (Stalin 1946–1952, 4:75–76).

This was followed by a series of meetings attended by Stalin linking the new definition of intranational relations with the discussion on the constitution in which all nations within the USSR were portrayed as equal. His interpretation of the friendship of peoples as unbreakable was then applied to the defense against foreign enemies. Although Stalin conceded that each nationality within the Soviet Union had fully developed into a nation over time in an uneven fashion, he asserted that the process had taken place more rapidly under Soviet power. During the Second World War, the idea of the essential character of nations was exploited to define and denigrate enemy nations, first and foremost Germany. Although all nations in the Soviet Union were deemed equal, Stalin, as early as 1929, singled out the Russian nation as "the most Soviet of all nations" (Stalin 1946–1952, 6:186); in 1933 he elevated Russia to "the most talented in the world;" and finally "the most Soviet and revolutionary" (Stalin 1946–1952, 13:12).

These pronouncements spelled an end to the affirmative action theme, which singled out "Great Russian chauvinism" as the primary internal enemy in his definition of relations among nations. Perhaps the final step in this long journey came at the end of the Second World War. In his victory speech, Stalin toasted the Russian people as "the leading force" in the victory against fascism (Stalin 1946–1952, 2:203–4). Although Stalin, in the end, rigorously endorsed the idea of immutable elements in national cultures, he was equally insistent in how changing historical circumstances could alter the pace of development into a nation.

Consistent with this view, Stalin in his late major theoretical work, "On Marxism in Linguistics" pointedly rejected the erroneous conclusion that Marxist formulas derived from one period of historical development were correct in all periods of historical development. This kind of error he attributed to any attempt to monopolize thought. It resembled, he wrote, the mentality of an Arakcheev, an example significantly plucked from the tsarist past. He then took the occasion to demolish one of the last bastions of determinism that survived in the rather obscure field of linguistics, by arguing that language did not belong wholly to either the economic substructure or to the cultural and political superstructure. The Russian language remained the same throughout different periods of history, yet it was open to change as society evolved toward socialism. One implication drawn from many debates by historians, philosophers, and scientists was that once again the superstructure under socialism represented by the party would play a role in the evolution of the most fundamental character of human beings—their language—culminating in a universal language that was neither Russian nor any other existing language but an amalgam of all.

Similarly, in his lengthy and complex involvement in the preparation of a textbook on political economy that appeared on the eve of the Nineteenth Party Congress in 1952 titled *Economic Problems of Socialism*, Stalin wrote of his desire to produce a work that would combine theoretical and practical observations in a historical context. He was seeking an interpretive work that would educate the public and be prepared by economists engaged in an exchange of views in a closed debate. This would take the form of discussion (*diskussiia*), a device to which he frequently resorted when he sought to inform himself of alternative ways of formulating policies. His primary aim in this case was to explore the relationship between the objective laws of political economy that determined history's movement toward socialism and the "economic policy of the directing bodies" that would overcome the last obstacles to the achievement of communism. In a slight deviation from his historical views on the evolution of language, he sought to find a satisfactory explanation of the relationship between a universal and immutable law based on the economic substructure with a formula to organize rationally the productive forces to achieve the law governed ends. To put it another way, Stalin was determined to maintain the scientific foundations of Marxism–Leninism while at the same time recognizing that historically determined change had produced new conditions, which then required political intervention to bring a changing society into a corelationship with the laws of economic development.

Stalin's views on the superactive role of the superstructure as exercised by the leadership of the state and Communist Party frequently led him to focus on the history of Russia, as he defined its spatial and temporal parameters, in his theoretical statements and his editorial interventions in works he commissioned or written by academic scholars. His emphasis on the particular over the universal in historical analysis had the additional effect of diminishing his interest in the history of the class struggle either in general or even in tsarist Russia as a subject worthy of his close attention. Moreover, this preoccupation with the unique character of Russian history that had produced the first society engaged in building socialism, was prominent in his justification of his aims in foreign policy and his negotiations with foreign capitalist powers to achieve them.

The term legalist as applied to Stalin is bound to be more controversial. What is meant here is his use of juridical norms in his domestic policy, primarily to eliminate enemies of the people and in his foreign policy, primarily to negotiate and implement treaties with capitalist states. In domestic policy he resorted to trials, investigative techniques, and the promulgation of a constitution to mobilize public opinion and legitimize his rule by demonstrating that the Soviet system was law governed rather than arbitrary and despotic. In foreign policy this was linked to an adaptation of all the traditional forms of diplomacy and generally by adhering strictly to conditions and obligations, which the Soviet Union was committed to fulfill in signing international agreements. To be sure, there were exceptions. But even when he denounced a treaty, which was rare, it was done in accord with the procedure provided by the text of the treaty. Stalin's legalism exhibited a paradoxical quality. In theory he was committed to a radical overthrow of the institutional forms, originating in the capitalist world, which he accepted in practice. Stalin's attempt to resolve the paradox derived from his concept of socialism in one country and its corollary of capitalist encirclement. That is, while building socialism by its own efforts in a hostile world, the state was obliged to adopt a defensive posture to prevent foreign intervention and a war for which it was not yet prepared to fight. This further required the state to mask its radical transformative aims and even to give the impression that they had been relegated to some future time. Finally, the adaptation of traditional diplomatic methods was the most effective way of conducting a foreign policy that aimed to divide the capitalist world by siding first with one and then with another side in the imperialist rivalry which Lenin had already identified as characteristic of the final stage of capitalism.

Two examples taken from his use of legal forms to advance both his domestic agenda and foreign policies were the show trials and the constitution of 1936. The Bolsheviks introduced and applied the idea of revolutionary legality from the outset of their taking power, but it was not until 1928 that Stalin had recourse to the public trial as a means of mobilizing public support of his policies. In this case the Shakhty Affair aimed at discrediting the nonparty industrial experts by accusing them of sabotage in the interests of foreign intelligence. The accusation played with the workers who harbored resentment against the bourgeois specialists and echoed in the party bureaucracy as a contest between the industrial and education commissariats. The extended public discussion also corresponded to the first of the war scares that Stalin used to discredit the Right Opposition. Finally, the trial opened the way to attributing failures in industrial planning, about to be launched, to sabotage rather than mistakes of the planners. Thus, as guide to the future, this inaugural show trial fulfilled multiple purposes.

The three big show trials of the 1930s ratcheted up the rhetoric of denunciation to a level of hysteria in the strident voice of head prosecutor Andrei Vyshinsky. Acting as the sole arbiter of legal norms, Vyshinsky violated Soviet law in several respects, all harmful to the defense. But he was following Stalin's scenario. No doubt Stalin relished the theatrical aspects of his careful staging of the show trials, but the drama expressed serious political aims. The three trials differed in their primary focus. The first emphasized conspiracies to launch terrorist attacks on the leadership, especially Stalin. But it did not link these to foreign intrigues. The second broadened the conspiratorial level to include a plot to undermine the military potential of the country through "wrecking" and "sabotage." The third was all-encompassing, linking its various elements tied to the dangers of fascism and war (Chase 2005, 226–48)

All three show trials shared the aim of making enemies of the people a living reality, but the discourse and the objects of denunciation were designed to have an impact on several different audiences. A key element in the effort to reach and convince the mass of the population, still rooted or barely emerging from a premodern world, was the confession. Bukharin called it "the medieval principle." It hearkened back to the witch trials and persecution of the Schismatics in the seventeenth century. By invoking the evil forces (*nechistaia sila*) of peasant folk tradition with its demonic images, Vyshinsky portrayed the accused as subhumans. His frequent reference to them as animals was a device that was later used during the war with Germany to portray the nature of the "fascist beast." In cases where the NKVD could not extort a confession by physical or psychological torture, as in the case of Marshal Tukhachevsky and other Red Army commanders, a public trial was not held, and the accused were executed in secret. Although the device of show trials was subsequently employed by East European communists, the accusations were limited to Titoism, national communism, Zionism, and foreign intelligence. What they lacked from the Soviet example was the denunciations of wrecking, sabotage, and assassination wrapped in the demonological discourse.

Even as Stalin was preparing for the first show trial in an atmosphere of growing tensions following Kirov's assassination, he inaugurated a campaign in early 1935 to launch a new constitution. This was part of his campaign of cultural diplomacy that sought to influence major Western intellectuals of the progressive and indeed superior character of Soviet institutions and values to those that they admired in their own countries (David-Fox 2012). From the outset, he took an active part in chairing a commission that studied foreign constitutions and then commenting on subsequent drafts. A few years earlier, a Central Committee decree approved by him had already set down strict rules for the observation of "revolutionary legality." The discussions preceding the adoption of the constitution centered on new legal rights for Soviet citizens. The first draft was discussed in public forums attended by 52,000,000 people. It proclaimed an end to legal discrimination against "former people" (priests and kulaks), broadened social rights, and introduced universal secret suffrage in national elections. It substituted the word "people" for "proletariat," emphasizing once again the march toward socialism. He insisted on a referendum that overwhelmingly approved the final draft. His speech to the Seventeenth Party Congress in 1934 praised the constitution as the most democratic in the world, refuting the criticism of fascist propagandists. The speech was printed in 20,000,000 copies in two dozen languages. It is now possible to discern several audiences, first and foremost the Soviet population, by stressing a new historical era of stability and relaxation. Coming on the eve of two years of terror, this conclusion appears paradoxical, even improbable. Yet it was a typical Stalinist ploy, drawing a Manichaean division of the population between the loyal and obedient who were rewarded by the rule of law and material rewards and those soon to be identified as traitors, saboteurs, and murderers. At the same time, it functioned to enlist the population against the regional cliques and family circles within the party that resisted or evaded controls from the center and hampered the hunt for oppositionists. But there was also the foreign audience. Following the signing of the Franco-Soviet and Czechoslovak Soviet alliances, the Seventh Comintern Congress proclaiming a popular front, and the Soviet support for the Loyalists in the Spanish Civil War, the proclamation of a democratic constitution could only have reinforced the international reputation of the Soviet Union as a leader in the struggle against fascism. This facade of constitutional legality and democratic rights fit snugly into the justification of the terror as a defense against traitors and wreckers in the service of German and Japanese intelligence agencies as well as the further progress along the road to building socialism.

Along a parallel line of mobilization, Stalin employed history to elicit a different set of emotional responses within the party and the population at large. He was not a historian in the conventional sense. Unlike Churchill, he did not write book-length studies. When he did engage in historical writing, it was more in the role of editor of works by professionals or else in commissioning them to write on specific topics. As an editor, he was surprisingly attentive to detail, at times resembling a proofreader. But he was also capable of rewriting or excising whole passages. He approached the function of history from two perspectives. First, in the history of the Soviet Union and the communist party, he was more directive than in the prerevolutionary period. His editorial comments made clear that the purpose of history was to educate the party cadres and raise the consciousness of the general public in the ideology of Marxism-Leninism. Second, in his revisions of the prerevolutionary period, he emphasized the growth of centralized state power, the expansion of Russia, and its embattled relationship with its more economically developed competitors. On Soviet subjects, he frequently toned down his participation in historical events or what he considered obsequious praise by party historians without eliminating his leading role entirely. His interventions can now be closely traced in writing the histories of the Russian civil war, the Communist Party of the Soviet Union (CPSU [b]), the origins of the Second World War, the Great Fatherland War, and his biography. One may conclude that in all these productions he sought to fine-tune a uniform interpretation of history that incorporated and justified his governing style (Roberts 2020, 190–209).

Stalin used citations and applied lessons he drew from history to instruct, inspire, chastise, and correct in political lectures, literature, art, music, and the cinema as well as textbooks and general works. Ever since he was a youth in Georgia, he was an avid reader in his native language and later in Russian. Romantic tales of Georgia's past with warrior heroes fascinated him. His reading was eclectic and remained so throughout his life. Summing up, three themes can be identified as figuring prominently in his reference to historical events and personalities: the necessity of a strong centralized power, an ideologically informed aesthetic, and an emotional bond with the fatherland (*otechesvto*) and motherland (*rodina*) (Suny 2020, 37–48, 66–70).

Stalin's most dramatic, paradoxical invocation of history as a guide to action came in his oft-cited statement in February 1931 on Russia's historical backwardness as a justification for a crash program of industrialization and transformation of the country to catch up with the advanced countries. (An English translation cannot capture the accents of incantation reminiscent of a traditional chant of the Orthodox Church.) Powerful as the speech was, it expressed a version of Russian history that was close to that of the Mensheviks, on the one hand, and Trotsky, on the other; within a few years Stalin would reverse the thrust of the argument.

Although Stalin did not write a history of the USSR, he entered discussions from time to time on the need to introduce a history textbook and to intervene in controversies over discrete events and personalities in Russian history. The first of his major interventions came in 1934 after his angry attack on a spate of experiments in the writing of history. Together with his closest associates, Andrei Zhdanov and Sergei Kirov, he criticized four major shortcomings in the historiographical interpretations in previous drafts of a textbook. The summary failed on three counts: to emphasize the annexationist colonizing role of tsarism, to emphasize the counterrevolutionary role of tsarist foreign policy, and to reflect the role of West European bourgeois-revolutionary and proletarian-socialist movements in Russia. It was characteristic of Stalin's manipulation of the lessons of history to match changing circumstances that all three of these criticisms were later abandoned and reversed. By the end of the 1930s, they had been sacrificed on the altars of Russocentrism and Soviet patriotism. The problem remained, however, of reconciling the contradiction between the progressive elements in Russia's past that served as the foundation of the first proletarian revolution in world history and the backward elements that required a major transformation of the economy and society to overcome them. The recurrent dilemma that faced the interpretation of history was to demonstrate in an ideologically convincing manner the interaction between the determinist and voluntarist, the class-based and leadership function, embodied in a narrative that would educate the party cadres and the new generation to become loyal and obedient servants of the state.

Stalin took advantage of a competition for the best textbook, which produced a prize winner in the 1937 *A Short History of the USSR*, to introduce an important innovation in the treatment of the history of the nationalities. It was a rather crude attempt to resolve the difficulties over the process of state-building. In referring to the Russian acquisition of Georgia and Ukraine, Stalin introduced the term "the lesser evil" to distinguish this imperialist expansion from the alternatives of Persian or Ottoman domination. Invoking the "concrete historical circumstance of the time" Stalin's implication was clear. Absorbed by tsarist Russia, these national cultures benefitted in the long run from being swept up in the Russian Revolution and the building of socialism rather than vegetating in semifeudal conditions. This formula subsequently became enshrined in the histories of the national republics.

Except for the history of the party and his biography, Stalin took a more active role in the history and historians of foreign policy than domestic history. But once again his interventions did not add up to a comprehensive and consistent interpretation. He did not create a union of Soviet historians as a means of exercising control over them. Instead, historians were included in the Academy of Sciences where their election was in accord with the rules of the academy carried out in secret. But historians were forced from time to time to denounce their colleagues, recant their views and, exceptionally, suffer imprisonment. As Stalin's dictates shifted emphasis, many became victimizers as well as victims (Zelnik 2005, 12–80). The so-called Academic Affair involved the arrest of three distinguished historians. S. F. Platonov died in prison; B. A. Romanov served five years in a camp; but E. V. Tarle was exiled to Alma Ata for three years. Romanov was rehabilitated, and Tarle was restored to favor by Stalin, who appointed him to the Litvinov Commission on planning for postwar Europe. These moves were part of a fundamental revision of Stalin's view of history.

Until the early 1930s, the central problem facing Russian historians was how to contain within a single explanatory scheme the condemnation of Russian imperialism under the tsars and the celebration of the Russian nation. Before the shift, the emphasis initially endorsed by Stalin had been to draw little distinction between Russian and West European imperialist designs. Romanov's error had been to go too far in embracing this internationalist position in his criticism of Count Witte as part of his strong condemnation of Russian imperialism in the Far East. Released from prison he revised his work to distribute equal blame among all the imperialist powers in the Far East. Tarle, too, had to learn the same lesson. Upon his return from exile, he was to revise his book on Napoleon's invasion of Russia to restore what he had earlier denigrated, namely the heroism of the Russian people and the generalship of Mikhail Kutuzov in 1812. Although the shift was marked by rivalries among individual historians and the so-called Moscow and Leningrad schools, the main thrust was undeniable. The trajectory of revision followed along the same lines as that of the nationalities question. Great Russian chauvinism was no longer the main culprit in the relations between Russia and the nationalities, but rather the lesser evil; Russian imperialism having been less predatory than that of the European imperialists. The key word here is "less." As in other areas of Soviet social thought, it was difficult in the process of writing history to keep the dialectical relationship between the policies of the ruling class that were not uniform in detail, and the achievement of national ideals that also changed over time. Stalin was prepared to restore the equilibrium when it became dangerously imbalanced. But he could not read every work of history. So, the controversies continued to be carried on within professional journals.

Two important landmarks in Stalin's active intervention in restoring national pride in Russia's domestic history were the rehabilitation of Ivan Groznyi (Ivan the Terrible) and the discredit heaped on the work of M. N. Pokrovsky. The two developments were closely linked. In a follow-up to his speech, "we will not be beaten," Stalin revived an interpretation of Ivan Groznyi as a powerful state builder and undermined the reputation of Pokrovsky for political sins, including the denigration of leading figures in Russian history such as Groznyi. The two lines joined in the late 1930s when Stalin recruited Pokrovsky's former students to publish a two-volume work, *Protiv istoricheskoi kontseptsii M. N. Pokrovskogo: Sbornik statei* [Against the historical concept of M. M. Pokrovskii: A collection of articles] (Moscow, 1939–40), and exclusively devoted to denouncing the cosmopolitanism of their deceased mentor and in particular his dismissal of important figures such as Ivan Groznyi and Peter the Great. Stalin's restoration favored Ivan over Peter because, in his view, the latter drew heavily on Western models as compared to Groznyi's purely Russian perspective. The rehabilitation of Groznyi reached a climax in the first part of Sergei Eisenstein's film on the early years of the tsar in which Stalin took an active interest. In this case, Stalin's blatantly opportunistic use of history took a cruelly ironic turn. A much earlier attempt to rehabilitate Ivan as a far-sighted ruler had been made in 1924 by Platonov, whom Stalin had ordered arrested and executed. Like many of Stalin's manipulations of prerevolutionary Russian history, his rehabilitation of Groznyi was fraught with ambivalence, allowing ongoing debates over the progressive and reactionary elements that could be given varied emphasis by the vozhd to further his political aims (Platt and Brandenberger 1999, 635–54).

This exhumation of the indigenous Russian roots of Russia's growth as a great power was accompanied by Stalin's adherence to efforts to situate revolutionary Russia and the building of socialism in an international context defined by accepting established diplomatic norms and legal practices. Ever since the intraparty debate preceding the Brest-Litovsk Treaty, Stalin accepted the necessity of subordinating the pursuit of international revolution to concluding treaties with capitalist states involving mutual obligations. By the time of the Franco-Soviet Alliance in 1935, the Soviet Union had signed dozens of treaties on nonaggression and trade with most Western states and entered the League of Nations. Soviet diplomats adhered strictly to international protocol. Stalin treated the Comintern like a poor relation and after 1936 subjected it to a murderous purge. It was already expiring as an active force years before it was abolished in 1943. Even the signing of the Molotov-Ribbentrop Pact was no exception to the rule of legalism. It had been preceded by formal negotiations with both the Anglo-French and the German sides. Once he had accepted Hitler's more generous offer, Stalin adhered strictly to the obligation to deliver raw materials much needed by the Nazi war machine right up to the day the Wehrmacht invaded on June 22, 1941. To be sure, Stalin broadly interpreted in his favor the division of Eastern Europe into spheres of influence, as he was to do with the Yalta agreement. But he and Vyacheslav Molotov had taken advantage of the failure of their counterparts in Berlin to employ unambiguous language to define the extent of the mutual obligations of the signatories. The absorption of the three Baltic states, Estonia, Latvia, and Lithuania was preceded by formal agreements on the stationing of Soviet garrisons in these countries. The attack on Finland in 1940 was the sole exception and the only aggressive war by the Soviet Union under Stalin's rule. It, too, had been preceded by lengthy negotiations to obtain strategic bases protecting Leningrad.

In the history of foreign relations, Stalin took an active interest in providing the context for the three-volume *Istoriia diplomatii* (History of diplomacy) (Moscow 1940–45). He appointed a veteran diplomat, Vladimir Potemkin as editor in chief. Potemkin had served as a Soviet representative in Italy, Turkey and, most important, France during the Popular Front, and then as first deputy commissar of foreign affairs from 1937 to 1940. He was a survivor of the massive purge of the Litvinovtsy (Litvinov's people) in the foreign commissariat, probably because of his early association with Stalin when he served under him as a political officer during the Civil War on the southeastern front. Stalin also drew many of his military favorites from the group around him at that time. In 1940, Stalin substantially revised the draft of the first volume of *Istoriia*, from the nineteenth century to the origins of the Second World War, written by two professional historians commissioned by Potemkin—I. I. Mints and A. M. Pankratova. He eliminated many passages of a polemical character and deleted the frequent quotations from the works of Lenin and himself. What remained was an account that followed the trend he had established in the previous years: a general condemnation of imperialism in the years before 1914, with Russia trailing the pack, and an exemplary treatment of Soviet diplomacy in contrast to the continuous imperialist practices of the capitalist countries. In the revised postwar interpretation, the interwar years were vastly expanded from a chapter to 700 pages, again attributed to the same two professional historians and reflecting Stalin's editorial legacy. It was a dry, factual account that promoted Soviet diplomacy. Stalin then selected Tarle to write a highly polemical conclusion on "the methods of bourgeois diplomacy." The work was awarded two Stalin Prizes and translated into French. In the meantime, Potemkin was appointed commissar of education from 1940–1946 and elected to the Academy of Sciences in 1943. He died a much-honored figure. His work appeared to serve two purposes. First, it set a definitive standard for professional historians writing about foreign policy; second, the translation and dispassionate tone aimed to attract a sympathetic foreign audience, particularly within the Western powers. But Soviet historians took away different lessons. They concluded it was safer to avoid writing on topics of diplomatic history for the years from 1861 to 1914. In the historical journals between 1936 and 1952, only sixteen articles on foreign policy appeared on the period of imperialism. In the postwar period up to Stalin's death, only one monograph by F. I. Notovich, *Diplomaticheskaia bor'ba v gody pervoi mirovoi voiny* (Diplomatic struggle in the years of the First World War) (Moscow 1947) dealt with the broader questions of imperialist rivalries, without mentioning the word. The only two major monographs on diplomacy to be published focused on German and French foreign policy, with minimal mention of Russia in a passive role. Such was the work of A. S. Erusalimskii's *Vneshnaia politika i diplomatiia germanskogo imperialzma v kontse XIX veka* (Foreign policy and diplomacy of German imperialism in the late 19th century) (Moscow 1948) or A. Z. Manfred, *Vneshnaia politika Frantsii 1871–1891* (Foreign policy of France, 1871–1891) (Moscow 1952).

With the gathering of war clouds, Stalin took numerous occasions to awaken historical memories of Russia's military traditions under the tsars. The climax was reached during the Great Fatherland War with the enshrinement of tsarist generals Alexander Suvorov and Kutuzov (whose portraits flanked Lenin's in Stalin's private office), Prince Alexander Nevsky and Admiral Pavel Nakhimov. Medals were struck in their name and veterans of the First World War were allowed to wear publicly their decorations. Gold braid and terms of address among the ranks were reinstituted. The Moscow Suvorov Military School was inaugurated in 1944 for youngsters. The title guards regiments was revived and assigned to heroic units. It was more difficult to find appropriate historical heroes among the nationalities because so many had earned their heroic status in fighting against Russians. All of these shafts of light penetrating into the no longer uniform darkness of Russia's imperialist past, strengthening the emotional attachment to the country that invariably accompanies a sense of continuity.

STALIN AS HISTORIAN AND LEGALIST

In wartime negotiations with his allies, Stalin frequently invoked the lessons of history combined with ethnic considerations in justifying Soviet postwar spheres of interest and territorial claims. At the same time, he sought to carry out his aims by acting within the broad outlines provided by international agreements. Examples of his historical references abound. With the Poles he argued that the Soviet annexation of their eastern marches, the *kresy* (Galicia and Western Belorussia) would be compensated by their acquisition of East Prussia and Galicia, thus restoring Poland to its historical boundaries under the Piast dynasty. When Anthony Eden tried at Yalta to argue against the detachment of the same provinces, Stalin reminded him that he was merely accepting the ethnic boundary proposed by the Allied leaders in 1919: "What do you want, that we be less Russian than Curzon and Clemenceau?" Similarly, he rejected the idea of dismembering Germany by referring to Napoleon's error in pursuing a similar policy, which had merely stimulated a surge of German nationalism.

In dealing with Hitler's defeated allies, Stalin relied heavily on the terms of the armistice agreements he had signed with them and the authority of the Allied Control Commissions (ACC) shared by the British and Americans to consolidate Soviet influence in Finland, Romania, Bulgaria, and Hungary. As Zhdanov, acting as chair of the ACC in Finland made clear to his staff: Soviet policy stood for a strict legal point of view. In line with this approach, Stalin counseled the local communist parties to avoid illegal activities which might justify the intervention of the British and Americans.

In prewar negotiations with Japan and with his Western Allies at Yalta, Stalin insisted on recovering what Molotov called "the lost territories" (Southern Sakhalin and the Kurile islands), referring to the historic Russian defeat in the war with Japan in 1905. At the same time, he sought to apply pressure on Chiang Kai-shek during negotiations in 1945 to recover Russia's influence in Manchuria, which had also been lost in 1905. Despite allowing the victorious Soviet Army to turn over small arms captured from the Japanese to the Chinese communists, he continued to recognize the Nationalist Government until its collapse in 1949; another example of his adherence to legal principles, albeit in pursuing political aims.

Few incidents illustrate better Stalin's view of adding history to his ideological arsenal than his reaction to the publication by the US State Department in 1948 of the pamphlet *Nazi Soviet Relations*. Translated into Russian, it sparked an immediate reaction. The draft of a response by Soviet historians, which Vyshinsky sent to Stalin, aroused his anger. He edited the draft, added fifteen pages, and retitled it "Falsifiers of History." He took the opportunity to rework the diplomatic history of the coming of the war. He justified the negotiations with Hitler as a means to construct a vast buffer zone from the Baltic to the Black Sea, an Eastern Front, citing Churchill's approval at the time (Rieber 2015, 200–204).

In Stalin's consistent, indeed obsessive dedication to achieve, maintain and expand his power in the struggle to control domestic and foreign affairs, which Pierre Bourdieu has called the "field of force," he marshaled a wide range of ideas (Grenfell 2012). Despite his self-representation, he was, however, not an intellectual. He had little respect for the integrity of ideas. They were in his view means to explain, persuade and, in his application of them, coerce. He drew on them as if they stocked an armory of propaganda and agitation; indeed, he can be said to have weaponized ideas. This chapter has dealt with only two of these, history and legality. There are others, most notably aesthetics and science. He was careful not to adopt a single, dogmatic interpretation of history. Rather he preferred to apply a flexible version of historical materialism by invoking the dialectic to accommodate changing conditions which he called the balance of forces. With his firm grip on power, he could permit, and at times even encourage discussion within and outside the party on the historic events until he was satisfied that one or another interpretation best suited his immediate political aims. To this end, he could then brutally intervene to endorse one and dismiss or denounce the alternatives and their sponsors. This tactic had advantages for him. To cite one that has not been given due recognition—the appearance of flexibility helped him to dismiss the image of an Oriental despot, which Marx had derided as a product of a backward, agrarian society lacking the dynamic character of a class struggle.

Born, raised, and schooled in an imperial borderland where the local Georgian intelligentsia aspired to preserve and gradually expand a distinctive cultural identity, young Stalin (Koba) early recognized that successful state-building of a multinational polity depended on preserving and cultivating the historical roots of ethnicity and language in the borderlands under the aegis of a superordinate authority. Georgia, like other South Caucasian societies, had long been the object of a three-way struggle between the Russian, Ottoman, and Persian empires. Stalin quickly grasped the advantage of embracing the Russian option. For him it opened the way to a closer relationship with the advanced industrialized civilization of Europe. This helps explain the basis of his Soviet nationality policy, preserving local cultures under the aegis of Russian political hegemony within a socialist structure. Similarly, by endorsing Lenin's (and Trotsky's) justification of a social revolution in a backward, agrarian society and then accepting the unanticipated result of an isolated state encircled by hostile capitalist powers, he shifted his international gaze, never strongly fixed. Once he endorsed the construction of socialism in one country, the state assumed the dominant place in his field of force. This meant that he faced the challenge of reconceptualizing the history of Russia as the ideological foundation upon which a social transformation could be built. Elements of the superstructure had to be incorporated into the substructure. This created a series of problems for the interpretation of Russian history. How to reconcile the contradiction between portraying imperial Russia as a comparatively underdeveloped state with an autocratic government and a weak bourgeoisie with the idea that Russia and Russians had developed under these conditions the basis for constructing a wholly new and superior socialist civilization? A task for the most ingenious application of the dialectic. As Stalin's engagement with history shows, he not only sought to reconcile Marxism with state patriotism. He was obliged repeatedly to readjust, even at times to fine-tune history to keep the balance between glorifying a revolutionary tradition that aimed to overthrow the state and uproot the Orthodox faith while acknowledging the achievements of imperial Russia as a state-builder, a great power in competition with powerful rivals, and as a major contributor to European science, literature and the arts that were often subsidized by the state or inspired by religious ideals. As the war clouds gathered in the late 1930s, Stalin gave greater emphasis to the historical importance of imperial Russia to rally the population behind the defense of the country. This theme in Soviet propaganda reached its climax during the Great Fatherland War. At the same time, during his negotiations with foreign powers, the Axis and the Western allies, he and Molotov frequently resorted to historical precedents to justify and defend their policies.

Parallel to his ongoing recalibration of history, Stalin advanced a new concept of revolutionary legality and promoted progressive social and political rights at home linked to international norms in his dealings with foreign countries. The elaborate system of show trials, the justification of the Gulag as an advanced form of social rehabilitation, a constitution promising radical egalitarian rights, and the promotion of progressive education were all designed to reassure a restless public at a time of great upheavals and fears. Although these highly touted aims lacked any real commitment to the rule of law or human rights, they provided a facade behind which those who accepted them or pretended to were able to rationalize their participation in building socialism in its Stalinist form. At the very least, they provided a source of hope for the future evolution of the state. Finally, they played a role, perhaps less successfully, in convincing sympathetic observers abroad, who were willing to accept the promise for the real, as the basis for international cooperation. Judging by the enormous expenditure of time, energy, and money invested in promoting these aims, Stalin believed that his control and manipulation of history and legality would contribute mightily to his image as the supreme architect of socialism and its transition to communism as well as mobilizing the country in the process of achieving these ends.

Works Cited

Brandenberger, David. "Stalin and the Muse of History. The Dictator and His Critics on the Editing of the *Short Course.*" In *Ideological Storms: Intellectuals, Dictators and Totalitarian Temptations*, ed. Vladimir Tismaneanu, 871–90. Budapest: Central European University Press, 2019.

Chase, William. "Stalin as Producer: The Moscow Show Trials and the Construction of Moral Threats." In *Stalin a New History*, ed. Sarah Davies and James Harris, 266–48. Cambridge: Cambridge University Press, 2005.

David-Fox, Michael. *Showcasing the Great Experiment. Cultural Diplomacy: Western Visitors to the Soviet Union, 1921–1941*. Oxford: Oxford University Press, 2012.

Grenfell, Michael. *Pierre Bourdieu: Key Concepts*. 2nd ed. London: Routledge, 2012.

Platt, Kevin M. F., and David Brandenberger. "Terribly Romantic, or Terribly Tragic. Rehabilitating Ivan IV under I.V. Stalin." *Russian Review* 58, no. 4 (October 1999): 635–54.

Rieber, Alfred J. "The Historiography of Imperial Russian Foreign Policy: A Critical Essay." In *Imperial Russian Foreign Policy*, ed. Hugh Ragsdale, 360–44. Cambridge: Woodrow Wilson Center Press and Cambridge University Press, 1993.

Rieber, Alfred J. *Zhdanov in Finland*. The Carl Beck Papers, Russian and East European Studies. Pittsburgh: University of Pittsburgh Press, 1995.

Rieber, Alfred J. *Stalin and the Struggle for Supremacy in Eurasia*. Cambridge: Cambridge University Press, 2015.

Roberts, Geoffrey. *Stalin's Library: A Dictator and His Books*. New Haven: Yale University Press, 2022.

Stalin, I.V. 1946–1952. *Sochineniia*. 13 vols. Moscow: Gospolitizdat..

Van Ree, Erik. "Stalin as Marxist: The Western Roots of Stalin's Russification of Marxism." In *Stalin: A New History*, ed. Sarah Davies and James Harris, 159–80. Cambridge: Cambridge University Press, 2005.

Zelnik, Reginal E. *The Perils of Pankratova: Some Stories from the Annals of Soviet Historiography*. Donald W. Treadgold Studies on Russia, East Europe, and Central Asia. Seattle: University Washington, 2005.

CHAPTER 10

Stalin as Revolutionary Social Democrat

LARS T. LIH

My adviser Robert Tucker was devoting full time to his classic Stalin biography when I was a graduate student at Princeton, and so I have never had a time in my scholarly career when the Soviet dictator was not a looming presence. My direct entry into Stalin studies was also due to Tucker: he recommended me to Yale University Press as American editor for one of the first "now it can be told" archival publications: Stalin's letters to Molotov from the late 1920s and early 1930s. Basing myself on the great archival work of O. V. Naumov and Oleg Khlevniuk, I provided a commentary in which I tried to define Stalin's overall "definition of the situation."

I take this phrase from Tucker's *Politics as Leadership*, in which he argues that the essence of leadership is defining the current situation in a way that mobilizes action (Tucker 1981). Only many years later did I realize two things about this line of thought. First, Lenin and Stalin explicitly had the same theory of leadership—so much so that I wonder if Tucker partly picked it up from his subjects of study of long-standing. But I also realized that this phrase is a pithy label for what I am seeking—certainly not ideology, which gives me a musty, confining, overintellectual vibe—rather, the overall Bolshevik definition of the situation, the actual message about the world and what to do about it that they broadcast to the relevant audiences.

In this chapter, I argue that Stalin's basic definition of the situation was informed by Revolutionary Social Democracy. I remember long ago giving a talk

177

at the Michigan State University at the invitation of Lewis Siegelbaum and telling the audience that I was quite struck in my reading of Lenin by the phrase Revolutionary Social Democracy since Lenin used it as a positive self-identification. In today's world, Revolutionary Social Democracy is an oxymoron. As I told my audience, I had set myself the task of finding out what Lenin meant by the term. Well, a couple of decades later, I think I have an adequate answer. Revolutionary Social Democracy was the left wing of the prewar Second International whose prominent spokesmen were people like Rosa Luxemburg, Julies Guesde, Otto Bauer, and—far and away the most significant—Karl Kautsky. Revolutionary Social Democracy defined itself in contrast to nonrevolutionary Social Democracy, labeled "opportunism" by its foes on the left.

Lenin and the Bolsheviks saw themselves as the Russian representatives of Revolutionary Social Democracy. In a typical comment from 1909, Lenin stated flatly that "Bolshevism pursues the tactics of Revolutionary Social Democracy in all fields of struggle, in all fields of activity." The Bolsheviks also had a strong sense of the clash between Revolutionary Social Democracy and opportunism, not only in Russia, but internationally. When Lenin insisted in 1918 on changing the name of his party from Social Democrat to Communist, it was in no way a renunciation of Revolutionary Social Democracy. On the contrary, it was a defiant affirmation of loyalty to a banner he felt had been besmirched by the stand on the war taken by the Western Social Democratic parties. Lenin concluded that any coexistence with opportunism had by now become impossible. By purging the opportunists, a new International could arise consisting solely of a purified Revolutionary Social Democracy.

Like most of us, Stalin acquired his essential political identity in his youth and remained loyal to it throughout his life. In his case, this political identity was the detailed and explicit outlook of Revolutionary Social Democracy. But it turns out that Stalin is key to answering another question: Why did I not have any idea about the meaning of Revolutionary Social Democracy, and why could I not find any useful explanation in the standard scholarly literature? Why did such a central concept simply disappear? The person most responsible for this outcome is Stalin because in his presentation of "Leninism" and of party history, he simply airbrushed Revolutionary Social Democracy and its spokesman Kautsky out of the picture. But on this topic, although he fooled others, he did not fool himself.

In making this case, I will be commenting on his early published writings, on *Foundations of Leninism*, first published in 1924 (Stalin 1947) and on various products of the personality cult. One final document requires a little more explanation since it has always been among us and yet, at the same time, valiant archival work was required to bring it to light. We now know that the famous *Short Course* of party history published in 1938 had an extraordinary origin. In 1938, a high-level committee produced a draft of a much-delayed textbook of party history, which Stalin suddenly and unexpectedly decided to edit in a drastic fashion. He made hundreds of detailed excisions, alterations, and changes in wording, but more than that, he wrote completely new sections and even new chapters of considerable length. The mammoth spade-work needed to separate out Stalin's interventions from the original committee text was taken on by David Brandenberger and Mikhail Zelenov; in the English-language edition published by Yale University Press, Brandenberger provides a detailed account of the impact of Stalin's interventions on the original committee text (Brandenberger and Zelenov 2019).

Basing myself on this monumental archival work, I have extracted a text that is almost purely by Stalin himself. My methodology was simple: any intervention by Stalin that consisted of a page or more in the Yale edition was included. I worked on the assumption that if Stalin took it upon himself to replace a whole section, he must have been concerned about getting that particular topic right. The result is a document of something like 150 pages. Surprisingly, the extracted text can and (in my view) should be regarded as an integral whole with a unity and an argument all its own. I hope to publish this text under a title such as *Stalin's Credo*; this chapter is my first public unveiling of this project.

The revolutionary party of the proletariat must be "free of opportunism as well as irreconcilable in relation to the agreementizers (*soglashateli*) and to the capitulators"—this, for Stalin, is the most important lesson of party history. To those not well versed in "reading Bolshevik," these three epithets may seem like indistinguishable abusive labels. In reality, they point to specific types against which Stalin defined his own political identity. The extracted text divides into three parts, each featuring one of these types as a central character. Part I details the clash between Revolutionary Social Democracy—disguised here as 'the party of a new type'—versus its original foes, the opportunists. Part II describes the revolutionary victories of October and beyond. For Stalin, these victories came about because of the successful isolation of the agreementizers. Part III takes up the story after Lenin's death. The not-so-subtle main topic of this discussion is Stalin's great leadership qualities, as revealed principally by collectivization as well as by his concomitant battle against the skeptical, defeatist capitulators within the party. As we see, in each case victory over the deviation ensures the victory of the correct line.

Exorcizing Kautsky

Before embarking on our exploration of Stalin's view of party history, we need to first get our bearings by looking at his efforts to exorcise Karl Kautsky from the Bolshevik heritage. Why is recovering the Kautsky-Bolshevik link so vital? Kautsky is the key to the Bolshevik self-identification as the representative of Revolutionary Social Democracy in Russia. Not only was Kautsky the recognized spokesman of Revolutionary Social Democracy as an international movement, but he had a particular interest in Russia. His 1906 article "Driving Forces and Prospects of Revolution in Russia" is the classic statement—recognized as such by the Bolsheviks—of hegemony or proletarian leadership of the peasantry. Furthermore, Kautsky was a symbol of the split and the deep opposition between Revolutionary Social Democracy and "opportunism" (the right wing of international Social Democracy).

In past writings, I have called Kautsky the mentor of the Bolsheviks and even an honorary Bolshevik, and these descriptions would not have been considered hyperbolic by informed people at the time. Bolshevik reading groups had a steady supply of legal and illegal Russian translations of Kautsky's works (some prepared by Lenin). I have looked at enough reading lists of such groups to assert that Kautsky was by far the most important author, more so than any Russian Social Democrat. In *State and Revolution*, Lenin made the point:

> Undoubtedly, an immeasurably larger number of Kautsky's works have been translated into Russian than into any other language. It is not without justification that German Social Democrats sometimes say jokingly that Kautsky is more read in Russia than in Germany (we may say, in parentheses, that there is deeper historical significance in this joke than those who first made it suspected; for the Russian workers, by making in 1905 an unusually great and unprecedented demand for the best works of the best Social Democratic literature and editions of these works in quantities unheard of in other countries, rapidly transplanted, so to speak, the enormous experience of a neighboring, more advanced country to the young soil of our proletarian movement). (Lenin 1977, 104)

When Kautsky disappointed the Bolsheviks in 1914 and later when he became a virulent critic of Bolshevism and Soviet power, he imposed a massive case of cognitive dissonance on the Bolsheviks and Lenin in particular. To paraphrase B. B. King, the way he loved Kautsky back then, that's the way he hated him now. Lenin coped with this cognitive dissonance by affirming that Kautsky was a renegade, someone who had betrayed his own past views. This meant that the Bolsheviks had not been wrong to admire and learn from Kautsky in the past.

STALIN AS REVOLUTIONARY SOCIAL DEMOCRAT

Stalin adopted a more complicated strategy. *In foro interno*, he hewed here as in all else to the Lenin line: Kautsky was a renegade from his previous status as an authoritative spokesman of Revolutionary Social Democracy. But for obvious political reasons—Kautsky's post-October notoriety as an aggressive anti-Soviet critic—this could not be publicly acknowledged. Kautsky had to be airbrushed out of the Bolshevik self-portrait. Or rather, to update our metaphor: Stalin photoshopped the Second International by removing Kautsky—the real theorist of Revolutionary Social Democracy—and pasting in Lenin. Stalin thus created a deep fake that had immense direct and indirect influence over the years.

This daring operation was carried out in *Foundations of Leninism*, composed immediately after Lenin's death in January 1924 (Stalin 1947, 69–188). What does *Foundations of Leninism* have to say about the Second International? This question turns out to be unexpectedly productive. The Second International is ubiquitous in *Foundations*, and Leninism is defined against the Second International as its ideological other. Every section begins with a catalog of the sins of the prewar International, and then Lenin's corrections are presented. Using the litany-style repetitions that he no doubt picked up in his seminary education, Stalin gives us long lists, with each item beginning with *Ran'she, priniato bylo govorit'* (Earlier, it was the accepted thing to say). His whole exposition is thus structured around the New Testament contrast: You have heard that it was said . . . but I say unto you.

In Stalin's telling, the Second International was all of a piece: opportunist, reformist, feeble, afraid of conflict, contemptuous of the global East—in two words, utterly unrevolutionary. The occasional radical-sounding resolution only adds revolting hypocrisy to the list of sins. Nevertheless, despite his seeming endorsement of a unitary model of the Second International, Stalin is thoroughly imbued with Lenin's sense of a great clash between Revolutionary Social Democracy and opportunism, but the former has now been renamed Leninism. Revolutionary Social Democracy is presented not as a militant tendency within the Second International but as a challenge from outside to the Second International as a whole—a conflict between the decrepit and reformist Second International versus robust and revolutionary Leninism.

To carry out this operation, Stalin had to airbrush all non-Bolshevik Revolutionary Social Democracy out of the picture. According to Stalin, Leninism is thoroughly revolutionary because "it grew and became strong in clashes with the opportunism of the Second International, the fight against which was and remains an essential preliminary condition for a successful fight against capitalism" (Stalin 1947, 70). Stalin sums up by alluding to the muck-filled Augean stables that Hercules cleaned up by diverting whole rivers: "The honor of this general verification [*proverka*] and general purification [*chistka*, purge] of the Augean stables of the Second International fell to the lot of Leninism" (Stalin 1947, 81).

The paradoxical result is that *Foundations of Leninism* is not such a bad guide to Revolutionary Social Democracy since it succinctly sets forth many of its basic tenets. Only—to use a Bolshevik metaphor—we have to rip off the mask. This is not the place to undertake the instructive task of going through *Foundations of Leninism* and documenting how each stand labeled as Lenin's original contribution can be found in prewar writings of Kautsky and other spokesmen of Revolutionary Social Democracy. A look at Stalin's own pre-October writings will show why he could never be completely successful in exorcizing Kautsky. We can easily come up with a long list of complimentary references to Kautsky in Stalin's works. Here we will look at one article in particular in which Stalin defends the hegemony scenario that became permanently a central part of his outlook. Kautsky's 1906 article "Driving Forces and Prospects of the Russian Revolution" set forth in full the rationale behind Bolshevik hegemony (although Kautsky does not use this term), and as such it was enthusiastically endorsed with extensive commentary by Lenin, Stalin, and non-Bolshevik Trotsky. Kautsky's endorsement of Bolshevik tactics was ruefully noted by Menshevik leader Iulii Martov: "Kautsky, in his final conclusion, is in agreement with com. Lenin and his fellow thinkers who proclaim the democratic dictatorship of the proletariat and peasantry" (Stalin 1946, 12).

In his commentary, Stalin first asks: Who will be the leader of the revolution, who will be the *vozhd'* of the rebellious *narod*? Stalin cites the Menshevik writer Aleksandr Martynov: "The hegemony of the proletariat is a harmful utopia." Stalin defiantly replies: "The hegemony of the proletariat is not a utopia, it is a living fact, the proletariat is actually uniting the discontented elements around itself":

> The only *vozhd'* of our revolution, interested in and capable of leading the revolutionary forces in Russia in the assault upon the tsarist autocracy, is the proletariat. The proletariat alone will rally around itself the revolutionary elements of the country, it alone will carry through our revolution to the end [*do kontsa*]. The task of Social Democracy is to do everything possible to prepare the proletariat for the role of the *vozhd'* of the revolution (Stalin 1946, 62).

What about the liberals? Can they at least be allies of the proletariat? The Bolsheviks answered no, because the only reliable allies are the poorest peasantry or just plain peasantry (Stalin uses these terms interchangeably). Only the peasants can "conclude a solid alliance with the proletariat for the whole period of the current revolution." Stalin expanded on this conclusion in a later article:

> Our bourgeoisie is terrified by the revolutionary spirit of the proletariat; instead of marching at the head of the revolution it rushes into the embrace of the counterrevolution and enters into an alliance with it against the proletariat. Its party, the Kadet Party, openly, before the eyes of the whole world, enters into an agreement [*soglashenie*] with Stolypin, votes for the budget and the army for tsarism to use against the *narodnyi* revolution. Is it not clear that the Russian liberal bourgeoisie is an antirevolutionary force against which the most relentless war must be waged? And was not Comrade Kautsky right when he said that where the proletariat comes out independently the bourgeoisie ceases to be revolutionary? . . .
>
> Thus, the Russian liberal bourgeoisie is antirevolutionary; it cannot be the driving force of the revolution, and still less can it be its *vozhd'*; it is the sworn enemy of the revolution and a persistent struggle must be waged against it. (Stalin 1946, 62)

By contrast, the Mensheviks overestimate the revolutionary qualities of the liberals and seek an agreement with them both during Duma elections and in general. For the sake of this agreement, they are ready to compromise on programmatic demands, even to the extent of accepting the goal of a constitutional monarchy instead of demanding a democratic republic. Thus the liberals seek agreements with the tsarist establishment, and the Mensheviks seek agreement with the liberals, while the Bolsheviks opposed both kinds of agreementizing on principle.

Another question separating Bolsheviks from Mensheviks: What is the class essence of the victory of the revolution, or, in other words, which classes must claim victory in our revolution, which classes must conquer the power (*vlast'*)? According to the Bolsheviks, victory in the revolution entails a worker-peasant *vlast'*. By contrast, Mensheviks want the *vlast'* to be incarnated in a liberal-dominated Duma legislature: a dictatorship of the Kadets (the main political party of the liberals). But according to Kautsky (Stalin triumphantly asserts), any such government would be counterrevolutionary. The Bolsheviks would be willing to participate in a revolutionary government—if it truly embodies a worker-peasant *vlast'*: "If in the struggle on the streets the proletariat together with the peasants destroys the old order, if the proletariat sheds blood alongside the peasants, then, naturally, the two should go together into the provisional revolutionary government in order to carry the revolution to the desired results" (Stalin 1946, 11).

To back up his case, Stalin again quotes someone he regards as an incontrovertible authority:

> What does Kautsky say about this issue? "It is quite possible that in the further course of the revolution victory will be attained by the Social Democratic party. . . ." But this does not mean that "the revolution being experienced by Russia at present will lead to the installment in Russia of a socialist mode of production, even if it provisionally gives the helm of the *vlast'* to Social Democracy."
>
> As you see, according to Kautsky, participation in a provisional revolutionary government is not only permissible, but events may even so turn out that "the helm of the *vlast* is provisionally" but nevertheless entirely transferred into the hands of Social Democracy alone. (Stalin 1946, 12)

What is important for Stalin in Kautsky's argument, is not the obvious limitation (the revolution is not yet socialist) but rather the daring perspective of Social Democracy taking over the helm of the *vlast'*. Stalin got great satisfaction by being able to conclude this article on hegemony by saying: "As you see, Kautsky, the most authoritative theoretician of Social Democracy, and the Bolsheviks are in complete agreement with each other" (Stalin 1946, 12).

(A brief polemical digression that applies to Lev Kamenev as well as Stalin. Kamenev and Stalin were the leaders of the Petrograd Bolsheviks in March 1917, prior to Lenin's return in early April. At this time—so we are told by the prevailing historical consensus—these two ceded the leadership role in the revolution to the bourgeois Provisional Government, they were ready to support various agreements with the liberals, and they renounced in principle any aspiration for an exclusive worker-peasant *vlast'*. In other words, they embraced the very views they had just spent a full decade mocking and deriding! The prewar writings of Kamenev and Stalin are indeed marked by a steady drumbeat of invective against both the treacherous liberals as well as the Menshevik traitors to Marxism who are ready to make deals with the liberals. But all these arguments were promptly forgotten in March 1917, due, presumably, to the euphoria unleashed by the February events—or so we are told. Spoiler alert: the Bolshevik message prior to Lenin's return in early April 1917 has been stunningly misdescribed.)

In *Foundations of Leninism* and elsewhere, Stalin made a valiant effort to exorcise Kautsky and to assign Kautsky's role as the authoritative spokesman of revolutionary Marxism over to Lenin. As far as the outside world was concerned, he was entirely successful. But in the privacy of his own memories, he remained aware of a more complicated portrait of the great spokesman of Revolutionary Social Democracy who turned to the bad in 1914.

"Party of a New Type": Against the Opportunists

We now turn to the text extracted from the *Short Course* to see how Stalin negotiated his political identity as (so to speak) a closeted Revolutionary Social Democrat. I have divided this text into three parts: prerevolutionary, the victory of the revolution in 1917 and in the civil war, and the post-Lenin period marked by what Stalin saw as another great victory, namely, collectivization. Each of these three parts is further defined by avatars of the eternal ideological Other: opportunism before the revolution, agreementizing during the revolution, and capitulationism in the post-Lenin period. (As discussed earlier, the extracted text consists of Stalin's personal large-scale interventions to the canonical *Short Course* of party history published in 1938. I have not yet published this text, but it is based directly on the archival work presented in Brandenberger and Zelenov 2019; translations from the Russian are my own.)

Part I of this text, covering pre-October party history, presents Lenin's struggle to create a party of a new type against opportunism, his constant foe. Thus the party of a new type plays the same role as Leninism in *Foundations of Leninism*: a stand-in for Revolutionary Social Democracy that was manufactured in order to give Lenin and the Bolsheviks all the credit for this international revolutionary movement.

Party of a new type is an oft-cited phrase, and, for some reason, it seems de rigueur to put quotation marks around it, as if to say: not my phrase, but Lenin's actual words. And yet this phrase cannot be found in Lenin's writings. The phrase has its origin in the party histories of the late 1920s, where it is used in a narrow sense: the party of a new type was a post-1914 innovation that no longer tolerated the coexistence of opportunism and Revolutionary Social Democracy in a single organization. In the extracted text of 1938, Stalin took up the phrase and made it the centerpiece of a highly elaborated rerun of his earlier airbrushed portrait.

What Stalin is up to is perfectly clear when we look at the extracted text for part I: he gives us a pearl-string of Lenin's greatest hits, each presented as a stepping-stone to the shining goal of the party of a new type. Here is Stalin's climactic claim (demonstrating that he saw these various interventions, inserted passim in the canonical text, as a unified and integral argument):

> The Bolsheviks wanted to create a new party, a *Bolshevik* party, one that would serve as a model for all who wanted to have a genuinely revolutionary Marxist party. The Bolsheviks had been working to build up such a party ever since the time of the old *Iskra*. They prepared it stubbornly, persistently, in spite of everything. A fundamental and decisive role in this

preparatory work was such writings as *What Is to Be Done?*, *Two Tactics*, and so forth. Lenin's book *What Is to Be Done?* was the *ideological* preparation for such a party. Lenin's book *One Step Forward, Two Steps Back* was the *organizational* preparation of such a party. Lenin's book *Two Tactics of Social Democracy in the Democratic Revolution* was the *political* preparation of such a party. Finally, Lenin's book *Materialism and Empirio-Criticism* was the *theoretical* preparation of such a party. It may be safely said that never in history has any political group been so thoroughly prepared to constitute itself a party as the Bolshevik group was.

We find the following pattern in Stalin's various discussions of each of the texts that are included in this list. First, there is an extensive exposition of, say, *What Is to Be Done?* in its Russian context. These expositions are actually pretty good—in fact, considerably better than almost all Western discussions. And why not? Stalin had been a passionate participant in these polemics back in the day, and he retained a genuine interest in the issues. Despite or perhaps because of his hyper-partisan perspective, Stalin usefully presents intraparty debates as the Bolsheviks saw them.

After finishing this type of analysis, Stalin then adds: "But this does not exhaust the significance of Lenin's work *What Is to Be Done?*" (this phrase repeated almost verbatim with the remaining texts, as was Stalin's repetitious wont). This pronouncement introduces a tacked-on section making the claim that Lenin's argument in each of these works is a profoundly new innovation. Unlike the substantive opening section, this tacked-on section is always false and misleading. Unfortunately, it is the tacky tacked-on sections, not the earlier substantive exposition, that have influenced the standard interpretation of Bolshevism. The summary paragraph quoted earlier, which describes a process that climaxed in 1912 at the Prague Conference, is probably the most influential contribution to academic Lenin studies ever made. Its influence lives on, although (because?) the *Short Course* itself is dismissed and forgotten.

The overall party of a new type framework can be used without adopting Stalin's particular readings of Lenin's books. *What Is to Be Done?* is a case in point. According to the standard textbook interpretation of Lenin's 1902 publication, he reveals here what has been called his "worry about workers." Lenin gave up on the revolutionary inclinations of the workers and therefore aimed to create a conspiratorial party of professional revolutionaries from the intelligentsia. This reading has nothing in common with Stalin's account, and it has nothing to do with Lenin's actual life-long attitude. I have shown this at length in my monograph *Lenin Rediscovered* and elsewhere, so I will not say anything further on this topic.

Despite the fact that Western historians disagree with Stalin's reading of *What Is to Be Done?* (or rather, they would disagree if they were aware of it), they are in complete agreement with Stalin's narrative of a party of a new type created by the genius Lenin—only now the alleged innovations are described in such a way as to make Lenin look like an evil genius. In other words, historians reject Stalin's explanation on points where he is actually pretty good and embrace him when he is pretty bad.

To sum up: although he knew better, Stalin found it expedient in 1924 to airbrush out Revolutionary Social Democracy and its spokesman Karl Kautsky from his portrait of Bolshevism. Lenin himself was turned into something of an ersatz Kautsky and given exclusive credit for their shared outlook. In 1938, Stalin gussied up this portrait by creating a *gradus ad Parnassum* of Lenin's prerevolutionary works that moved inexorably toward the climactic goal of the party of a new type. This model has been immensely influential, especially among those on the left and on the right who self-identify as anti-Stalinist. Looking back at my own work on Lenin and Kautsky, I see now that it could be described as a process of rejecting the influential part of Stalin's portrait and resuscitating the forgotten but genuinely useful part.

The Victory of the Revolution: Against Agreementizing

Agreementizing is a new and unfamiliar translation for a word that will be familiar to any historian of 1917, namely, *soglashatel'stvo*, a term of political abuse that was coined from the common and straightforward word *soglashenie*, uncontroversially translated as agreement. Nevertheless, *soglashatel'stvo* is usually translated compromise or conciliationism (the very fact of two translations has helped to obscure the term's centrality in the political discourse of 1917). As it happens, compromise and conciliationism are separate and distinct Russian words (*kompromiss* and *primirenchestvo*).

Agreementizing in 1917 refers to a specific and concrete agreement between the Petrograd Soviet and the Provisional Government that stipulated that the government would carry out some fairly radical revolutionary measures in return for legitimization by the Soviet. As the central proagreement spokesman, Irakli Tsereteli, put it: "Comrades, it was not the proletariat alone or the army alone who adopted this path of agreement; but, I affirm, this path of agreement was adopted by an enormous part of the bourgeoisie—otherwise we would not have had the Provisional Government" (Tsapenko 1927, 147–50).

The Bolsheviks made rejection of this agreement the linchpin of their message to the soviet constituency throughout 1917: the agreement between Soviet and government would not work, revolutionary goals would not be met, a coherent response to the burgeoning crisis would not be forthcoming, due to the clashing interests of the parties to the agreement, namely, the *narod* versus the *tsenzoviki*, the people versus elite censitarian society.

Although the issue of the agreement was most prominent in 1917, opposition to agreementizing had strong roots in prewar Revolutionary Social Democracy, as we saw earlier in Stalin's writings. After the revolution, he insisted more than once that this theme connected Bolshevik tactics throughout both prerevolutionary and post-revolutionary periods. One such occasion was *Foundations of Leninism*, when Stalin looked at three stages of the Russian Revolution. He identified "the direction of the basic blow" at each stage:

> First stage, 1903 to February 1917: isolation of the liberal-monarchist bourgeoisie, striving to take over the peasantry and liquidate the revolution by means of an *agreement* with tsarism.

> Second stage, March 1917 to October 1917: isolation of the petty-bourgeois democracy (Mensheviks, Socialist Revolutionaries), striving to take over the toiling masses of the peasantry and finish the revolution by means of an *agreement* with imperialism.

> Third stage, starting after the October overthrow: isolation of the petty-bourgeois democracy, isolation of the parties of the Second International, who base their politics essentially on an *agreement* with imperialism. (Stalin 1947, 152–53)

Of note, Stalin put emphasis on the word "agreement" at each stage, thereby turning opposition to agreementizing into the main link between the various stages. We also see that opposition to agreementizing is closely tied to the hegemony scenario; the Bolsheviks isolate the agreementizers who are rivals for influence over the peasantry. This aspect will occupy us in the following section when we consider Stalin's views of collectivization.

Stalin had a consistent narrative about 1917: October was the result of the soviet constituency's progressive disillusionment with the agreement advocated by the Mensheviks and the SRs, a process speeded along by Bolshevik agitation but caused principally by the flow of events. We cannot pursue this fascinating topic further here, so let us turn now to the way that the hegemony scenario and the accompanying opposition to agreementizing informed Stalin's understanding of all-out collectivization.

Collectivization and the Capitulators

Up to now, the extracted text of 1938 followed in the footsteps of *Foundations of Leninism* in 1924, although in a more elaborate and systematic fashion. The prerevolutionary Lenin who creates a party of a new type while combating the opportunists and the revolutionary Lenin who leads the party to victory by taking on the agreementizers—these are familiar figures. But now we come to the 1924–38 period: Lenin is dead, but a new Lenin-like figure is waiting in the wings. The features of a genuine Bolshevik *vozhd'* had been carefully laid out: a leader whose creative use of Marxist theory allows him to successfully navigate the shoals of history, to face down defeatist capitulators among the Bolsheviks themselves (the latest incarnation of opportunism), isolate rivals for influence over the peasantry, and break through the roadblocks to put the Soviet Union on a new path. These features demonstrate why Stalin is the Lenin of today, and why collectivization is the new October.

In part III of the extracted text, we will have to pick apart a tangle of themes: the role of theory, political leadership, hegemony as the fundamental Bolshevik tactic, the steady (and overtly melodramatic) degeneration of the capitulators from *nashi* (our people) to traitorous saboteurs, and finally and centrally, collectivization. Let us look at each of these separately. Even during Stalin's lifetime, he was known to be the author of the *Short Course*'s famous section on dialectical materialism. Looking past all the abstractions about quantity turning into quality and the like, we find the argument that any leader who does not align themselves with the laws of history—no matter how talented, brilliant, and popular these leaders are—will go down to defeat and disgrace. Trotsky and Bukharin were just such leaders. By contrast, a leader who aligns himself with these same laws will be carried by the tidal force of history from obscurity to world leadership.

The paradigmatic example of bold creative theory versus shortsighted and envious capitulationism is collectivization. The chapter on collectivization is central to part III of the extracted text, and perhaps to the text as a whole. Stalin regarded collectivization as his proudest achievement and his particular claim to greatness. An indication of his feelings is found in the mirror provided by a collection of tribute articles issued on the occasion of Stalin's sixtieth birthday in 1939 (Molotov et al. 1940). The authors of these articles were his top lieutenants who had been with him for many years; the red courtiers understood Stalin's self-image and reflected it back at him.

Yes (said the eulogizers), Stalin led the industrialization drive, but this achievement, great as it was, merely carried out Lenin's plan. In contrast, collectivization was Stalin's brainchild. As Lazar Kaganovich described the collectivization campaign, using an overwrought "locomotive of history" metaphor, Stalin had to "theoretically plan out the track and lay the rails so that the locomotive could move on other routes for which the theoretical rails had not yet been laid, and for which even the track had only been generally indicated" (Molotov et al. 1940, 45). We further learn from these tributes that the collectivization drive was theoretically innovative, a new kind of revolution from above that was equal to the October Revolution, and a feat that made a truly socialist society possible. Kaganovich assures us, "we, Comrade Stalin's immediate pupils, can say without exaggeration that there is not a field of socialist construction into which Comrade Stalin has put so much energy, labor and care as he put in the field of collective farm development" (Molotov et al. 1940, 46). If Stalin knew that collectivization was deeply unpopular, it evidently did not faze him; he was happy to own it.

A question arises: If Stalin had it all planned out ahead of time, whence all the chaos, contingency, improvisation, and repression? Yes, there was some of that, admitted the eulogizers, but it was entirely due to the class enemy: "All the brutal remnants of capitalism, all the elements of ignorance and vileness left over from the old system were mobilized with the assistance of foreign imperialists to prevent the socialist reconstruction of our country . . . There was not a crime that these monsters hesitated to commit: terrorism, the assassination of some of our best people, blowing up factories, train wrecking, incendiarism, poisoning cattle—everything was brought into play" (Molotov et al. 1940, 46–47).

What, then, was the leadership theory behind collectivization? Reading the extracted text, we see that, in Stalin's mind, the collectivization drive was a brilliant application of Bolshevik hegemony: carrying the revolution forward by proletarian leadership of the peasants and by isolation of the rivals for influence over the peasants. A note before proceeding. In my view, Stalin was a sincere follower of Lenin who tried to answer, as best he could, the question WWLD: What would Lenin do? But this view does not mean I am trying to make Stalin look good (by associating him with Lenin) or make Lenin look bad (by associating him with Stalin). Lenin cannot be held responsible if his loyal follower came up with a clumsy, cruel, and incompetent application of Bolshevik tactics. Our goal here is to identify Stalin's definition of the situation in his own mind, not to evaluate either collectivization or Bolshevism.

Despite the triumphal language he used about collectivization in the extracted text, Stalin evidently still felt defensive about the critique of the Right Opposition even in 1938—partly, I speculate, because in his heart of hearts he respected them more than he did the Trotskyists, and partly because he knew that their doubts were still shared by wide circles in the party and among the people. These painful realizations led to a remarkable outburst, almost a *cri de coeur*, at a combined meeting of the Politburo with propaganda experts in October 1938:

> You know that the Rights explained our sharp turn to the collective farms by pointing to some sort of peculiar ideological itch on our part—this was the reason that we decided to get all the muzhiks into collective farms. From the testimony of the Rights we know that they declared: the Russian spirit has nothing in common with any sort of collectivization . . .
>
> [Chapter 11 on collectivization] is key: why did we go over to the collective farms? What was this? Was it the caprice of the leaders, the [ideological] itch of the leaders, who (so we are told) read through Marx, drew conclusions, and then, if you please, restructured the whole country according to those conclusions. Was collectivization just something made-up—or was it necessity? Those who didn't understand a damn thing about economics—all those Rights, who didn't have the slightest understanding of our society either theoretically or economically, nor the slightest understanding of the laws of historical development, nor the essence of Marxism—they could say such things as suggesting that we turn away from the collective farms and take the capitalist path of development in agriculture. (Zelenov and Brandenberger 2014, 494–95)

Stalin's rationale for collectivization is a vastly complicated topic, and my aim here is simply to show how he frames the issues in terms of the hegemony scenario learned during his days as a proud Revolutionary Social Democrat. Here is how Stalin sets out the problem in the extracted text: Modern productive agriculture requires large-scale enterprises, and these can be of two kinds, capitalist and socialist. In contrast to industry, in agriculture the choice between these two paths was still an open question at the end of the 1920s. Stalin asked himself: How can we ensure that the peasants arrive at the fated goal of large-scale enterprise by going down the socialist path, thus bringing the revolution to a final and victorious conclusion? His unsurprising answer: by proletarian leadership of the peasants. Stalin quotes his speech from 1927: "The way out is for small and very small peasant farms—not through pressure, but through example and persuasion—to be gradually but steadily united in large-scale farms."

Positive leadership of the peasants toward a revolutionary goal was only one side of the coin. As Stalin had stressed in all his earlier discussions of hegemony, this tactic also included isolation of any rival force that threatened to lead the peasantry toward some sort of agreement with capitalism. The liberals and the socialist agreementizers had earlier been assigned this role. And now, for collectivization, Stalin named a new candidate: the kulaks. Therefore, he recalls, "the transition to all-out collectivization proceeded not through a simple and straightforward entry of the mass of the peasantry into the *kolkhozy*, but through a mass struggle of the peasants against kulakdom."

Since the kulaks represent a leadership force whose overall influence is feared, not only must their land and equipment be expropriated, but they themselves are to be physically removed from the village. All in all, dekulakization is key to the successful solution of proletarian leadership of the peasantry, and thus it justifies the propagandistic claim that Stalin is the Lenin of today: "[Dekulakization] represented the most profound revolutionary turnabout [*perevorot*], a leap from the old qualitative condition of society to a new qualitative condition, equivalent in its consequences to the revolutionary turnabout in October 1917."

In 1918, Lenin made a somewhat similar claim: class struggle in the village was equivalent to or even more profound than October because the socialist revolution had moved to the village. But this claim was clearly premature, and Soviet power quickly (long before NEP) had to arrive at a modus vivendi with the middle peasant. But now Stalin used the logic of hegemony to do what Lenin had been unable to do. We earlier quoted Stalin's invocation from 1924 of the defeat of agreementizing at three stages of the revolution. Dekulakization allowed him to add a fourth item to this list, which would have read something like this: "Fourth stage, beginning in 1929–30: isolation of kulakdom that strives to lead the mass of the peasantry down the path to capitalism; defeat of the capitulationist Bolshevik Rights; successful proletarian leadership of the peasantry down the path to socialism."

In 1938, half a decade after the collectivization drive, Stalin realized that the peasants still needed to be convinced that economic necessity, not ideological caprice, lay behind collectivization: "It is very important to explain this to the muzhik." After running through the economic rationale (the inefficiency of small peasant farms, the tendency toward further division of the land, the need for larger production units, the horrors of the capitalist path), Stalin concluded, "how much expense, how much blood would have been demanded if we had taken the capitalist path! But the path of the collective farms meant less blood: not the impoverishment of the peasants, but their unification . . . All this needs to be explained to the muzhik, he'll understand it" (Zelenov and Brandenberger 2014, 494–95).

Collectivization was also central to Stalin's melodrama that portrayed the degeneration of the capitulators who were transformed from previously loyal party members into *dvurushniki* (doubledealers, hypocritical oppositionists who mask their real views) and from thence into traitors (on the outsize role of the *dvurushniki* in the Stalinist imaginary, see the essays collected in Lih, *What Was Bolshevism?* (2024). According to Stalin, the political degeneration of the capitulators was triggered by their incomprehension of the laws of history. Because they did not know these laws, they rejected the party line and predicted disaster. When their skepticism was belied by the success of the party line, they turned sour and became more and more embittered. The presence of these embittered opportunists within the party and state bureaucracy led to the painful necessity of the purification campaign of 1937–1938—or so Stalin saw it.

A snapshot of the process of degeneration can be found in Stalin's description of the oppositionists at the Seventeenth Party Congress in 1934, that is, after the main collectivization battles had been fought. The title of the relevant section is: "Degeneration of the Bukharinists into political *dvurushniki* [double-dealers]. Degeneration of the Trotskyist *dvurushniki* into a White Guard band of murderers and spies." Here we see two precisely delineated stages of degeneration: the opposition led by Bukharin is now degenerating into *dvurushnichestvo,* in contrast to the Trotskyists, who are already *dvurushniki* but who are now degenerating even further into a White Guard band of murderers and spies.

Instead of evaluating the success of the collectivization drive from the point of view of the *narod* (Stalin continues), the capitulationists saw only the collapse of their own policies; they evaluated everything from the point of view of their "pitiful factional group and were cut off from real life and thoroughly rotten" (this supercharged language of abuse is a specialty of Stalin's prose). To revenge themselves on the party and the people, they resort to wrecking activities: arson, explosions, and the like. At the same time, they hypocritically toady up to the party. Their speeches of praise for the party and its leadership at the Congress were acts of defiance that instructed their followers outside the Congress not to lay down their arms but rather to become *dvurushniki* like themselves.

The indicated remedy for capitulationism was "theoretical preparation." As he explained in late 1938 while discussing the just-completed *Short Course* and its ambitious goals:

> How do we explain that some of them [among the larger constituency of the Right Opposition] became spies and intelligence agents? I mean, some of them were our people and afterward went over to the other side. Why?—because they were politically ungrounded, they were theoretically uneducated, they were people who did not know the laws of

political development, and because of this they were not able to digest the sharp turn toward the collective farms . . .

Many of our cadres lacked grounding politically, they were poorly prepared theoretically, and so they thought that nothing would come of [the collectivization drive], and because of this we lost a fairly significant number of cadres, capable people . . . We have to lead the country through the government apparatus, and in this apparatus are many people foreign to us—people who followed us before collectivization and who went away from us during collectivization. (Zelenov and Brandenberger 2014, 479)

Let us put Stalin's collectivization narrative into a wider framework. When we consider young Stalin as Old Bolshevik, we find that his early self-identification as a representative of Revolutionary Social Democracy in Russia is plentifully documented in the first three volumes of his Collected Works that take us up to October 1917. In *Foundations of Leninism* (1924), Stalin superficially denied this identity (by renaming it 'Leninism'), but more fundamentally affirmed it. Many other features of Revolutionary Social Democracy not discussed in this chapter continued to have a great influence in the Stalin era, in particular, campaignism (the permanent campaign inaugurated by Ferdinand Lassalle) (Lih 2019), Kautsky's global scenario of interactive revolutions (Lih 2014), and the cult of party leaders.

We focused here on two key features of Revolutionary Social Democracy in Russia: the hegemony scenario and opposition to agreementizing. In the text extracted from the *Short Course* that could well be called Stalin's Credo, he made these two themes central to the creation of a party of a new type, to revolutionary victory in October, and to his own crowning achievement, namely, collectivization via dekulakization. Revolutionary Social Democracy had always defined itself against opportunism, but Stalin turned this contrast into mortal combat. Thus his whole saga is punctuated by various avatars of the same enemy: opportunism, agreementizing, capitulationism. Stalin's life-long 'definition of the situation' cannot be understood without Revolutionary Social Democracy—and conversely, Revolutionary Social Democracy cannot be recovered without awareness of Stalin's role in airbrushing it out of the historical picture.

Works Cited

Brandenberger, David, and Mikhail Zelenov, eds. *"Kratkii kurs istorii VKP(b)": Tekst i ego istoriia v 2 chastiakh*, pt. 1. Moscow: ROSSPEN, 2014.

Brandenberger, David, and Mikhail Zelenov, eds. *Stalin's Master Narrative*. New Haven: Yale University Press, 2019.

Lenin, V. I. *Polnoe sobranie sochinenii*, 5th ed. Vol. 33. Moscow: Gosizdat, 1977.
Lih, Lars T. "'A New Era of War and Revolution': Lenin, Kautsky, Hegel and the Outbreak of World War I." In *Cataclysm 1914: The First World War and the Making of Modern World Politics*, ed. Alexander Anievas, 366–412. Leiden: Brill, 2014.
Lih, Lars T. "Campaignism and the Fate of Political Freedom in Russia." In *The Fate of the Bolshevik Revolution: Illiberal Liberation, 1917–1941*, edited by Lara Douds and James Harris, 31–46. London: Bloomsbury Academic, 2019.
Lih, Lars T. *What Was Bolshevism?* Leiden: Brill, 2024.
Molotov, V. M., L. M. Kaganovich, et al. *Stalin*. New York: Workers Library Publishers, 1940.
Stalin, J. V. *Sochineniia*. Vol. 2 Moscow: OGIZ, 1946.
Stalin, J. V. *Sochineniia*. Vol. 6. Moscow: OGIZ, 1947.
Tsapenko, M. N, ed. *Vserossiiskoe soveshchanie sovetov rabochikh i soldatskikh deputatov: stenograficheskii otchet*. Moscow: Gosizdat, 1927.
Tucker, Robert C. *Politics as Leadership*. Columbia: University of Missouri Press, 1981.

Part Five

The Spacial

CHAPTER 11

Power, Violence, and Rurality in the Soviet Union in the 1930s

LYNNE VIOLA

In the past fifty years, the historiography on Stalinism has been dominated at various times by the totalitarian model, modernization, and then modernity studies, Stalin-centered "great man" approaches, and revisionist studies in social and political history. What many of these studies have had in common is their Russocentric orientation and neglect of the rural sector of the population—that is, the majority of the Soviet Union's population in the 1930s. Our grand theories of Soviet historical development have often been based on fifteen percent of the population at best.

There have been important exceptions. The work of Moshe Lewin dominated the field in the 1980s and 1990s. Lewin brought a Marxist perspective to his studies of the peasantry, a perspective that was not always an easy ideological fit for a traditional agrarian society. While his knowledge of peasant society in its particulars was vast, his primary arguments always revolved around Stalin's role in collectivization and the issue of an alternative to Stalinism, something that begs counterhistorical logic (which is not logical, by the way). In a sense, Lewin blamed the peasantry for the rise of what he called the Leviathan state built as it was on a "quicksand society" unmoored and destabilized by the civil war and collectivization. (Lewin 1975; 1985, 209–40, 258–86) At about the same time, R. W. Davies advanced our empirical understanding of rural society and agriculture through prodigious research that remains without parallel. Far less given to historiographical grandstanding than his American colleagues, Davies succeeded in demonstrating the complex interplay between politics, society, and economics in understanding state violence against the peasantry (Davies 1980, 2004).

Yet perhaps the most important work on the peasantry came from the pen of Teodor Shanin, a sociologist steeped in the literature of peasant studies. Drawing on the work of Chaianov from the 1920s, *The Awkward Class* demonstrated a profound understanding of the dynamics of rural society employing Chaianov's notion of household cyclical mobility to understand the instability of social categorizations in the village and the difficulties of applying traditional Marxian notions of class in the countryside. Shanin also stressed the solidarity of the village in the face of attacks from without. In this sense, his work deeply influenced my own scholarship on peasant resistance to collectivization and the social and political dynamics of dekulakization (Shanin 1972).

My work has focused on extraction and internal colonization as ways to understand state-peasant relations and violence in the 1930s. The Soviet Union was an extraction state. In this, it resembled colonial empires. In the Soviet Union, however, the peasantry became a substitute for overseas colonies, serving as a primary source of extraction for grain, labor, soldiers, and internal colonization. Collectivization became a means toward this end as well as a control mechanism to manage the rural population and its economy. Other industrializing nations also exploited the peasantry and countryside for resources, but nowhere was the time frame as compressed, the scope as vast, and the violence as intense as in the Soviet case. The forced deportation of peasants under the kulak label was a further step in this direction as close to 2,000,000 peasants were shipped off to colonize the far north and east and to extract resources for the needs of industrialization in 1930 and 1931 alone. Forced labor dominated these remote and forbidding parts of the Soviet Union, where free workers refused to go. The special settlements which these peasants built would come to hold roughly half of the Gulag population through the Stalin era (Viola 1996, 2007).

Stalin provided the justification for internal colonization in a July 1928 speech to the Central Committee plenum:

> In capitalist countries industrialization was usually based not only on internal accumulation but also on the plundering of other countries, the plundering of colonies or vanquished countries, or on substantial loans from abroad. You know that for hundreds of years England used to drain all its colonies, from every continent, and in this way injected additional investments into its industry.... Our country differs from the capitalist countries, by the way, in that it cannot and must not engage in the plundering of colonies or in the plundering of other countries in general.

Therefore this path is closed to us. But our country doesn't have loans from abroad either. Consequently, this path is closed to us as well. In that case what is left for us? One choice is left: to develop industry, to industrialize the country on the basis of internal accumulation. . . . But where are the sources of this accumulation? As I said, there are two such sources: first, the working class, which creates valuable output and moves industry forward; and second, the peasantry. (Viola, Danilov, Ivnitskii, and Kozlov 2005, 98–99)

State violence became the primary lever of Stalin's internal accumulation, and it was aimed squarely at the peasantry, the primary source of extraction. Needless to say, internal accumulation was not the only causal factor in the state's decision to collectivize agriculture. A cultural disdain for the peasantry as well as ideological notions of rural class struggle and the supposed danger of the kulak also played their part. And the continuous threat of war and fear of a Fifth Column served as backdrop. This violence then rebounded in other types of state violence against kulaks and key ethnic diasporas, especially on the borders of the Soviet Union, as well as serving as a causal agent for the repression of the late 1930s.

The centrality of the rural context in Soviet violence was not a coincidence. Oxford political scientist, Stathis N. Kalyvas, coined the term "rurality" to encapsulate the ways in which rural contexts shaped violence. In *The Logic of Violence in Civil War*, Kalyvas explains:

"Rurality" is a proxy for various causal mechanisms, including the ability of combatants to hide without being denounced because of rural norms of solidarity and honor; higher levels of tolerance among rural people to threats of violence; a tradition of rebellion reinforced by norms of reciprocity, which leads to mass participation in antistate activities ranging from contraband to banditry to full-fledged rebellion; and the fact that an economy based on subsistence farming tends to favor armed resistance more than one based on wage labor. Perhaps most important, the dispersion of the population settlements, in rural environments impedes policing.

Although not every component of Kalyvas's description fits the Soviet countryside in this time period, the concept of rurality offers a useful context for understanding the dynamics of Soviet violence (Kalyvas 2006, 136).

In 2012, Charles King, a Georgetown political scientist, employed Kalyvas's concept of rurality in a brilliantly argued article entitled, "Can there be a political science of the Holocaust?" In this article, King took up the challenge of understanding the mass shootings of Jews in the East, arguing that they differed radically from the "industrial killing" of the German death camps. Making use of the concept of rurality, King writes: "The intensely local logic of killing as well as the relationship between selective violence and territorial control, both stressed in the work of Kalyvas, seem to map reasonably well the reciprocal horror committed by Nazi and Soviet forces during their sequential occupations of Eastern Europe." For King, rurality—the rural setting—shaped the dynamics of mass murder, collaboration, resistance, and partisan struggles (King 2012, 325).

Rurality is a useful tool for understanding the context of many aspects of violence in the Soviet Union in the 1930s. Although the Soviet Union was not engaged in actual war before 1939, the state saw itself at war with parts of its own population, making use of civil war metaphors and a continuing cast of enemies featuring most prominently the kulak and remnants from the civil war—prerevolutionary elites (*byvshye liudi*) and political parties, clergy, bandits, petty traders and artisans, Ukrainian nationalists, and the like. Although the list of enemy categories widened during times of mass violence and, at times, differed according to "local conditions," these categories stayed fairly uniform through the mass operations of the Great Purges.

In Stalin's Soviet Union, violence was preemptive, at times reactive, and always centered around the fear of a Fifth Column arising in the event of war. On January 11, 1930, OGPU boss Genrikh Iagoda penned a memo to his top lieutenants, calling for a purge of "kulak elements" from the countryside. "The kulak," he wrote, "must be destroyed as a class. . . . [The kulak] understands that he will perish with collectivization and therefore he renders more and more brutal and fierce resistance, as we see already, [ranging] from insurrectionary plots and counterrevolutionary kulak organizations to arson and terror. [The kulak] will and is already burning grain, murdering activists and government officials. If we do not strike quickly and decisively . . . we will face a whole series of uprisings" (Viola 2007, 14). Likewise, in 1937 on the eve of the launch of the mass operations, the Politburo issued a decision "On the discovery of counterrevolutionary insurrectionist organizations among exiled kulaks in Western Siberia" (Getty 1999, 469–72). In both cases, it made no difference that there was no real threat emanating from kulaks. In the case of collectivization, peasant violence was reactive, a response to state violence. Still, Stalin had not forgotten the lesson of the civil war and the threat of peasant rebellion.

Stalin struck first, and he did so through the agency of an unwieldy and inert bureaucracy. The undergovernment of the Soviet countryside is of central importance to understanding how rurality shaped violence in the Soviet Union, both during collectivization, the war, and, to a lesser extent, the Great Purges.

The Soviet state ruled the villages from the raion (or district), the stronghold and last bastion of rural government, party organizations, and the OGPU/NKVD in the countryside. At the start of the collectivization drive in 1929, for instance, there was only one *sel'sovet* (the lowest form of Soviet governance) for every 8.31 rural settlements in the Russian Republic and some 1,447,928 *sel'sovet* members for a rural population of around 125,000,000 people. At about the same time, there were only 339,000 communists in the countryside, the majority of whom were not peasants. Policing at the village level was almost nonexistent. The only policing agents in the village were the *sel'skie ispol'niteli*, a rotating, voluntary position among villagers that was more akin to a guard than police, with responsibilities for protecting the village from theft, fire, and fights.

The weaknesses of rural administration could only be overcome by mobilizing outside forces from the raion level. In the 1930s, these mobilizations assumed the form of military-like campaigns to take grain, organize collective farms, and arrest "enemies." It was virtually impossible for these campaigns not to become exercises in excess (*chrezvychainost'*) and arbitrary violence, as they overrode the authority of local officials and practiced the equivalence of an undeclared martial law, implementing policy at breakneck speed and in a slapdash manner, without regard for human life. In the countryside, governance see-sawed between this kind of campaign-style intervention and sheer inertia.

In collectivization and the Great Purges, Moscow ruled vertically, making use of a system of outside plenipotentiaries to instruct, cajole, and punish local authorities, while keeping some written orders secret and continually pushing for results—higher tempos of collectivization, larger numbers of arrests. Each layer of the regional-administrative hierarchy sent its plenipotentiaries down to the next level, from center to region to raion to village or town. The potential for what Stalin always labeled "excesses" increased as policy was implemented down the line in similar ways to the game of telephone, distorting the original message as it is passed along. In reality, policy was radical from the start as well, especially in collectivization, often vague and contradictory in regard to how to carry it out. During both collectivization and the mass operations, there were major personnel shortages, leading to the recruitment of a wide variety of less than qualified auxiliaries from the militsia and other organs, which only created further chaos. In both collectivization and the mass operations, Stalin issued the order from the top. His cadres tried desperately to fulfill and overfulfill these orders, competing in cruelty and excess. Once Stalin felt he had achieved a breakthrough in policy, he issued orders for a retreat as in "Dizzy with Success" and the November 1938 directive that halted the mass operations. In both cases, Stalin declared success and scapegoated select officials for "mistakes" and "excesses." These were simply "bad apples," leaving Stalin innocent of any problems (Viola 1996, 2017).

During collectivization, the preemptive nature of state violence and the undergovernment of the countryside combined with peasant traditions of solidarity and rebellion made for a lethal setting. State violence sparked peasant violence in what became a deadly crescendo. In 1930, the most dangerous year for peasant rebellion, there were close to 14,000 mass disturbances with nearly 2,500,000 participants. The largest number of mass disturbances occurred in grain-producing areas with dense populations like the Central Black Earth Region, the Lower Volga Region, and the North Caucasus. The largest number of revolts per capita with the largest number of participants occurred in Ukraine, where the supposed kulak threat came together with the equally supposed threat of Ukrainian nationalism. Border areas, especially in Ukraine and Belorussia, were also subject to intense violence and viewed as naturally dangerous settings. Banditry, another feature of rurality, also spread at this time. It erupted during the civil war and was not completely extinguished through the 1920s. At the end of the 1920s, approximately 9,000 exiled criminals escaped into the woods and joined up with peasant rebels. In the fall of 1929, Siberia was declared "unsafe due to banditry." Banditry would only increase as the collectivization campaigns spread and as peasants, especially young men, fled to the forests or mountains for survival, often relying on local villages for support (voluntary or otherwise) (Viola 1996).

Traditions of solidarity in the village do not necessarily equate to a monolithic or united village society. That was not the case. Instead, villagers came together as a result of the brutal intervention of outside forces and the violation of peasant moral economy. It was no coincidence, moreover, that most cases of violence against officials (beatings, murders) were aimed against locals who had broken solidarity and sided with the outsiders against village interests. This was a kind of "intimate violence," to use Kalyvas's words, that occurred in rural settings at war or in this case at war with their own state (Viola 1996).

Collectivization resulted in a massive famine, hitting key grain-producing regions and non-Russian republics like Ukraine and Kazakhstan. This was extraction onto death, with death rates reaching the multimillions as well as leading to an enormous geographical mobility as people left the villages in search of food. In Ukraine, where Stalin feared Ukrainian nationalism, the state was determined to silence its practitioners as well as the Ukrainian peasantry. In the cities, peasants poured in, leading to a host of urban problems as well as exacerbating the housing and food crises in the cities. The massive population booms resulted in more repression, this time in the cities, as the state attempted to register its population with passports while purging "socially alien elements" in what David Shearer and Paul Hagenloh have identified as campaigns of repression that would lay the groundwork for the mass operations and turn the police into agents of social purging. The continuum of violence from the collectivization drive through to the Great Purges maintained similar enemies and featured similar types of "social policing" (Shearer 2009; Hagenloh 2009).

The dynamics of the Great Purges can also be partly understood within this conceptual framework of rurality. The mass operations—both NKVD order 00447 (the "kulak operation") and the various national operations—targeted peasants, who constituted the majority of the victims of the Great Purge. The implementation of these deadly operations was structured in a vertical of rule. Moscow issued its detailed directives, and its plenipotentiaries, up and down the regional line, set off to translate policy into action through a combination of persuasion, threats, and force. Within regions, there were additional verticals as republic-level officials served as troubleshooters throughout Ukraine. A. I. Uspenskii mobilized the entire NKVD Ukraine with his excursions to regional NKVD offices in the summer of 1938; following Uspenskii's visits, other officials from NKVD Ukraine traveled out to the regions to order, cajole, and threaten. Within the regions, regional NKVD leaders traveled to the raion levels to do the same. Because they often had no more than one or two NKVD officials, local NKVD offices were forced to mobilize a multitude of additional forces to implement these repressive policies. In many villages, the NKVD sought out witnesses, generally local party and state officials labeled officially as simple peasants, to provide witness testimony concerning the biographical background of supposed enemies. Most agreed under considerable pressure and the promise that they would not be required to appear in court—that is, their neighbors would not know they had testified against them. In the village, the mass operations were public affairs; despite official secrecy, it was nearly impossible to carry out arrests without the rest of the village being aware (Viola 2017).

In both collectivization and the mass operations, the center unleashed radical policies that gained momentum as they descended the regional hierarchy of the NKVD and party-soviet administration. Although the center did not exactly lose control, the momentum of these policies in the far-flung towns and villages of the Soviet Union were not easy to regulate. Stalin opened the floodgates; closing them was more difficult. In both collectivization and the mass operations, he resorted to widely announced retreats once he had achieved his policy initiatives.

In both campaigns, enemies who were not shot were channeled into the Gulag. While deported kulaks entered the special settlements, other enemies would pour into the labor camps, the more familiar of the Gulag penal institutions.

The Gulag would continue to be used as an agent of colonization, pushing into the hinterland where it was difficult, if not impossible, to maintain a free workforce and continuing the work of extraction as the products of the Gulag (the extraction of raw materials for industrialization, labor for construction and agriculture) continued to play a key role in the economic development of the Soviet Union.

The various components of rurality also help us understand the conduct of war, both German and Soviet, during the Second World War. From the beginning, the Soviets strategically took advantage of the broad expanses of the countryside to retreat into the interior. They laid waste to what was left behind in Stalin's scorched earth policy. The Germans did the same when they retreated, burning down villages, especially in Belorussia. When they occupied the country, the Germans soon realized the difficulties of rule in this vast and undergoverned rural nation. They, too, ruled from the raion, relying on the collaboration of locals, forced or not, to implement their murderous policies, including the murder of Soviet Jews. As the war wore on, the Germans became increasingly reluctant to go out to the villages, especially once the Soviet partisan movement grew. As King noted, rurality is a central factor for understanding the dynamics of the partisan movement, collaboration, resistance in the Soviet Holocaust, and the wholesale violence of retributive politics and scorched earth practices on all sides of the conflict. Additionally, rurality aids us in understanding the vast differences between the industrial killings of European Jews in the German death camps and the mass shooting of Soviet Jews in the small towns and villages where they lived.

We have long assumed that violence in the Soviet context was tantamount to the Soviet state (or Stalin) achieving full control or power over its population. An understanding of rurality, however, clearly raises the issue of violence and power and what these terms actually mean. In *On Violence*, Hannah Arendt wrote about the inverse relation between power and violence: "Power and violence are opposites; where the one rules absolutely the other is absent" (Arendt 1970, 56). Debates in the field over strong states and weak states miss the point of what violence means. In the Soviet context, the state employed all means of violence in radical attempts to transform, control, and exert the will of the dictator. The results were often destructive, pyrrhic victories, whether in the collectivization of the countryside or the social purge of the nation. As Arendt wrote, "To substitute violence for power can bring victory, but the price is very high; for it is not only paid by the vanquished, it is also paid by the victor in terms of his own power" (Arendt 1970, 53). Socialized agriculture proved the Achilles' heel of the Soviet economy, and the extraction state centered in the Gulag fostered the state's reliance on forced labor to mine raw materials for industrialization into the postwar years and the use of premium-paid free workers as the Gulag declined in the Brezhnev years. The Gulag, moreover, was an economically costly institution dependent upon the inefficient work of forced labor (Gregory and Lazarev 2003).

Arendt's dictum helps us understand that violence does not translate into power or authority. It also helps us to understand the vast chasms between Soviet planning and reality, as I have written in a discussion of the kulak special settlements (Viola 2003). Special settlements were pencil points on a map chosen not for their suitability for settlers but for their proximity to raw materials needed for industrialization. Located in the furthest reaches of the Soviet hinterlands, the state could neither supply nor administer these places, resulting in high mortality, massive escapes, and investment into settlements of larger amounts than what the state managed to extract originally from the kulaks. Planning as such became a dystopian exercise in socialist realism aiming for perfection and order. The impossibility of implementing policies in an ordered way resulted in waves of violence in a context that resisted change. Violence was a cudgel in the attempt to establish order; it was a substitute for administration (especially in the countryside), an instrument for the mobilization of labor and resources for industry, and a tool of colonization. Rurality was the context for much of this violence.

None of these conclusions are exclusive to Stalinism or even to the Soviet experience. They are instead phenomena most likely to occur at times of extreme stress of war or conflict in rural settings, according to Kalyvas's concept of rurality. We should also not be surprised to see evidence of these phenomena in the prerevolutionary Russian Empire or in today's Russia under Putin. As I write, Russia is at war with Ukraine. This is an unprovoked war that has unleashed wholesale violence and destruction throughout Ukraine. Rurality may help us to understand Russia's current difficulties in occupying and maintaining control over Ukrainian territories, as well as the stubborn and heroic resistance of Ukrainians in small towns and villages throughout the nation. Russia's lack of local knowledge and its ignorance of the reality on the ground resulted in initial humiliating defeats for Russia's army. Russia's response has been to echo Stalin's scorched earth policy in practices of total war. Russia also continues to be an extraction state with an overdependence on oil production. According to the *Washington Post*, Ukraine holds "some of the world's largest reserves of titanium and iron ore, fields of untapped lithium and massive deposits of coal," in addition to being an agricultural powerhouse. To date, Russia "has seized 41 coal fields, 27 natural gas sites, 14 propane sites, nine oil fields, six iron ore deposits, two titanium ore sites, two zirconium ore sites, one strontium site, one lithium site, one uranium site, one gold deposit, and a significant quarry of limestone previously used for Ukrainian steel production." Ukrainian grain also remains a contested item, following Russia's blockade and continued obstruction of grain shipments. Extraction, not "liberation," animates this war under the cloak of imperial pretensions, paranoia about NATO, and a disregard for humanity that cannot but remind us of the Soviet 1930s (Faiola and Bennett 2022). The cultural contempt that Russia has displayed toward the sovereign nation of Ukraine is not at all unlike the cultural disdain that the Soviet state held toward the peasantry and the seemingly ubiquitous but largely fictional Ukrainian nationalists who were subject to repression repeatedly through this decade.

Works Cited

Arendt, Hannah. *On Violence*. New York: Harcourt Brace, 1970.
Davies, R.W. *The Socialist Offensive: The Collectivisation of Soviet Agriculture, 1929–1930*. Cambridge: Harvard University Press, 1980.
Davies, R.W., and Stephen G. Wheatcroft, eds. *The Years of Hunger: Soviet Agriculture, 1931–1933*. London: Palgrave Macmillan, 2004.
Faiola, Anthony, and Dalaton Bennett. "In the Ukraine War, a Battle for the Nation's Mineral and Energy Wealth." *Washington Post*, August 20, 2022.
Getty, J. Arch, and Oleg V. Naumov, eds. *The Road to Terror: Stalin and the Self-Destruction of the Bolsheviks, 1932–1939*. Trans. Benjamin Sher. New Haven: Yale University Press, 1999.
Gregory, Paul R., and Valery Lazarev, eds. *The Economics of Forced Labor: The Soviet Gulag*. Stanford: Hoover Institution Press, 2003.
Hagenloh, Paul. *Stalin's Police: Public Order and Mass Repression in the USSR, 1926–1941*. Baltimore: Johns Hopkins University Press, 2009.
Kalyvas, Stathis N. *The Logic of Violence in Civil War*. Cambridge: Cambridge University Press, 2006.
King, Charles. "Can There Be a Political Science of the Holocaust?" *Perspectives on Politics* 10, no. 2 (June 2012): 323–41.
Lewin, M. *Russian Peasants and Soviet Power: A Study of Collectivization*. Trans. Irene Nove. New York: Norton, 1975.
Lewin, M. *The Making of the Soviet System: Essays in the Social History of Interwar Russia*. New York: Pantheon, 1985.
Shanin, Teodor. *The Awkward Class. Political Sociology of Peasantry in a Developing Society: Russia, 1910–1925*. Oxford: Clarendon Press, 1972.
Shearer, David R. *Policing Stalin's Socialism: Repression and Social Order in the Soviet Union, 1924–1953*. New Haven: Yale University Press, 2009.
Viola, Lynne. *Peasant Rebels under Stalin: Collectivization and the Culture of Peasant Resistance*. New York: Oxford University Press, 1996.
Viola, Lynne. "The Aesthetic of Stalinist Planning and the World of the Special Villages." *Kritika: Explorations in Russian and Eurasian History* 4, no. 1 (Winter 2003): 101–28.

Viola, Lynne. *The Unknown Gulag: The Lost World of Stalin's Special Settlements*. New York: Oxford University Press, 2007.

Viola, Lynne. *Stalinist Perpetrators on Trial: Scenes from the Great Terror in Soviet Ukraine*. New York: Oxford University Press, 2017.

Viola, Lynne, V.P. Danilov, N.A. Ivnitskii, and Denis Kozlov, eds. *The War Against the Peasantry, 1927–1937*. Trans. Steven Shabad. New Haven, CT: Yale University Press, 2005.

Chapter 12

How I Learned to Read Stalin's Time in Space

Karl Schlögel

Post-Soviet Moscow has staged itself and brought in lighting artists from America. The lavish illumination follows the motto "Learning from Las Vegas." The once planned capital of the future has become a historical backdrop. The architectural heritage is being restaged. Bookstores are full of literature on the architecture and aesthetics of the Stalin era. At the same time, a wave of demolitions is sweeping through the city, mostly affecting buildings from the eighteenth and nineteenth centuries. Citizen protests by organizations like Archnadzor, which work to save historic buildings, have to watch helplessly. Even iconic buildings such as the Hotel Moskva, built in 1937 by Alexey Shchusev, with all its interiors and historical details, fell victim to the demolition promoted by Mayor Yuri Luzhkov. What can be seen there today is a copy that has only the facade and name in common with the original.

Almost all foreigners working in Moscow were housed in one of the iconic buildings of the late Stalin era, the Lomonosov Moscow State University (MGU) complex on the Lenin Hills. I remember MGU as a monumental complex, a city within a city, with magnificent foyers, theater halls, a baroque-like *stolovaia* (cafeteria) with sculptures of Russian scholars, porticoes with chandeliers, richly ornamented stucco ceilings, elevators in their original state. Everything seemed built for eternity. But I was late in realizing the privilege of the place. I found these rooms bombastic and oppressive, even tasteless. I was more interested in the achievements of the Soviet avant-garde, the buildings of Constructivism, which had also been rediscovered in the West since the 1960s; my Moscow friends could not understand my enthusiasm for the often-run-down workers' clubs, dormitories, and public baths from the 1920s, which reminded me of the Bauhaus. The architecture of the Stalin era became an object of reflection for me only much later, when I realized that the built city could also be read and interpreted as history turned to stone.

Ways into Soviet Russia

One is not born a historian, and one is not destined to spend almost a whole professional life with Stalin and his time. There have been many reasons, a peculiar pull, a kind of fascination, if one has done it anyway. For me—and presumably not only for me—the preoccupation with Stalinism was not a matter that arose primarily from a logic of research, from an immanent development of research, or from a sensational find of sources, but has to do with my horizon of life and experience, more precisely with the politicization of the 1968 generation and the questions of the New Left. The reference to one's own life story is not free from the risk of retrospective stylization. I can say up front that what is called the year 1937 was at the beginning of my questions. It was the question with which everyone was incessantly confronted around 1968, how the tragedy of millions of human fates could go together with a history of socialism. It was not primarily a matter of filling a research gap but an existential question of finding an answer to the why of 1937.

Before the politicization in the student movement of 1968, there was no point of reference to Russian, Soviet, or even Stalinist history stemming from family circumstances. The years that my father had spent as a soldier in the Wehrmacht in Russia—and it was not only Russia but also Ukraine—were not talked about in my youth, and even less so after the break with the family, which was connected with 1968. Even the teachers at the high school did not talk about what they had seen in places like Orsha, Kharkiv, Kramatorsk, Stalino, or what they had experienced as prisoners of war. I saw "Russians" for the first time in the early 1960s on the then-obligatory school trip to West Berlin, where one was supposed to learn about real socialism while looking over the Wall. Also, the first trip to the Soviet Union, organized by us students in 1966, was more about Russian culture, Dostoyevsky, the theater, the churches of Zagorsk (today again Sergiev Posad), the sights of Moscow, as they were listed in the travel guides of Intourist (Red Square, St. Basil's Cathedral, MGU, VDNKh, etc.).

What we were concerned about in the 1960s was to get our own picture, to finally get out of the experiences of the war generation and the ideological and factual blockades of the Cold War. The New Left was on the lookout for alternatives to the bureaucratic workers' state, to the betrayed revolution, and looked rather to Cuba or to the China of the Cultural Revolution. All the factional struggles of the Left of the 1920s were played out once again in the New Left—this time more as a farce. But there was a strong impulse in this: namely, to get away from the discourse of totalitarianism, which in Germany could easily be misunderstood as an apologia for the failure of the Germans under the Nazi regime and instrumentalized in the ideological struggle between East and West. The Soviet Union readings of those years were fascinating and endlessly rich: from Trotsky to Hannah Arendt, Arthur Koestler to Barrington Moore, the texts of the prerevolutionary intelligentsia to Aleksandr Solzhenitsyn. The island of West Berlin was a place where the experience of socialism beyond the Wall came together with the antitotalitarian experience of academic teachers who had returned from emigration, such as Ernst Fraenkel and Richard Loewenthal. West Berlin, with its contested status, was not only the capital of agents but also of cultural transit and transfer. I still remember Viktor Shklovsky's visit in the early 1970s to the city from which he had returned to the Soviet Union after a brief exile fifty years earlier.

In my memory, a central role in the confrontation with Stalinism was played not, as one might have thought, by the Frankfurt School, not by Theodor W. Adorno's and Max Horkheimer's *Dialektik der Aufklärung* but by Maurice Merleau-Ponty's *Les Aventures de la dialectique*, published in German in 1968, which, of course, was easily explained by the rampant neo-Hegelianism. His interpretation of the show trials and the increasing informativeness about what the Chinese Cultural Revolution really was beyond its benevolent sympathizers—all this helped to reopen the field of research. If I remember correctly, the late reading of Sheila Fitzpatrick's volume *Cultural Revolution in Russia, 1928–1931*, published as early as 1978—and everything that followed—was a kind of initial spark, the electrifying discovery of a scarcely explored continent. One had somehow arrived beyond the discourse of totalitarianism and modernization. In the Soviet Union, with the dissident movement, an intellectual space had emerged that allowed—however marginally—a free approach to one's own past, long before the erosion of the established Soviet academia. I learned a lot from meeting Soviet dissidents in Western exile in the 1970s. Something new could begin.

Reading the City, Looking for a Narrative of Simultaneity

Often (unplanned) side results are as important as the planned project. The goal of my research stay at MGU in 1982 was to reconstruct the Vekhi (Landmarks) debate. Out came the monograph on *Petersburg—Laboratorium der Moderne 1909–1921* (1986) and more important, the side book *Moskau lesen* (1984). Outwardly, it was a description of the city, an archaeology of Moscow. But as it turned out, it was for me a new approach to unlocking and telling history. Not the texts or the documents in archives and libraries were the main material, but the visible surface of the city itself, the texture with everything that belonged to it: public spaces, houses, facades, styles, and monuments. They could all be uncovered in their history and made to speak, a kind of archaeology that deciphers the different historical layers, like palimpsests.

The starting point for this approach was not a plan but the subjective impression and immediate experience of the city. This kind of navigation in space opened up a city beyond the history already known and described in Intourist guidebooks and overwritten again and again. As a result of this—often aimless—wandering, a different city and a different historical space emerged: industrial architecture, empty spaces where churches had once stood, the Moscow of Constructivism, the salons of the Silver Age, and finally: the sites of all those events that had played a role in Stalin's epoch from 1929 to 1953. The eye was trained by reading city maps, memoirs, travelogues of fellow travelers and testimonies of survivors of the Terror, architectural guides, and so on.

One walked through the city with entire libraries in one's head, and everywhere scenes and contexts showed themselves in a new light. I came to Moscow with books that had just been published at that time: Walter Benjamin's monumental and historically significant *Passagen-Werk*, a two-volume study of Paris as the capital of the nineteenth century, which has remained a torso, as well as his *Moskauer Tagebuch* from 1926/1927, published in 1980, in which one could learn what exact city observation and city description could be. Carl E. Schorske's great study *Fin-de-siècle Vienna—Politics and Culture* (1980) was also important for sharpening the view. The reading of this work was something like the training of the historical sense, which from now on in the following decades was to guide the exploration of other—mostly Eastern European—cities (Lodz, Kaliningrad, Lviv, Vitebsk, etc.). It was precisely not the genre of the travel guide—guidebook, *putevoditel'*, Baedeker—but another form of historical narrative tied to the exploration of historical sites. The central figure of this kind of observation is Benjamin's *flâneur*, who says of himself, "I have nothing to say. I only have something to show," and who uses the method of montage. I later elaborated on this in my book *Im Raume lesen wir die Zeit. Über Zivilisationsgeschichte und Geopolitik* (2003). It is a theoretical treatise rehabilitating the importance of space for historiography but also a warning against the new reductionism of a "spatial turn."

The implications of this new attention to the spatial and the solution from the almost exclusive fixation on the temporal dimension were—for me at least—not yet foreseeable. It amounted to a problematization of the almost taken-for-granted predominance of the chronological narrative and demanded a new form of representation. This, however, as we know, is not merely a question of literary-rhetorical genre but an epistemological question: What is the form of telling the story which takes place not only in chronological order but also in simultaneity, at the same time at the same place—a problem that in my view remains unsolved.

The main form of representation in historiography is a narrative in time, a narrative of temporality, the sequence of events, and the chronology. Time is sequential, reflects the process, is dynamism, "dialectics" (Michel Foucault). Space, fixed in maps, is static, nondynamic, and nondialectic. Maps are representations of simultaneity. Of course, this dichotomy and counterposition is to a certain degree exaggerated, artificial, only *idealtypisch*, as Max Weber would say. All historiography needs maps, implicates descriptions of sites, locations, and distances, as expressed literally in the basic saying: all history takes place.

Though I am convinced of the spatiality of historical processes, I have to find a way of researching and telling the story not only in chronological order but simultaneously in a given moment at a given site or place. I think we must learn from other forms and modes of narration. I have in mind cinema, the techniques of sharp cuts, of Sergei Eisenstein's montage, in short: to develop the rhetoric of simultaneity. I think that above all the technique of montage will help us to find the proper ways of mastering the problem of "simultaneity of non-simultaneity" (Ernst Bloch's "Gleichzeitigkeit der Ungleichzeitigkeit").

A Russian tradition existed of telling the story in spatial terms. I have in mind the work of Vasilii O. Kliuchevskii, Petr Tian-Shanskii, Nikolai Antsiferov—contemporaries of Vidal de la Blache in France, Karl Lamprecht in Germany, Frederick Jackson Turner in the United States, and the founders of the Annales school in France. In Russia the tradition was broken; after a certain transition period geography, geohistory, and geopolitics were heavily criticized and disappeared from the academic field. The link between geography and the social sciences was cut. Class, class relations, and social structures took over, geography did not matter anymore, geography was viewed as deterministic. The

Marxist heritage in spatial thinking—Karl August Wittfogel, for instance—was eliminated, and a strong economistic reductionism took over. In the West there was a late comeback of space in Marxist thinking with Henri Lefebvre's *La production d'espace social* and in postmodern thinking with Edward Soja's works.

It has become clear that scholarship on Soviet Russia has to take up this issue again. There cannot be a history of the late Russian Empire without rethinking the production of "imperial space" through administration, industrialization, railway construction, telegraph, and other means of communication; in short, without the production of imperial space. There cannot be a history of the Russian Revolution and Civil War excluding the dimension of fragmentation of the empire, disruption and degradation of the infrastructure—railways, ships, trains, automobiles, telegraph, waterways—and so on. And there is no history of Stalinism beyond the violent transformation of the spaces of the former empire. Almost all elements have been analyzed: the construction sites of communism—Magnitogorsk; the tractor and automobile plants in Cheliabinsk, Stalingrad, and Gorky; the new canals and artificial waterways—Belomor and Volga-Moskva; the great infrastructural and transport projects, including the Metro in Moscow, the Turksib in Central Asia, the Salekhard-Igarka Railway in Siberia. But we have not yet transformed all these studies into a more general topography of power and society in Russia. There should be many more pioneering works like Stephen Kotkin's study of Magnitogorsk (1995) or Yuri Slezkine's *The House of Government: A Saga of the Russian Revolution* (2017). How can we continue our discourse on totalitarianism without knowing how distances in this immense territory have been mastered. There is no history of total power without raising the question of where this power was based or executed. That is, without placing and spacing Russian history. Russian history has to include what Vladimir Kaganskii (2001) called "spatial hermeneutics."

In Search of a Narrative of Simultaneity

The question of the narrative of simultaneity arose for me in Moscow in 1937. What became apparent in even a cursory survey of the events of that year was the extreme density, indeed condensation, of events all occurring simultaneously in one place: the adoption of the new constitution in December 1936, the census in January 1937, the second great show trial and the Pushkin anniversary in February, Ordzhonikidze's suicide, the conquest of the North Pole, the mass killings starting in August 1937 and the unfolding of the campaign for the Soviet elections, the premiere of spectacular entertainment films and the start of major construction projects, and so on. In the given case, it was a matter of finding a narrative form in which the juxtaposition of violence and enthusiasm, of state of emergency and normality, of breathtaking social advancement and extermination furor, of targeted mass killings and social anomie could be captured. Both existed simultaneously and in the same space—and not in the retrospective construction of historians, but in the experiential horizon of the "Generation 1937," as one can easily gather from the countless testimonies of contemporaries.

To grasp this coexistence of extremes, a stereoscopic-panoramic overview was just as necessary as a specific and individual point of view. Everything took place not only in a moment—a year is condensed time—but also in a place, almost within sight and hearing. The Pushkin celebration took place in the House of Trade Unions, the old noble assembly, that is, in the place where the show trials were also staged; in Red Square, sportsmen's parades alternated with mass marches demanding death sentences for the enemies of the people; in the film studios, actors who had been exposed as spies disappeared; the International Geological Congress visited the large-scale project of the Moskva-Volga Canal, which was in fact a forced labor camp for 200,000 prisoners; and democracy was propagated while almost a million people were arbitrarily and systematically killed. The specificity of this juxtaposition of all these events and processes, demanded a specific narrative form. If one wanted to reconstruct the horizon of experience of the contemporaries—perpetrators as well as victims—then one could not avoid exposing oneself to their confusion and paralysis through precisely this simultaneity of extremes.

One could only competently join in here if one knew something of the dissolution of boundaries and the loss of judgment or at least suspected something. Our ideas, shaped by the Nazi terror with its clear distinctions of friend and enemy, of who belongs and who must be destroyed, were of little help here in getting at the arbitrary-random, indeed the enigmatic, of 1937 and of the whole Stalinist universe in which anyone could become an enemy. It was a matter of finding a form of representation appropriate to the process of self-destruction and the dissolution of the friend-enemy distinction. Here, concepts such as Benjamin's montage, Robert Musil's space of possibility, or Mikhail Bakhtin's chronotope perhaps help.

The City as Text. The Legibility of the City

My discovery of Moscow as a historical space began not with Stalin's Moscow but with that of the Soviet avant-garde and the Art Nouveau, Russian *style mod-*

erne, that preceded it. This line of vision was prepared by the rediscovery of Soviet modernism in the West, signaled in the exhibition "Paris-Moscou 1900–1930" at the Centre Pompidou. The exhibition Berlin-Moscow (1995) followed a long time later due to the precarious status of Berlin. It was, as it were, the reestablishment of a connection that had fallen into oblivion as a result of the Second World War and the Cold War.

Among the common places of rediscovery and rehabilitation of the Soviet avant-garde were Vladimir Tatlin's Tower of the III International, the fellow travelers on the Paris-Moscow axis, Rodchenko's photography, Kazimir Malevich's Suprematism, the buildings of Constructivism. All interest on my part was aimed at exploring the topography of Russian-Soviet modernism. The buildings that belonged to this *parcour* of the avant-garde were in poor condition, neglected and almost ready for demolition: Moissei Ginzburg's Narkomfin building, Konstantin Melnikov's Rusakov Club, Ivan Fomin's Dinamo apartment building, Mosselprom's "skyscraper," the Vesnin brothers' Likhachev Palace of Culture, Nikolai Kolli and Le Corbusier's Tsentrosoyuz building, the large housing estate on ulitsa Usacheva. Buildings of this type can also be found in Leningrad, Gorky, and Sverdlovsk.

The buildings that dominate Moscow to this day were not envisaged on the modernist *parcour*, but rather the reverse: the seven skyscrapers that dominated Moscow's silhouette were seen as evidence of confectioner's buildings, of stylistic regression. Even the magnificent metro stations were perceived as too pompous and dysfunctional. It took me a long time to become interested in the signal buildings that marked the rise and end of the Stalin era. These buildings were somehow always present but did not deserve special attention. Masterpieces—like the Lenin Mausoleum in Red Square—were contaminated by the rituals and annual parades on May 1 and November 7. The pavilions at the Exhibition of the Achievements of the National Economy were considered eclectic "kitsch" because of their often exotic and bizarre ornamentation.

The gap in the city's perception was embodied by the large swimming pool in the center of the city, which was an attractive place to swim during the lunch break, especially for foreign scholars who worked in the Lenin Library in Reading Room 1. Few knew at the time that the swimming pool was a replacement in the 1960s for the failed construction of the Palace of Soviets, the planned largest building in the world, and was that point to which the seven skyscrapers that dominated the Moscow cityscape were related. At that time, apart from professional journals for architects and urban planners, there was no discussion or reference to this imaginary center, to the empty center, and only gradually did the void fill in, which today is part of the general knowledge of every visitor to Moscow: that in the place where today stands the new

Cathedral of Christ the Savior, built between 1995 and 2000, there had previously stood the Cathedral of Christ the Savior, blown up in December 1931 to make way for the construction of the Palace of the Soviets. Gradually it became clear that the vacuum left by the demolition was the central site for the competitions in which the international architectural elite—Le Corbusier, Erich Mendelsohn, Naum Gabo, and others—had participated and that the building, which was not realized due to the German attack on the Soviet Union, was in a sense to become Stalin's signature world capital.

Once this point was understood, the layout of the new capital, defined in the General Plan of 1935, unfolded before the eye. From that moment on, the city layout and silhouette, which changed fundamentally and in characteristic ways between 1929 and 1953, became legible as a text, as built history. While architects had usually analyzed these buildings only from a stylistic-architectural-historical point of view, historians usually did not perceive them as historical documents sui generis.

Constructivism—Post-Constructivism—Soviet Art Deco—Stalin's Imperial Style

Periodization and analysis of stylistic vocabulary are not easy and remain controversial to this day. Political decisions and caesuras, such as party congresses, do not necessarily coincide with the change of styles, whose genesis and decay have their own time. Architecture, urbanism, fashion, and literary genres are not planned or even decreed but have their own incubation period. This is also related to the inertia that is peculiar to planning and construction time. Thus, there are purely Constructivist buildings such as the Likhachev Palace of Culture (the Vesnin brothers), which were completed only when Constructivism was already theoretically obsolete in 1932, with the decision to dissolve the competing associations of architects. Thus, master buildings of the late Stalin period—MGU, Hotel Ukraina, Ministry of Foreign Affairs—were completed only after Stalin's death and Khrushchev's secret speech, event time (*temps événementiel*) and long time (longue durée) do not coincide, as is well known.

And yet there is a correspondence between political and urban-stylistic development, as anyone who has been around Moscow and the other major Soviet cities knows. The sparse, laconic, even ascetic style that characterizes the first metro line—from Park Kultury to Sokolniki—differs radically from the lush neobaroque of the ring line built during and after the Great Patriotic War—Kievskaia or Komsomolskaia-Koltsevaia, for example. And even more different are the new lines built after Stalin's death with their rather modest decor. Each ride through the Moscow underground thus becomes an object lesson in the evolution and metamorphosis of styles, a ride through time. One can extend this real ride by visiting all the projects that never became reality but which say something about the ideas of the Stalin era—here, above all, the numerous competitions for the central buildings of the New Moscow: Palace of Soviets, House of Radio, People's Commissariat of Heavy Industry and others.

The evolution that Soviet capital architecture underwent between the signal buildings of Constructivism, on the one hand, and the signal buildings of Stalin's Imperial style, on the other, is one of the most exciting subjects of art historical and historical analysis because it involves transitional forms, ambivalent formations, hybrids, in which the dynamism of postrevolutionary new construction is combined with the static and representativeness of established power, which at the same time is still far removed from the monumentalism and eclecticism of the skyscrapers that began to dominate the capital in the late 1940s. In my memory, Vladimir Paperny's book *Architecture in the Age of Stalin: Culture Two*, earlier published in 1985 as *Kul'tura Dva*, was a great inspiration for the resumption of the architectural-historical discourse.

It is not clear how to appropriately describe this hybrid form, this hermaphrodite, this transitional form; what is certain is that it is a hybrid and transitional form, and that therein lies its aesthetic and functional attractiveness. If one directs one's gaze from the prominent buildings of Constructivism and Stalin's Empire for a moment to the mass of buildings erected between 1929 and 1953, it becomes apparent how much the city was shaped by the extraordinary building volume of those years. What types of buildings are we talking about?

Quantitatively, the most important construction projects were those related to the construction and new building of infrastructure, that is elementary facilities such as water supply and sewerage with associated transformer and pumping stations, the construction of bridges and embankments, locks and canal constructions, airports and river ports, the construction of the metro and trolley bus lines, and last but not least the new magistrals and prospects, which changed the scale of the city and the perception of the city.

The construction of new schools, kindergartens, scientific institutes, libraries, and palaces of culture represented a large part. The city, bursting at the seams due to immigration, urgently needed housing, so large model housing estates with municipal facilities were built throughout the city. These included new buildings of hospitals, public baths, post offices, and department stores. For recreation and leisure, already existing facilities were expanded or newly built: cultural parks, stadiums, cinemas, and concert halls. The buildings of state power and administration, organizations and people's commissariats were to be outstanding and striking. This overview of the reconstruction and new building of Moscow may seem exaggerated, but it is necessary to emphasize this because the view is usually only directed to the outstanding buildings of those years, such as the Gosplan building, Ivan Zholtovskii's model building for Intourist, Hotel Moskva, the Military Academy, the widening of Tverskaia/Gorky Street, the Lenin Library, the Northern river port, and last but not least the House on the Embankment. But anyone who visits, for example, the locks along the Moskva-Volga Canal immediately understands that this is a technogenic landscape, created in a short time and with terrible human sacrifices. The effect of these new buildings must have been particularly striking in view of the fact that the mass of residential buildings still consisted of wooden houses: a piece of utopia in the present. On a large scale, in addition to the new buildings, prerevolutionary buildings were extended by floors, and entire buildings were moved by a hundred meters.

This process of radical and accelerated urban redevelopment can also be observed outside the capital, or more precisely: what has been exemplified in Moscow should also set standards outside in the provinces. A kind of aesthetic homogenization of space is beginning. As a rule, the general plans and projects came from planning and architectural offices in Moscow and Leningrad. Identical plans for universities, stadiums, housing estates, cultural parks, Soviet houses, and so on can now be found throughout the former Soviet Union—from Kiev to Dushanbe, from Gorky to Magadan.

Moscow is an exemplary construction site, where massive demolition goes hand in hand with construction and rebuilding. The old city is described as chaotic, anarchic, cumbersome, and hostile to life, while the new city is described as clear, planned, healthy, and people-friendly. Central topoi in the debate about the general line, which have been extensively documented and analyzed since the perestroika and glasnost periods, are the rejection of international style, functionalism and constructivism, the search for a form and style of one's own, the emphasis on pictoriality and the preciousness of materials, and not least the emphasis on monumentality. Buildings should not only be functional, not only satisfy Louis Sullivan's motto "form follows function," but they should also be beautiful. The proletariat was to take the best from the wealth of forms of the old cultures, not in a simple adoption but in critical appropriation. The white or gray cubes of the new building were followed by colonnades, columns, pilasters, domes, and rotundas. There was to be an end to the idealization and fetishization of the machine; the shaping, artistically designing architect was to take first place again over the engineer.

The class struggle should also be fought out in the field of architecture. Buildings should not only be useful but should reflect something of the joie de vivre and harmony of the new society. Pictoriality instead of abstractness, preciousness of material instead of asceticism. There was a new appreciation for ensembles, interiors, and details—even down to the design of doorknobs, textiles, and furniture. Where constructivist architects had been content with white surfaces, there were now to be frescoes, reliefs, and mosaics. Department stores were now no longer just sober stores but something like palaces with foyers, spacious staircases, columns, chandeliers, another form of shopping malls, displays of opulence, even if it was out of reach for most. The park was now no longer just a green space for walking, but recreational and cultural space for the new, physically healthy, and educating New Man, an alternative to the capitalist Lunapark.

The debate about building and urban planning was conducted with great intensity, even acuteness, and from the midst of the architectural community. The struggle for the general line did not always run along generational lines and established schools and associations. Many architects who had set the tone in the 1920s moved to the second row or to the margins—Moissei Ginzburg, the Vesnin brothers, and Konstantin Melnikov. Others who had made careers before the revolution but lost their influence after the revolution made a comeback with the building boom of the Second Five-Year Plan—Vladimir Shchuko and Zholtovskii. Militant critics of Constructivism, especially from the younger generation, now began their great careers, which extended into the period after Stalin's death—Karo Alabyan, for example. Boris Iofan, who had designed the compound of the House of the Government (where he also had his studio until his death), the winner of the competition for the Palace of Soviets, was probably the one who had most closely translated the spirit of the times into his buildings: completed in the Soviet pavilion at the 1937 Paris World's Fair, unfinished in the Palace of Soviets, which was not executed.

Stalin's terror also raged within the professional group of master builders and architects, as the fates of Mikhail Okhitovich and Vyacheslav Oltarzhevskii testify. In my impression, they were less affected—similar to the group of engineers and technicians—because of their indispensability in the construction, but this would have to be statistically proven by a portrait of that cohort of architects and urban planners.

The search for a Soviet style that was distinct from Constructivism and the International Style but also different from Stalin's Imperial style after World War II resulted in a style in which the dynamism and thrust of the 1920s are still effective and combined with the force of increased power representation.

It seems to me that Soviet Art Deco could be the most appropriate characterization, the name for the specifically Soviet form of an international trend in the 1930s.

Was Soviet Art Deco also a reaction to a crisis as in the capitalist West? The 1925 Exposition internationale des arts décoratifs et industriels modernes in Paris, where, incidentally, Soviet architects were prominently represented by Konstantin Melnikov's Makhorka Pavilion, signaled a new appetite for wealth, exclusivity, and luxury in all areas of life, after the gloom of war and postwar. In America, stream-lining modernity came just as the boom of the 1920s collapsed with the Black Friday of 1929, and the state intervened in economic and public life in the New Deal in a hitherto unknown way: with infrastructure and job creation programs, public buildings, and state support for the arts. Art Deco America was also about turning away from the Machine Age, about imagery, beauty, even monumentality, a promise of the future. The neoclassical government buildings in Washington, DC are also monumentalist, while the skyscrapers of New York are fascinating in their technical perfection and flawless elegance. There, too, it was not just a matter of pure functionality but of beauty, ornamentation, preciousness of materials, marble in the lobbies, and a preference for windows and doors set in chrome.

The construction site of Radio City, that is, Rockefeller Center in the 1930s, was the attraction of numerous delegations of Soviet architects and engineers who wanted to get an idea of the new state of the art and the world of the future. Boris Iofan, chief architect of the Palace of Soviets, was fascinated during his visits to America, drawing incessantly, and getting the technical details of Radio City—air conditioning, escalators, elevators—for his palace design. He was not the only celebrity to make a pilgrimage to America, and it is an irony of history that it was a Russian-Soviet architect who was able to study the construction of Rockefeller Center at close range and help design Moscow's skyscraper landscape after World War II.

Vyacheslav Konstantinovich Oltarzhevskii (1880–1966) received an excellent education before the revolution in Moscow and for a time also with Otto Wagner in Vienna. After the revolution and the Civil War he was involved in the planning of the All-Union Agricultural Exhibition in 1923 together with other prominent architects before he went to the United States on official assignment to familiarize himself with the theory and practice of high-rise construction. He recorded his impressions and his conception of the modern city in a magnificent volume of architectural drawings entitled "The New Babylon," almost parallel to his American colleague Hugh Ferris. He admired the skyscrapers of America but believed that they would find their true meaning only in a society beyond capitalist anarchy, land speculation, and chaotic city-building; beyond gloomy street canyons, traffic chaos, and monotonous facades. Returning to the Soviet Union in 1935, he was charged with planning the All-Union Agricultural Exhibition, which was to open in 1937, but he was indicted on suspicion of alleged espionage and wreckage and sentenced to a camp in the North. He returned from Vorkuta, where he was able to work as an architect, at the end of the war and was immediately appointed to the committees responsible for the construction of the seven Moscow skyscrapers. Under his direct participation, Hotel Ukraina and the representative volume, in which the overall planning is set out, are created. The relationship between the American and Soviet careers of Vyacheslav Oltarzhevskii / Oltar-Jevsky is first analyzed in Jean-Louis Cohen's study of Soviet Americanism (2020) and by Katherine Zubovich in her monograph on *Soviet Skyscrapers and Urban Life in Stalin's Capital* (2021) based on Moscow archival sources.

In Oltarzhevskii's work, emphasis is placed on the semantic distinction between skyscraper and high-rise—*neboskreb* versus *vysotnoe zdanie*—but above all, the Soviet skyscraper is derived exclusively from European and Russian tradition: from church and bell towers like Ivan Velikii in the Kremlin, fortress buildings and palaces like the Admiralty in Saint Petersburg. Among the pioneers of high-rise construction, the names of Russian master builders alone are mentioned. "The principles of building Soviet skyscrapers are diametrically opposed to the principles of building American skyscrapers, which are diametrically opposed to the principles of savage capitalist competition, which are diametrically opposed to the capitalists' desire to extract as much profit as possible from every piece of urban land. The victims of the capitalists' greed are the interests of the entire urban population. Moscow's high-rise buildings do not displace residential neighborhoods. These buildings are erected at the most suitable points of the city area, are surrounded by sufficient open space, they serve the whole city, our whole Soviet people." The Moscow high-rise buildings embody the great Russian building tradition,

> "the free rise of monumental and strong volumes, their impressive upward aspiration, the ideal penetration of the architectural form, the bold combination of architectural forms with sculptural elements. The skyscrapers erected in Moscow are the multiform embodiment of the main principles of Soviet architecture. Free construction of the silhouette, the powerful rise of the multilevel structures, grandiose simplicity and associated vitality are characteristic of all high-rise buildings of Moscow. The fundamental importance of the skyscrapers is given by the fact that each of them is the architectural center of the surrounding territory, creating the possibility of new architectural ensembles and shaping to the highest

degree the architectural form of the city as a whole. The architectural form of these monumental buildings embodied the creative power of Soviet culture, the greatness and beauty of Stalin's epoch. (Oltarzhevskii 1953, 3, 4)

The main part of the publication is devoted to the documentation of individual buildings: Moscow State University on Lenin Hills, the administrative buildings (Ministry of Heavy Industry in Zaryade, Ministry of Foreign Affairs on Smolenskii Square; Administrative Building on Krasnye vorota); hotels (Ukraina, Leningradskaia). Ukraina is the only high-rise project Oltarzhevskii built, together with Arkadii Mordvinov; residential buildings (Kotel'nicheskaia naberezhnaia and ploshchad' Vosstaniia). The preference for the tower-shaped silhouette is justified with reference to Leon Battista Alberti and Ivan Velikii's bell tower, the tower of San Marco in Venice, and that of Palazzo Vecchio in Florence. The American skyscrapers and what Oltarzhevskii learned there are no longer mentioned in this splendidly illustrated volume. The photographs documenting the process of erecting the Moscow high-rises are all the more explicit, similar to Margaret Bourke-White's photographs of construction workers on the top of the Empire State Building. They are reinforced concrete skeleton constructions of, for instance, the Ministry of Foreign Affairs under construction, or the MGU, which enlighten us about the origins of this kind of technology, logistics, and aesthetics: the skyscrapers of Chicago and New York. A little later they are covered by stone facades, ornaments, and sculptures that are said to be borrowed from the heritage of Russian master builders. "These gigantic, grand buildings, rising above Moscow with their austere silhouettes, are the new monument of our socialist epoch, the epoch of the genius builder of communism, the great Stalin" (Oltarzhevskii 1953, 211, 213, 214).

Postscript

The Moscow skyscrapers had not yet been completed when sharp criticism of this form and style of construction took off. Even before Khrushchev's secret speech in February 1956, with which he exposed the system of the cult of personality and Stalin's crimes and fortified his power, criticism of the exaggerations in planning and building had already begun at the end of 1955—the starting signal for de-Stalinization before official de-Stalinization. Finally, what was obvious to most citizens and many architects was brought up for discussion: the gap between the extreme housing shortage (especially after the destruction of the war) and the neglect of housing construction for the mass of the population, and a pompous building activity that spared no expense and was reflected in exuberant ornaments, porticoes, precious materials, senseless floor plans, turrets, cornices, frescoes, mosaics, and reliefs. What was demanded now was the rapid and systematic development of type dwellings, of prefabricated houses on a large scale, in order to remedy the dramatic housing situation. This marked the beginning of mass housing construction in the second half of the 1950s, exemplified in the prefabricated buildings of the Cheryomushki District in Moscow. Criticism of the facade-ness and pomp of the workers' palaces, which were reserved for the Soviet elite, was accompanied by the rediscovery of pre-Stalin Soviet modernism and the reconnection with now the international urban and architectural discussion. The story of this second Soviet modernism of the 1960s and 1970s remains to be told. Their original and innovative creations were largely unknown for a long time, partly because they were in poor condition.

Since then, the glass towers of Moscow City have been pushing their way into the skyline of the center of post-Soviet Moscow, where they have become now targets in the war, unleashed by Russia against Ukraine. Nearby and at the same time gigantic compounds such as Triumf Palace on Leningradskoe shosse have taken shape, resuming the Imperial style of Stalin's high-rises, brightly illuminated and obviously representing much more than just a postmodernist quotation.

Works Cited

Baron, Nick. "New Spatial Histories of Twentieth Century Russia and the Soviet Union: Surveying the Landscape." *Jahrbücher für Geschichte Osteuropas* 55, no. 3 (2007): 374–401.

Bassin, Mark, Christopher Ely, and Melissa K. Stockdale. *Space, Place, and Power in Modern Russia: Essays in the New Spatial History*. De Kalb: Northern Illinois University Press, 2010.

Benjamin, Walter. *Moskauer Tagebuch*. Aus der Handschrift herausgegeben und mit Anmerkungen von Gary Smith. Mit einem Vorwort von Gershom Scholem. Frankfurt am Main: Suhrkamp 1980.

Benjamin, Walter. *Das Passagen-Werk*, hrsg. von Rolf Tiedemann. 2 vols. Frankfurt am Main: Suhrkamp, 1983.

Chan-Magomedow, Selim O. *Pioniere der sowjetischen Architektur*. Dresden: Verlag der Kunst 1983.

Cohen, Jean-Louis. *Building a new New World. Amerikanizm in Russian Architecture*. New Haven: Yale University Press 2020.

Fitzpatrick, Sheila. *Cultural Revolution in Russia, 1928–1931*. Bloomington: Indiana University Press 1978.

Gershkovich, Yevgeniya, and Yevgeny Korneev. *Stalin's Imperial Style*. Moscow: Trefoil Press 2006.

Goldman, Wendy Z. *Terror and Democracy in the Age of Stalin: The Social Dynamics of Repression.* Cambridge University Press: 2007.

Hudson, Hugh D., Jr. *Blueprints and Blood: The Stalinization of Soviet Architecture, 1917–1937.* Princeton: Princeton University Press, 1993.

Kaganskii, Vladimir. *Kul'turnii landshaft i sovetskoe obitaemoe prostranstvo.* Moscow: NLO 2001.

Kopp, Anatole. *L'Architecture de la période stalinienne.* Grenoble: Presses universitaires de Grenoble, 1978.

Kotkin, Stephen. *Magnetic Mountain: Stalinism as a Civilization.* Berkeley: University of California, 1995

Merleau-Ponty, Maurice. *Les Aventures de la dialectique.* Paris: Gallimard 1955.

Nikologorskaia, Ol'ga. *Ol'tarzhevskii.* Moscow: Molodaia gvardiia, 2013.

Oltarzhevskii, V. K. *Stroitel'stvo vysotnykh zdanii v Moskve.* Moscow: Gosizdat literatury po stroitel'stvu i arkhitekture, 1953.

Paperny, Vladimir. *Architecture in the Age of Stalin: Culture Two (1985).* Cambridge: Cambridge University Press, 2002.

Schlögel, Karl. *Moskau lesen.* Berlin: Siedler 1984.

Schlögel, Karl. *In Space We Read Time. On the History of Civilization and Geopolitics.* Trans. Gerrit Jackson. Chicago: Chicago University Press 2016.

Schorske, Carl E. *Fin-de-siècle Vienna—Politics and Culture.* New York: Vintage 1980.

Selivanova, Aleksandra. *Postkonstruktivizm. Vlast' i arkhitektura v 1930-e gody v SSSR.* Moscow: Buksmart 2019.

Solovieva, Elena, and Tatiana Tsareva. *New Houses. The Architecture of Housing Estates Built in Moscow in the 1920s and 1930s.* Moscow: Plan 2012.

Vystavochnye ansambli SSSR 1920–1930-e gody. Materialy i dokumenty. Moscow: Galart, 2006.

Zubovich, Katherine. *Moscow Monumental: Soviet Skyscrapers and Urban Life in Stalin's Capital.* Princeton: Princeton University Press 2021.

About the Contributors

William J. Chase is Emeritus Professor of History, University of Pittsburgh.

Donald Filtzer is Emeritus Professor of Russian History at the University of East London in the United Kingdom.

Sheila Fitzpatrick is Professor at Australian Catholic University and Distinguished Service Professor Emerita of the University of Chicago.

J. Arch Getty is Distinguished Research Professor of History at the University of California at Los Angeles.

Wendy Z. Goldman is Paul Mellon Distinguished Professor of History at Carnegie Mellon University.

Lars T. Lih is an independent scholar who lives in Montreal.

Alfred J. Rieber is University Professor Emeritus at the Central European University and Professor Emeritus at the University of Pennsylvania.

Gábor T. Rittersporn is Research Director Emeritus at the Centre National de la Recherche Scientifique in Paris.

Karl Schlögel is Professor Emeritus of East European History at European University Viadrina, Frankfurt/Oder, Germany.

Lewis H. Siegelbaum is Jack and Margaret Sweet Professor Emeritus of History at Michigan State University.

Ronald Grigor Suny is William H. Sewell, Jr. Distinguished University Professor Emeritus of History and Professor of Political Science Emeritus at the University of Michigan and Emeritus Professor of Political Science and History, The University of Chicago.

Lynne Viola is University Professor Emerita at the University of Toronto.

INDEX

affective disposition, 9, 119–21, 125, 127, 131–32
April Revolution, 9, 85–6, 90
archives: access to, 1, 5, 7, 8, 17, 20, 22, 28, 34, 111, 137, 155; and archivists, 149; revolution in, 1, 5–6, 20, 33, 42, 69–70, 111
Arendt, Hannah, 10, 154, 206–7, 212
army. *See* Red Army

Belorussia, 173, 204, 206
Benjamin, Walter, 213, 216
Beria, L. P., 142, 147
Berlin, 103, 105–9, 113, 140, 171, 211–12, 217
Bolsheviks, 9, 15, 18, 21, 34–5, 86–7, 92, 101, 105, 109, 113, 120, 121, 132, 137–38, 143, 182–83, 189; and Civil War, 86, 123–25, 126; and revolutionary legality, 165; as Revolutionary Social Democrats, 178–80, 184–85, 188
Brezhnev, L. I., 42, 50, 61, 153, 207
Bukharin, N. I., 126–27, 142, 165, 189, 193
bureaucracy, mid-level, 17, 165, 193, 202

capitalism and capitalist system, 43, 56, 57, 61, 62, 127, 129, 133, 164–5, 181, 190–92; and oppression, 18, 47, 50, 53, 54, 63; post-Soviet, 51, 53
Cheliabinsk, 147, 215
children, 34–36, 39–41, 43, 128, 131
Churchill, Winston, 119, 167, 174
Civil War (1918–21), 123–24; experience of, 139, 143, 147, 150, 202; and October Revolution, 69, 85–87, 199
Clemenceau, Georges, 143, 173
Cold War, 2, 4, 15, 24, 68–69, 212, 217
collective farms (kolkhozy), 20, 88–90, 97–98, 153, 190–92, 194, 203
collectivization: of agriculture, 26, 30, 35–36, 79, 93, 144, 146, 147, 188, 189–94; as internal accumulation, 199–205;

violence of, 9–10, 18–20, 76, 77, 80, 89, 94, 101, 126, 140
Comintern, 106, 111, 144, 162, 167, 171
Communist Party of the Soviet Union (CPSU): cadres of, 9, 35, 38, 43, 87, 88, 92, 93, 94, 95, 96, 98, 167, 168, 194, 203; Central Committee of, 42, 77, 91, 93–94, 95, 102, 127, 133, 139, 140, 142, 145, 146, 148, 166, 200; Control Commission of, 71, 74, 146; Eighteenth Congress of (1939), 38; local organizations of, 17, 70–72, 74–76, 78, 87–88, 89, 93, 95–96, 140, 145, 146, 151, 152, 173, 203, 205; Nineteenth Congress of (1952), 163; and Old Bolsheviks, 102, 104, 142, 148–49; oppositions within, 72–79; Politburo of, 39, 42, 70, 75, 77, 78, 88, 103, 108, 112, 113, 127, 137, 139–40, 143, 146, 147–48, 152, 191, 202; regional secretaries, 75; Seventeenth Congress of (1934), 19, 88, 93, 166, 193
Constitution of 1936, 77, 90, 100, 112, 162, 164, 165, 166–67, 175, 215
constructivism, 210, 213, 217, 218, 219, 220, 221
Cultural Revolution, 16–17, 35, 212; in China, 212

dekulakization, 10, 26, 35, 36, 76, 79, 81, 96–97, 126, 146, 147, 192, 194, 200, 201
de-Stalinization, 7, 39, 41–42, 218, 224
Dunham, Vera, 28, 38

Eisenstein, Sergei, 84, 170, 214
enemies of the people, 30, 95–98, 112, 132–33, 164, 165, 216
engineers. *See* specialists
ethnic minorities. *See* nationalities
Ezhov, N. I., 71, 72, 96, 101, 109, 110, 141, 142, 144, 145, 146, 147, 152
Ezhovshchina. *See* Terror

229

INDEX

Fainsod, Merle, 37, 136, 154
February Revolution, 2, 9, 84, 184, 188
Figes, Orlando, 125, 131
Five-Year Plans: First (1928–32) 18, 34, 35, 36, 37, 55, 129; Second (1933–37) 35, 221
Foucault, Michel, 23, 153, 214
Foundations of Leninism, 10, 178, 181–85, 188–89, 194

Georgia, 142, 167, 169, 174
German Communist Party (KPD), 105–6, 109
Gestapo, 105–6, 109, 110
glasnost, 5, 17, 220
Gorbachev, Mikhail, 38, 43, 58, 81
Gorky, 106, 108, 215, 217, 220
GPU (State Political Administration). *See* political police
Great Fatherland War. *See* World War II
"great man" history, 151, 154, 199
Great Patriotic War. *See* World War II
Great Purges. *See* Terror
Great Retreat, 17, 37, 129
Great Terror. *See* Terror
Gulag, 42, 101, 175, 200, 205–7

Hellbeck, Jochen, 22, 23, 127, 130–31
historians and historiography: labor, 17–20, 24; revisionist, 4, 16–17, 37, 40, 69, 199; senior, ix, 1, 7, 17; social, 4, 6, 7, 8, 15–30, 42, 49, 69–82, 151; Soviet, 37, 169, 172–73; Western, 4, 18, 42, 187
Hitler, Adolf, 79, 111, 119, 137, 140, 143, 144, 151, 171, 173
Hoffmann, David, 20, 23
Holodomor, 26, 94, 126, 204
Hough, Jerry, ix, 37, 43

Iagoda, G. G., 71, 72, 103, 104, 108–13, 147, 202
ideology, 3, 10, 50, 51, 55, 68, 80, 123, 127–28, 177
industrialization, 30, 72–73, 162, 168, 189, 215; extraction of raw materials for, 200, 206, 207; impact of, 23, 47, 57, 76, 77, 79; pace of, 19, 35
industry, 24, 56–61, 73, 88, 94, 191, 201, 207
intelligentsia, 28, 34, 35, 37–43, 50–52, 55, 123, 131, 174, 186, 212. *See also* specialists
Iofan, Boris, 221–22

Kaganovich, L. M., 72, 144, 148, 190
Kalyvas, Stathis, 10, 201–2, 204, 207
Kamenev, L. B., 103, 126, 184

Kautsky, Karl, 10, 63, 178, 180–84, 187, 194
Kemerovo, 72–73
Khlevniuk, Oleg, 43, 177
Khrushchev, N. S., 7, 39, 40, 41, 50, 61, 140, 148, 149, 153
Kirov, S. M., 71–72, 100, 136, 139, 166, 168
Koenker, Diane, 18, 27
Komsomol, 19, 28, 34, 44
Kotkin, Stephen, 21, 23, 215
Kutuzov, M. I., 169, 172

Landau, Kurt, 105–7
Lenin, Vladimir: Marxism-Leninism, 2, 5, 23, 34, 122, 125, 134, 161, 165, 185; as Revolutionary Social Democrat, 178, 180–82, 185; and Stalin, 10, 121, 174, 177, 180–84; and Terror, 134, 149, 153; and totalitarian school, 15
Leningrad, 71, 81, 136, 139, 140, 169, 171, 217, 220
Lewin, Moshe, ix, 6, 16, 20, 30, 154, 199
liberals, 2, 182–84, 188, 191
Luxemburg, Rosa, 63, 178

managerial and technical personnel. *See* specialists
Magnitogorsk, 25, 91, 215
Mao Zedong, 122, 151
Marx, Karl, 43, 46, 47, 50, 51, 55–62
Marxism and "marxists": East European, 26, 51; Soviet, 23, 34, 35, 49, 51–52, 121–22, 125, 133, 137, 167; role of superstructure in, 10, 20, 56, 161–64, 175; Stalin's, 10, 51, 121–22, 161–64, 175, 184, 185, 189, 191; Western, 2, 7, 8, 17, 25, 36, 37, 46–50, 53–54, 199, 215
McNeal, Robert, ix, 136
Melnikov, Konstantin, 217, 221–22
Mensheviks, 96, 168, 183, 188
middle class (Soviet), 28, 38
Moch, Leslie, 29, 30
Molotov, V. M., 125, 127, 139, 140, 144, 145, 148, 171, 173, 175, 177
Moscow Metro, 81, 215, 217–19
Moscow State University (MGU), 38, 210, 211, 213, 218, 224
Muraveva, Nadezhda, ix, 149–50
Murphy, Kevin, 26, 82

nationalities, 4, 7–8, 43–44, 77, 138, 162, 168–72, 174
NEP (New Economic Policy), 57, 125, 150, 192

New Left, 67–69, 211–12
NKVD (People's Commissariat of Internal Affairs). *See* political police

October Revolution, 15, 16, 84, 86–89, 123, 124, 131, 188, 189, 190, 192
OGPU (Joint State Political Administration). *See* political police
Olberg, V. P., 100, 103, 105–13
Oltarzhevskii, V. K., 221–24
Order 00447. *See* political police
orientalism, 43, 174
Orwell, George, 136, 149, 154

Palace of Soviets, 217–18, 219, 221, 222
peasants and peasantry: and 1917, 85–86; leadership of, 182, 183, 184, 190, 191, 192; resistance of, 133, 138, 139, 140, 146, 148, 150, 151, 200, 202, 204; violence against, 201, 202, 204–5; and worker promotion, 34–43. *See also* April Revolution; collectivization; dekulakization
Peter the Great, 80, 170
Petrograd, 84, 184, 187
political history, 3, 6, 8, 28, 42, 151, 199
political police, 90, 151, 153; GPU (State Political Administration), 107; NKVD (People's Commissariat of Internal Affairs), 74–76, 78, 101, 103, 104, 106–13; OGPU (Joint State Political Administration), 26, 126, 202, 203; and order 00447, 112–13, 146, 205
Potemkin, V. P., 171–72
proletarian promotion, 7, 33, 34–36, 38, 39–44
Provisional Government, 123, 183–84, 187
Putin, Vladimir, 2, 6, 153, 207

raion (district), 149, 203, 205, 206
Red Army, 28, 140, 143–46, 154, 166
religion, 55, 138, 146, 151
revolution: from above, 16, 190; from below, 16, 17; Stalin, 20
Revolutionary Social Democracy, 177–85, 187, 188, 194
"rurality", 3, 10, 201–2, 205–7
Russian Orthodox Church, 138, 168, 175
Rykov, A. I., 127, 138

Second International, 178, 181–82, 188
Sedov, L. L., 103–7
Serp i Molot, 72, 78
shock work (udarnichestvo), 18, 19, 55

Short Course (History of the Communist Party of the Soviet Union (Bolsheviks)), 179, 185–86, 189, 193, 194
show trials. *See* Terror
Siberia, 202, 204, 215
Slezkine, Yuri, 39, 41
Smirnov, I. N., 100, 103–5, 107, 108, 110, 112
social democracy. *See* Revolutionary Social Democracy
social history, 4, 6, 7, 8, 16, 17, 19–20, 22, 24, 27, 29, 30, 49, 69–72, 76, 78, 79–80, 151
socialism: collapse of, 24, 70, 81; in One Country, 10, 111, 138, 162, 164, 174, 175; senior historians and, 4, 19, 29, 47, 63, 211, 212; Soviet faith in, 127–31, 149, 161, 163, 164, 166, 192
socialist competition, 19
social mobility, 3, 7, 36, 40, 54–55, 80, 90
Sokolov, Andrei, ix, 21
Spanish Civil War, 143, 167
specialists, 35, 92, 98, 165
special settlements, 26, 146, 200, 205, 207
Stakhanovism and Stakhanovites, 21, 22, 24, 25, 27, 55, 94, 131
Stalin, I. V.: and fear, 138–41, 153; as historian, 161–64, 167–75, 179; as legalist, 164–67, 175; political identity of, 178; psychology of, 71, 98, 119, 120–22, 125–26, 133, 142, 148–49; and revolution from above, 16, 20; 43, 44; and Revolutionary Social Democracy, 177–94; social mobility under, 34–40; and Terror, 75, 78, 80, 88, 96–99, 101, 120, 141–47, 151–52, 155, 202–3, 205, 206, 221; and Trotskyist threat, 102–13
Stalinism: affective disposition of, 120, 131; in Eastern Europe, 52; and internal colonization, 200–201; origins of, 1, 3–4, 16, 53, 125; social history of, 20, 25–26, 30, 68, 151; subjective experience of, 22, 54, 132–33; and totalitarian model, 70, 101, 154, 199; Western understanding of, 47–48, 68, 80, 100, 211–12. *See also* de-Stalinization
Strauss, Kenneth, 20, 26
superstructure. *See* Marxism and "marxists"
Sverdlovsk, 40, 97, 121, 217

Tarle, E. V., 169, 172
Terror, The: denunciations in, 39, 70–74, 78, 94, 133, 140, 165–66; executions during, 70, 75, 79, 97, 102, 110, 133, 140, 145;

Terror (*continued*)
Ezhovshchina, 9, 101; "Great Purges", 9, 17, 37, 101, 202, 203, 205; mass operations in, 10, 76–77, 138, 146, 147, 152, 202, 203, 205; and show trials, 9, 71–73, 94–95, 110, 143, 150, 165, 166, 175, 212, 215, 216; and wrecking, 72–73, 79, 94, 104, 126, 165–67; and troikas, 144–47; zaiavleniia (declarations) in, 74, 76, 78
Thompson, E. P., ix, 19
Ticktin, Hillel, 8, 48, 49, 59
Timasheff, Nicholas, 17, 37
totalitarianism and totalitarian theory, 2, 4, 6–7, 15–16, 23, 36–37, 47, 52, 68–71, 128, 136–37, 149, 154, 199, 212, 215
trade unions, 24, 27, 35, 52
Tromly, Ben, 38, 41
Trotsky, L. D., 9, 16, 48, 81, 103–7
Trotskyists, 48–49, 72, 101–11, 113, 139, 143, 147–48, 190, 193
Tukhachevskii, M. N., 144–45

Ukraine, 2, 26, 43, 53, 78, 106, 162, 169, 204, 205, 207, 208, 211, 22
upward mobility. *See* proletarian promotion

Vesnin brothers, 217, 218, 221
violence: and affective disposition, 120, 124; preconditions to, 141, 150–51, 154; centralized control of, 142, 146, 147, 149, 150, 153, 206–7; against the peasantry, 200–206
Volga, 136, 138, 204
Volga-Moskva Canal, 215, 216, 220
Vorkuta, 109, 223
Vyshinskii, A. Ia., 76, 81, 103, 105, 107, 110, 112, 146

West Berlin, 211–12
White Army officers, 146, 70, 77, 96, 122–25, 139, 148, 193
workers: and Communist Party, 91, 129; industrial, 18, 20, 35, 72, 91, 128; women, 18, 27, 34, 35, 36, 68, 85
working class, 21, 24, 29, 37, 39, 40–43, 47, 50–52, 55, 62, 90, 124, 201; as ruling class, 34–35, 50, 57, 86, 91. *See also* proletarian promotion
World War I, 2, 63, 172
World War II, 2, 16, 24, 27–28, 38, 81, 111, 143–44, 150, 162–63, 167, 172, 173, 175, 206, 218

Yalta, 171, 173
Yeltsin, Boris, 5, 43, 44

Zhdanov, A. A., 168, 173
Zholtovskii, I. V., 220, 221
Zinoviev, G. E., 103, 124, 126, 148